Under Polaris ✶

An Arctic Quest

for Dean and Tomi McManus — Appreciatively,

Tahoe Washburn

Now, in 2000, the Inuit
live in villages and much of their
land is officially theirs — Nunavut!

Under Polaris

An Arctic Quest

TAHOE TALBOT WASHBURN

A McLellan Book

University of Washington Press SEATTLE AND LONDON

This book is published with the assistance of a grant from the McLellan Endowed Series Fund, established through the generosity of Martha McCleary McLellan and Mary McLellan Williams.

Copyright © 1999 by the University of Washington Press
Design by Pamela Canell Chaus
Printed in the United States of America

Published simultaneously in Canada by McGill-Queens University Press, Montreal and Kingston

ISBN 0-295-97761-2

Library of Congress Cataloging-in-Publication Data can be found at the back of the book.

The paper used in this publication is acid-free and recycled from 10 percent post-consumer and at least 50 percent pre-consumer waste. It meets the minimum requirements of American National Standard for Information Sciences—Permanence of Paper for Printed Library Materials, ANSI Z39.48–1984. ♲ ∞

*T*his book is dedicated to my husband, Link,
in gratitude for sixty-three marvelous years,
including our numerous travels
in the lands of my childhood dreams;
and also to all our beloved friends of the North.

Maps

Contents

Foreword

$\mathcal{T}$his is an account of a people who had learned to live in harmony with nature long before established villages existed in the Arctic. For thousands of years, Native people survived in a land that alternated between the harsh and the beautiful, and they developed values and skills to deal with that environment.

Tahoe Washburn, as a small child, was enchanted with the people of the Far North and became an enthusiastic traveling companion of her husband, Link, as he pursued his doctoral studies in the Arctic between 1938 and 1941. The two decided to spend a full year in the Arctic, and in preparation for this they lived for a time with the Inuit. They marveled at the humor of their arctic friends: "a situation that would make us angry made them laugh, and what one could not change made them just consider it, then laugh about it." They became fully aware of the meaning of "traditional knowledge" as they learned to build a snow house, prepare skins for clothing and bedding, train and care for dogs, and perform a multitude of other tasks required to sustain themselves on the land. They learned that to survive in those harsh conditions meant you had to share your food and possessions.

On April 1, 1999, the Northwest Territories as the Washburns knew it will be split into two separately governed areas. Nunavut, the newly named eastern portion, will gain self-determination. *Under Polaris* is a record of the cultural heritage and achievements of some of the men and women, still revered in communities today, who have been the stewards of the Far North. These people and their way of life are what will allow Nunavut to succeed. At the end of the twentieth century, few people, including Native people, enjoy the experiences related in these pages. Some, not many, still travel in the traditional manner, to hunt, to picnic, to teach their children, and to retain their culture, but they do not need to do so to survive.

As we watch future developments in the Far North, those of us who have known the region and the way of life over many years are grateful to have been a part of that history. *Under Polaris* is a true, unembellished story of that former time.

kuannapuk–thank you, Tahoe.

George D. Hobson
First Director of Canada's Polar Continental Shelf Project
July 1998

Preface

$\mathcal{F}$or many years, friends have urged me to make my husband Link's and my day-to-day experiences in the Canadian Arctic available in book form. Link's geologic report of our Arctic work during the years covered by the present volume was published in 1947 as Memoir 22 of the Geological Society of America.

Under Polaris is based on my daily journals, written in tents, in snow houses, on board small Inuit schooners, the Hudson's Bay Company *Fort Ross*, the RCMP *St. Roch*, and in friendly homes at the posts. It presents brief descriptions of our fieldwork and relates the manner in which we met the varied challenges of each day.

I hope the Glossary may clarify the meaning of unfamiliar terms and that the Appendix Chronology will provide a quick source of information with respect to the dates, locations, and names of most of the people we met.

Because there are so many Inuit dialects, with alternate ways of spelling Inuit place names and personal names, I have in most instances used the spellings given me by George Porter in 1938, Ikey Bolt in 1939, and Patsy and Jorgen Klengenberg in 1940.

I trust that the maps will make it easier to track our travels, and that the photographs, most of which were taken by Link, will help the reader to visualize the places we visited and the many people who became our friends.

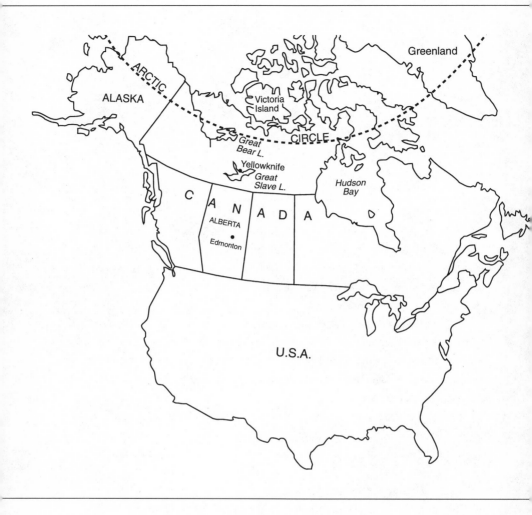

MAP 1. North America

Under Polaris

An Arctic Quest

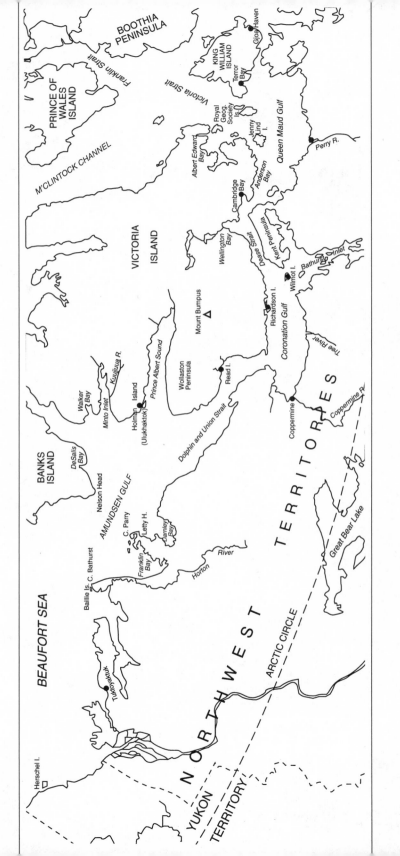

MAP 2. General Area of Our Travels

Introduction

*W*ith small nose pressed against the glass of a big case in the American Museum of Natural History in New York, I stared at models of an Inuit (Eskimo) family. Dressed in fur, they stood beside their snow house together with dogs, sledge, bow, seal spear, and other accoutrements.

"Who are they?" I asked my father. "Eskimos," he replied. I liked their faces and thought how warm and soft their fur clothes must feel. The next case held miniature figures depicting the seasons of their nomadic life as they traveled from one area to another, hunting, fishing, or gathering roots and berries, or willow fuzz for their kudliks, as their soapstone stove-lamps were called. I became one of them in my imagination, trudging across the tundra or running beside their dog teams on the ice.

When we returned home I asked my parents where those people lived, and on a globe Father pointed out the Arctic lands, saying that they lived under Polaris, the North Star. He had already shown me Polaris in the sky, in the constellation of the Little Dipper, and I remembered that it looked very faint and far away. That was in 1916, and a dream formed at the back of my mind. One day I would find the "People of Polaris."

In 1936, my husband Link and I traveled to Alaska with Bradford Washburn, an old friend but not a relative. Brad had asked Link to accompany him on the first photographic flight over Mount McKinley. After the successful flight, Link and I continued north up the Yukon and Porcupine Rivers to Old Crow in the Yukon Territory of Canada and by air to Aklavik, a small settlement in the enormous maze of the Mackenzie River Delta. From there we flew out to Richards Island and on west to Herschel Island, in the Beaufort Sea.

At last at Herschel Island I found the friendly Inuit, the real "People of

Polaris." Among them was Jorgen Klengenberg, whose father, Christian, had been a whaling captain. Jorgen was trading his fox skins with Captain C. T. Pedersen, who had turned to trading with the Inuit when whaling ended. We returned to San Francisco with Pedersen on the MS *Patterson*, picking our way through the ice as the winter pack moved in. Jorgen left on his schooner, *Polar Bear*, for his home at Terror Bay, on King William Island, about 1,500 miles to the east. Little did we know then that four years later we would spend three months there with him and his brother Patsy and their families.

Nellie Kunellik, a western Arctic Inuvialuit woman and an excellent seamstress, agreed to make heavy white wool duffle attigis, or parkas, for Link and me. They were beautiful, with wolverine fur around the hoods to protect our faces from freezing winds and as an edging at cuffs and bottom. Bands of colored tape were added as trim, and the cloth covers were similarly decorated. I wanted to hug her but smiled instead, shook her hand, and thanked her. Together with waterproof sealskin boots, these attigis kept us warm as we walked up over the flower-filled tundra of the island.

It was already early September, and from the height of land we looked out over the endless expanse of the ice-choked Beaufort Sea. Slowly, stealthily, the ice was closing its grip around Herschel Island, pressing on toward the mainland coast. The jagged points and peaks of the multiyear ice cast intense blue shadows across the pale pink and blue of the snowy surface. Fresh water pools sparkled like bright blue tourmalines on the old ice floes while the underwater ice was light jade green. Incredible. The power of the scene cast its spell on us. We both knew that we would return to the Arctic.

Link had only a year to wait. He had entered Yale University's Graduate School to study geology, which he felt might lead us north again. He was right. In January 1937 his professor, R. F. Flint, asked him to be his field assistant on explorer Louise Boyd's expedition to the magnificent fjord region of Northeast Greenland during the following summer. I was devastated not to be with him. Louise Boyd, a Californian, had made several previous visits to Northeast Greenland using a Norwegian sealing boat. Later, during World War II, she turned over all of her photographs and data to the U.S. government.

That summer strengthened Link's determination to work in the Arctic. Four school years in the Swiss Alps and four years at Dartmouth College, where he majored in geology and was a member of the Outing Club and Ski Team, had given him a love of the out-of-doors. Back at Yale he discussed with Professor Flint the possibility of basing his doctoral thesis on a study of several of the southern Canadian Arctic islands, to further record their geology and to discover whether they had in fact been covered by a North American Pleistocene ice sheet. The southern limit of glaciation across the northern United States was reasonably well known, but the northern extent was the center of hot debate between botanists and geomorphologists at that time. Botanists were sure the continental ice could not have covered the islands because the Arctic flora must have had a refuge. But the geomorphologists felt sure that the ice had covered at least the most southern islands. Link and I discussed the possibility of flying to the Canadian Arctic to find out, thereby hopefully resolving the debate. Professor Flint agreed with the idea and Link came home with a twinkling look in his eyes, saying, "How would you like to spend a summer in the Arctic?" Asking only, "When do we leave?" I threw my arms around him.

Link got out his maps of Canada, and it was decided that, if possible, we would make a charter flight from Yellowknife on Great Slave Lake to Coppermine on Coronation Gulf at the Arctic coast of the continent. From there we would continue east along the coast to Cambridge Bay on the southeastern coast of Victoria Island, to spend two or three days looking for any evidences of glaciation. After that we would fly west along the southern coast of Victoria Island, then south to Coppermine. The following day we would fly northward along the mainland coast and across Dolphin and Union Strait and the Wollaston Peninsula of Victoria Island to Prince Albert Sound, observing any signs of glaciation. We would then return to the southern coast of Victoria Island to land by the Hudson's Bay Company post on little Read Island. We hoped to find an Inuk who would guide us inland on Wollaston Peninsula to search for any signs of former glaciation.

1 / North!
Cambridge Bay, Victoria Island
Hike to Mount Pelly
July 17–20, 1938

*T*o work in the Canadian Arctic we had to get permission from the Canadian government. This entailed several visits to Ottawa, where we found everyone interested in Link's project and more than helpful. We procured the most recent map of the Canadian Arctic that included Banks Island, Victoria Island, and King William Island, along the coasts of which we planned to work. We also called upon the famous Arctic explorer Vilhjalmur Stefansson, who had led the Canadian Arctic Expedition of 1913–18. Dr. Rudolph M. Anderson was second-in-command. Stef gave us much valuable information about climate, possible methods of travel, clothing, and food, and impressed upon us that we must be equipped for all emergencies and never put ourselves in a position of having to call for help. Both of us had years of camping and climbing experience, but never in the Arctic.

Finally the necessary government papers were in hand. We then got in touch with W. R. "Wop" May at the Edmonton headquarters of Canadian Airways, to make arrangements for the charter flights. Wop had made our flights to Aklavik and Herschel Island possible in 1936, and we looked forward to meeting him in person. Beyond the arranged charter flights we would have to discover means of travel when we reached the Arctic. We were told that we might be able to find an Inuk who would give us a lift on his schooner or whaleboat, or guide us inland on foot.

Gradually we gathered clothing, dehydrated food, tent, Primus stoves, a Brunton compass (a compact instrument that can be held in a hand to read horizontal and vertical angles, for leveling, and for reading the magnetic bearing of a line), and other equipment, including my small amateur radio transceiver, which was required by the Canadian government. They had to keep track of our movements. At last, everything was packed and loaded on

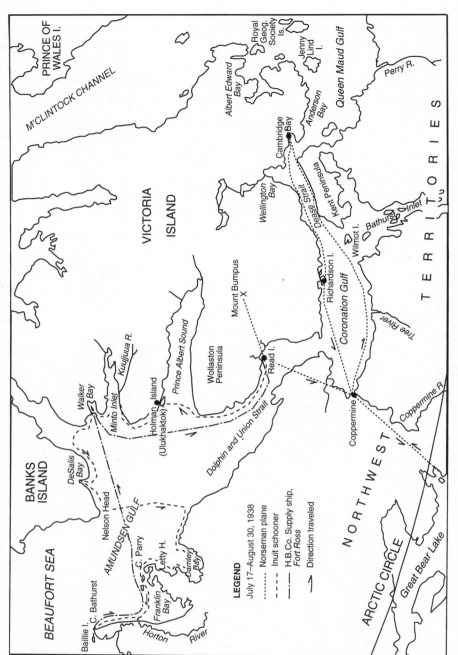

MAP 3. July 17–August 30, 1938

the train with us for Edmonton. When we arrived July 17th, we discovered Wop to be a keen, warm man with a great heart. Not only did he see that our needs were met, but he also gave us many valuable bits of information about the areas we hoped to visit. It would have been impossible not to return his warmth.

During the night before our departure for Yellowknife, a violent thunderstorm swept over that rapidly expanding prairie city of Edmonton. Startled awake by a blaze of lightning and crash of thunder, we wondered if we would be able to fly. The storm abated, however, and at 5:00 A.M. our pilot Harry Winnie arrived to pick us up. A tall fellow with a firm, assured carriage and a nice sometimes quizzical expression, he had that special aura that inspires confidence. We found the early Canadian bush pilots to be outstanding men individually and as a group. Harry assured us we would fly, and en route to Cooking Lake, the local floatplane base for northern flights, I tried to review in my mind everything we had packed, hoping I had not forgotten some vital item. We knew we could buy coal oil for our single-burner Primus stoves and lantern at the small Hudson's Bay Company fur trading posts. Some other basic necessities might also be obtained there, but we were expected to provide the major portion of our own food and equipment.

In 1938 there were no airstrips at the mushrooming gold rush settlement of Yellowknife on Great Slave Lake, or the tiny Arctic Coast hamlets or trading posts at Aklavik, Tuktoyaktuk, Baillie Island, Coppermine, Walker Bay, Read Island, Cambridge Bay, Perry River, and Gjoa Haven. Aircraft were equipped with skis in winter and floats in summer. Air traffic came to a halt for four to six weeks each spring and fall when it was impossible to land because ice in lakes, rivers, and the Arctic Ocean was either breaking up or forming. However, the Government Weather Station at Coppermine on Coronation Gulf sent a radio message that there was sufficient open water both there and at Cambridge Bay, our second stop, for our plane to land safely.

Mert Wales, a vibrant, cheerful chap who affectionately called his wife "Haggy," was waiting on the dock beside a small floatplane when we arrived at Cooking Lake. He was to be copilot-mechanic on the roughly 900-mile flight to Yellowknife and had already loaded most of the freight. The single-engine, fabric-covered Norseman was the favored "workhorse" of the North at the time. I looked at the little plane as it rocked gently on the steel gray water. A 300-pound rudder destined for a schooner at Copper-mine was being tied down to rings bolted to the floor of the plane. As I watched, an image of the rudder zipping out through the fabric side flashed through my mind. I hoped the rings would hold fast.

Finally, we and two other passengers were asked to climb aboard, and go forward to lean on the tightly strapped load during takeoff. That kept all the weight forward, making it easier for the aircraft to gain sufficient speed and "lift." The few, small, armless seats faced the aisle. There were no seat belts or stewardess. Our pilot Harry flew beneath the trailing remnants of the storm, and not far below us the mosaic of Earth slipped by. Clusters of ranch buildings seemed remote, perhaps toys dropped and forgotten. Then there was only forest. A flood of excitement engulfed me, for we were actually on our way to the Arctic again!

At the time, the only navigation aids in the North were radio, compass, and natural landmarks. Bush pilots usually flew "contact," below cloud cover, in sight of water. To the extent that it was feasible, routes were planned along rivers and over lakes or along sea coasts. The compass was of less and less value the farther north one flew, due to the proximity of the North Magnetic Pole, which wanders and was moving northerly through Prince of Wales Island at that time, just east of Victoria Island. We landed briefly at the little settlement of Fort McMurray for lunch and later at Fort Smith on the Slave River to gas up. Smoke from forest fires became thicker as we neared the vast reaches of Great Slave Lake. The low-lying shorelines soon vanished behind us; finally a dim line delineated the northern shore. Yellowknife Bay and rocky, high-centered Latham Island, on which the gold mining settlement was growing, emerged ahead through the pungent veil of burning forest. We splashed down at 4:30 P.M.

Prospecting in the vicinity had commenced in the early 1930s, and the rush began after a number of gold strikes. Tents, a few log cabins, and board buildings were scattered among the trees and big rocks; more were under construction. The Wildcat Cafe offered a good meal and the little Corona Inn, a bed. We were given one of the three "separate" bedrooms— the remaining space comprising a kitchen, a general room for eating, sleeping, cards, and talk among the prospectors, and a hall bath. Bedrolls belonging to those too late to get a bunk were shoved against the wall until time to roll in, or out under the stars. All the partitions were made of thin boards and were left open a foot at top and bottom, economically allowing

Yellowknife, N.W.T., Canada. General view.

Yellowknife. Floatplane cove.

Yellowknife. July, 17, Corona Inn, the only place to stay at the time.

Yellowknife. August 30, Wildcat Cafe, the only place to eat, and Gordon Latham's new hotel.

hot air from the stoves to circulate. To our dismay, then amusement, we quickly realized that all sounds circulated equally well. Plenty of liquor was available, and the prospectors' remarks and conversations were interesting, frequently ribald, and often funny. Rudy Huess, another Canadian Airways pilot, came in to say he and Dunc McLaren would fly us to Coppermine and then to Cambridge Bay on southeastern Victoria Island the next day. Since the flight would be roughly 900 miles each way, they planned to use the Norseman "BDG" because it had an extra belly gas tank.

Early in the morning we headed north over a vast region of forest, lakes, ponds, and bogs separated by rocky outcrops thinly veiled by spiky spruce and muskeg. At last, Great Bear Lake stretched away to the west like an inland sea, then we were over the Barren Grounds, home of Inuit, great caribou herds, wolves, and Arctic grizzly bears. My heart skipped a beat as I realized we were north of the Arctic Circle. Low mountains rose ahead. Beyond them, we followed the Coppermine River as it made its crooked way through the ancient trap rock flows to Coronation Gulf.

When we passed over Bloody Falls, I shuddered as we recalled the early explorer Samuel Hearne's description of his terrifying experience there in 1771. On his third attempt to reach the Arctic Sea, and hopefully a Northwest Passage to the Orient, he was traveling down the Coppermine River with a band of Athapascans led by Matonabbee. There was bad blood between the Inuit and Athapascans at the time, so Matonabbee decided to attack during the night if Inuit were camped at the falls. Spies were sent ahead and when they returned to say that the Inuit were indeed camped there, Matonabbee ordered an attack that night while they were asleep in their tents. Hearne, whose own life depended on the Athapascans' frame of mind, could do nothing to prevent the ensuing massacre. A few Inuit escaped in their boats, but most were murdered. Hearne wrote, "My situation and the terror of my mind at beholding this butchery, cannot easily be conceived, much less described." The place became known as the Bloody Falls.

We could see the ice pack lying some distance offshore. Minutes later we were circling over Coppermine. As I eagerly looked down, the scene caught my breath. The ten or twelve little buildings spread along the coast, plus a few Inuit tents, magnified the isolation of the inhabitants. They represented the Anglican and Catholic missions, the Royal Canadian Mounted Police, the Hudson's Bay Fur Trading Company, and the Government Radio

Yellowknife. Canadian Airways Norseman, "BDG."

Yellowknife. Link and pilot Harry Winnie on "BDG."

Mainland Arctic coast, Coppermine and Coppermine River.

Communications and Weather Stations. There were only ten to fourteen Caucasians, along with six or eight Inuit families who assisted them.

The main Inuit population still lived out on the land. According to the season they moved camp to the best areas for hunting, fishing, and trapping foxes, wolves, and other animals. Polar bears, seals, and caribou provided food, as well as skins for clothing and many other uses. The Inuit seldom came to the trading posts except for Christmas and Easter, when they traded their fur skins for ammunition, coal oil, flour, sugar, tea, tobacco, cloth for attigi (parka) covers, tinned food, or other items. They also visited with their friends and enjoyed the festivities planned by the missions and the Hudson's Bay Company post manager. There were only two RCMP posts in the Central Arctic, one at Coppermine and the other at Cambridge Bay, so the areas under their authority covered thousands of square miles. The two missions vied with each other for the souls of the Inuit in this vast area, and both police and missionaries made extended sledge trips during the autumn and spring to check on and visit with the Inuit families.

The entire population of Coppermine waited on the bank to greet us. We shook hands with everyone and then accompanied the Hudson's Bay Company post manager, Mr. Nichols, his wife, and the others to the post. The Hudson's Bay Company inspector, Mr. Copland, and his assistant, Mr. Demment, were there, en route to inspect the four other posts at Perry River, Gjoa Haven, Cambridge Bay, and Read Island. The Anglican Missionary Reverend Harold Webster and his wife, Edie, were most welcoming, asking us to come for tea. Red Abraham of the RCMP, as well as the chief radio operator Mr. Deacon and his wife, and Oliver Howey, his assistant, were also full of inquiries about happenings "Outside," and the reason for our coming north. At the time, anyone living south of the Northwest Territories lived Outside. Our arrival was a novel experience for everyone. People not connected with government, churches, or the Hudson's Bay Company were rare visitors indeed, so our arrival was an "event."

After "tea," Link and I changed into our long woollies, heavy pants, shirts, and boots and were ready when Rudy called Mr. Copland and us for the three-and-a-half-hour flight to Cambridge Bay. From the relative comfort of the little plane we looked down with interest on the great number of small trap rock islands rising darkly from the ice-free waters. We thought of the first Inuit who had slowly migrated east from Alaska, and of the early explorers who had struggled along the same stretch of mainland coast as far as Turnagain Point on Kent Peninsula. In 1820, Captain John Franklin and his men, paddling two birchbark canoes, suffered through many harrowing experiences in the area because of storm-driven ice, as well as near starvation, for they were unable to kill sufficient game.

Eighteen years later Thomas Simpson and Peter Dease, Chief Factor of the Hudson's Bay Company, using two boats that had been built for the purpose at Fort Confidence on Great Bear Lake, struggled with their companions along the same ice-choked coast to Turnagain Point, where they, too, were stopped by impenetrable ice. However, Simpson led a party on foot to higher ground farther east. To the north, across the frozen strait they saw land, which they named Victoria Island. In 1839 Simpson, determined to explore the remainder of the coast east all the way to the mouth of Back River, again descended the Coppermine River. Partly because of perfect whether that summer, he and his companions succeeded. On the return voyage west they sailed along part of the southern coast of King

William Island and mapped 156 miles of the southern coast of Victoria Island.

As we flew east along the coast, the vastness of the Barren Grounds to the south, devoid of any sign of living creatures, stretched my mind. I knew Inuit were scattered there, along with millions of birds and animals, but it looked and *felt* empty. Below us and to the north we looked down on large floes of disintegrating ice, oddly beautiful patterns resembling a sparkling jigsaw puzzle spilled out on a huge table. Ahead, the almost flat, desolate wastes of western Kent Peninsula rose gently in a series of perfect, ancient raised beaches. This formation indicated emergence of the land, probably due to the melting of former glaciers whose weight had depressed land.

At the higher eastern end of Kent Peninsula, the sea ice was quite solid, with but few leads winding away. The patterns formed by water branching out from seal breathing holes and leads resembled delicate fronds of coral. As we flew north over Dease Strait, we saw Queen Maud Gulf, a blue-white expanse of ice stretching away to the east. I thought of Collinson, who wintered at Cambridge Bay in 1852–53, and of Rae, who in 1851 sailed through Dease Strait past Cambridge Bay, then, stopped by adverse winds, made his way north by foot up the east coast of Victoria Island as far as Gateshead Island, before returning to his boat. They, and many other gallant men, struggled against the fog, wind, cold, and unyielding ice in search of Franklin's last expedition, which was lost in 1847–48.

Cape Colborne loomed east of Cambridge Bay, and then we saw that the ice lay well up the bay. The big lakes were still frozen, but thousands of small lakes were scattered like sapphires on the beige tapestry of the land. Mount Pelly lay low in the distance, and open water sparkled at the head of Cambridge Bay, where we saw four well-separated groups of small buildings. As we circled before landing, Link and I wondered why the Hudson's Bay Company post here was a quarter mile from the Canalaska post, which had been Captain Pedersen's base for his trading with Inuit in the region and which the Hudson's Bay Company had purchased when Pedersen retired. The Royal Canadian Mounted Police barracks and Anglican mission, even farther removed, were on the east side of the largest of three streams at the head of the bay, and Slim Semmler's little trading post was half a mile farther along that side of the bay. It seemed odd to us, at the time, that the few inhabitants preferred to put so much distance between themselves and

Cambridge Bay, Victoria Island, N.W.T. Mount Pelly.

Cambridge Bay. Captain C. T. Pedersen's trading boat, *Nigalik,* with Royal Canadian Mounted Police post and Anglican mission in the distance.

their neighbors. As we thought about it later, we realized that the competing traders would naturally seek some privacy, and gradually we came to understand that the fewer the people, the greater may be the need for privacy.

The *Nigalik*, the small Hudson's Bay Company supply ship we had seen two years earlier at Herschel Island, was at anchor in front of the Post. On the bank were Mr. Bartlett, who was in charge of closing out the Canalaska holdings, Rudolf Johnson, Pete Brandt, Charlie Smith, and the crew, all of whom we had met at Herschel Island. The Reverend and Mrs. Roceby-Thomas, RCMP Constable John Cheetham, and the few local Inuit welcomed us with smiles, and Post Manager and Mrs. Milne invited us to join them, with Mr. Copland and Mr. Bartlett, for a delicious supper in their cozy little house. We answered their questions about our reason for coming north and asked them many questions about the local area.

As we left, Mr. Bartlett invited us to come on board the *Nigalik* for a snifter of rum and said we were welcome to bunks, thus making it unnecessary for us to put up our tent. We accepted with pleasure and enjoyed the rum and reminiscences of our voyage with him and Captain C. T. Pedersen from Herschel Island to San Francisco in 1936 on the MS *Patterson*. Maybe the rum, or the continuous early summer daylight, loosened our tongues, for it was three in the morning when we all finally sought our bunks.

We did not hear the plane take off that morning for Perry River with Mr. Copland and Mr. Demment aboard, but Rudolf wakened us at noon to say that Pete had hotcakes on the fire. Everyone crammed down as many as they could eat, and a few more, but Pete kept bringing them in. Feeling gluttonous, Link and I went on deck to stretch. Across the bay we saw the stern deck of a sunken ship sticking up out of the water. It was the wreck of *Baymaud*. Named *Maud*, she had originally belonged to Roald Amundsen, the famous Norwegian explorer who completed the first Northwest Passage in the ship *Gjoa* in 1905. After leading several dramatic expeditions to the Arctic and Antarctic, Amundsen's dream was to sail east from northern Norway along the coasts of the Russias to Bering Strait, thus completing the Northeast Passage. On July 18, 1918, he left Vardø in northern Norway on *Maud* and worked his way through the ice to the east. Two long years later, having been twice frozen in, *Maud* and her crew passed through the Bering Strait and reached Nome, Alaska, completing Amundsen's dream.

Sadly, Amundsen's finances depleted, *Maud* was impounded in Seattle

Cambridge Bay. Royal Canadian Mounted Police Corporal Kane and Constable
John Cheetham, Inuit, Hudson's Bay Company Post Manager Frank Milne, Tahoe,
Mrs. Milne, and Inuit.

Cambridge Bay. Hudson's Bay Company Post in the early 1930s. (F. R. Ross photo)

Cambridge Bay. Wreck of Hudson's Bay Company's *Baymaud*, originally Roald Amundsen's *Maud*.

for unpaid debts. Because she had been built to withstand the pressure of the ice, the Hudson's Bay Company purchased her, renaming her *Baymaud*. Used as an Arctic supply vessel, she later sank in Cambridge Bay. A sad ending for such a valiant and historic ship. Pete took us across the bay to see her. Clambering about on the remaining bits of steep-angled deck, marveling at the strength of her construction, we thought of the years the ship had fought its way through the monstrous ice of the polar seas. In the intervening years the Inuit had salvaged most of the superstructure. Finally we climbed back into Pete's whaleboat and he dropped us at the Anglican mission, where we checked the barometer to see if the weather was going to hold.

Link had decided that we should walk out to Mount Pelly to find the altitude of the raised beaches and summit of the long, low mountain. We donned our warm attigis and rucksacks and set off armed with our Brunton compass and Paulin altimeter. During an ice age the land is depressed by the enormous weight of continental ice sheets. As the ice melts, sea level rises and huge lakes are formed. At the same time, the now ice-free land also rises slowly, seeking an equilibrium. Link hoped to find fossil shells on the raised beaches which might give him the dates of emergence.

At three in the afternoon, our eyes on Mount Pelly lying low on the horizon seven airline miles distant, we started eagerly forth on a low ridge that jutted into the head of the bay. We were elated to find that the ridge was an esker, unmistakable evidence of earlier glaciation. Formed by a subglacial stream during the last ice age, it proved that at least this part of Victoria Island had been glaciated. The esker was composed of sand, silt, and clay, with numerous stones of various sizes, some having been split vertically by freezing. Some of the stones were erratics, brought by either sea ice or continental ice from the mainland.

Because of its coarse, gravelly nature, the ridge was dry and largely barren. However, the low areas between the esker and the myriad ponds and lakes were painted in the soft greens of grasses, sedges, mosses, Cassaiope, and almost prostrate willows, and were brightened by the blossoms of Saxifrages, poppies, Dryas, Pedicularis, and of many other small Arctic flowers.

To our dismay, our rocky highway petered out in an endless maze of lakes. A couple of islets in one small lake lured us as "stepping stones." Beyond, the water looked deeper, so we rolled up our pants, took off boots and socks, and waded in up to our hips. But our legs began to feel numb in the icy water and we wondered how much deeper it might get. Finally, out on the sunny bank, we pulled off pants and long johns, wringing them hard and waving them dry in the summery breeze while providing the hordes of mosquitoes with tasty meals. Reclothed at last, we went on and on over stony knolls and ridges, down through wet swales and over streamlets, now and again making cairns on high points to guide us on our homeward trek. The seven "airline" miles coiled themselves into a far longer, tortuous way. Distances, we found, are difficult to judge in the Arctic, for there is nothing of known height to use for scale. A "small" rock that seems to be nearby may actually be a very big boulder farther off; or a "low" hill, a distant mountain.

Marveling at the great numbers of eider ducks, Canada geese, tundra swans, Arctic loons, gulls, terns, and at least a dozen different land and wading birds, we gradually drew nearer the high hill. It was around eight in the evening when we finally stood at its base on the lowest well-marked ancient raised beach. There Link took a Paulin reading for altitude, which I noted in the log. I tried to visualize how the hill, a lonely island, appeared as it gradually rose from the sea with the melting of the continental ice.

My reverie was shattered, however, by the sudden appearance of five Inuit men coming over Mount Pelly's shoulder. In their winter-worn caribou-skin kuletaks (parkas), their black hair hanging to their shoulders, and strings of ducks and geese dangling down their backs, they somehow seemed wonderfully familiar—like the models I had seen as a child. They were even more surprised to see us, and we greeted one another with smiles and handshakes and spoken "hellos," each in his own tongue. We exchanged questions, though they could only be answered by smiles and laughter. We presumed that a camp we had seen earlier by a big lake was theirs.

We parted company after a few minutes, Link and I climbing up the sloping shoulder, taking altitudes of each raised beach. The summit, like all unknown summits, was always over the next rise, but after an hour we finally reached the top and took altitude readings, revealing the summit to be only 675 feet. The low-lying country, spread to distant horizons in all directions below us, was at least half water—a labyrinth of interwoven streams, puddles, ponds, lakes, creeks, and marshes. From our vantage point, it was impossible to trace a continuous dry path toward the head of Cambridge Bay. We started on, and near the bottom lined up our cairns to take a sight on the RCMP post with the Brunton compass. It looked at least a hundred miles away beyond the improbable maze of lakes. I took a deep breath as we sat down to devour "incomparable" canned bully-beef sandwiches, hungry after eight hours of hiking.

The low sun had become partly shrouded by ominous clouds, and when I stood up again I winced. The bottoms of my feet felt like two big blisters! I looked at Link. With wry expressions we started back. The sealskin boots were superbly waterproof, but our feet were city feet, accustomed to smooth pavements. We had not realized that besides the two pairs of thick socks which we wore, we also needed thick felt insoles and duffles or inner boot liners. The hard, dry ugyuk-skin soles had fooled us. Softened by wet ground and water as we walked, they gave us little protection. We now stepped gingerly, seeking out cooling marshes and shallow water by lakeshores, hour after hour. It became hard to fully appreciate the beauty of the rolling landscape and the multitudes of birds.

Finally, at five in the morning we reached the Anglican mission dock. All was quiet and serene, so we pushed the Thomases' jolly boat (a ship's small boat) into the water and rowed out to the *Nigalik*. It was Charlie's night to work the bilge pump, but he offered to accompany Link to the mission dock with the ship's dinghy, then row him back to the *Nigalik*. On their return, Charlie, having silently observed our careful steps, laconically handed us a bottle of White Liniment. As we applied it to the swollen bottoms of our feet, we thanked him most gratefully, then fell asleep.

In the morning we climbed into the Norseman and headed once again for Mount Pelly, just a few minutes away by air! Link needed to get aerial photos of the beaches and the area between the "big hill" and the bay before we turned west along the south coast of Victoria Island, then south over Coronation Gulf to Coppermine again, where we planned to spend the night.

2 / With George Porter and family on Fox

To Minto Inlet and on

July 21–August 30, 1938

*A*t Coppermine we dined at the Anglican mission with Harold and Edie Webster then returned to the Hudson's Bay Company post house, where we rolled out our sleeping bags on the floor. After breakfast with Mr. and Mrs. Nichols, I went to the Government Radio Station to check my transceiver with Oliver Howey to see if he could receive me. Once a week I had to report on our whereabouts and plans. The signal carried loud and clear.

That government requirement satisfied, we resumed our journey, flying north along the coast, then across Dolphin and Union Strait, over Read Island and on toward the Colville Hills on southwestern Victoria Island. The land there is higher and more irregular than in the vicinity of Cambridge Bay; and the highest peak, Mount Bumpus, or Wivyaruk as the Inuit called it, has an altitude of 1,500 feet. We continued north to Prince Albert Sound, which was full of ice, before turning back to Read Island. As we flew, the compass needle swung aimlessly back and forth, confused by the proximity of the Magnetic Pole, which was about northeast of us. It even pointed south at one point, though we were flying north.

When we reached the south coast of Victoria Island again, we landed at Read Island, where we met Post Manager Ray Ross, his wife Lillian ("Lin"), and baby Raymer ("Buddy"), as well as Mr. Chitty, who had been post manager of Captain Pedersen's Canalaska Company, together with the few Inuit who assisted them. The low island of limestone and dolomitic bedrock is only about two and a half miles long, and we were anxious to get to work looking for fossils to help us establish the age of the rocks. After a quick cup of tea with the Rosses, our pilots Rudy and Dunc departed for the south and Link and I set up our seven-by-seven-foot mountain tent and

Read Island. Hudson's Bay Company warehouse and Inuit.

Read Island. Hudson's Bay Company Post Manager Ray Ross, his wife, Lillian (Lin), and baby, Raymer (Buddy).

Read Island. Mr. Chitty, post manager for Captain C. T. Pedersen's Canalaska Company before Captain Pedersen closed his Arctic operations.

organized our belongings, later joining Ray and Lin for supper. Ray was a friendly, steady chap, with a quiet sense of humor, and Lin bubbled warmly with interest and enthusiasm. They treated us like old friends, which warmed our hearts.

We inquired if they knew of an Inuk who might be willing to go inland with us, as Link was anxious to check that area for eskers, glacial striae on bedrock, or other evidence of former glaciation. We were disappointed to find that all the people were out on the land at either their fishing or hunting camps, but Ray told us that George Porter, whose 35-foot schooner *Fox* was anchored near shore, was planning to leave for Tuktoyaktuk, east of the

July 21–August 30, 1938 ✶ *27*

Mackenzie River Delta, first going as far north as Walker Bay on Victoria Island. He thought George might be willing to take us with him.

George told us his father was a whaling captain, and a friend of Captain Pedersen, whose son Teddy and he went to school at the Jesse Lee Home in Dutch Harbor, Alaska. We told him we had met Captain Pedersen and Teddy at Herschel Island in 1936 and had sailed as crew with them on the MS *Patterson* for their return trip to San Francisco. George had spent a large part of his life Outside and could have stayed, but he liked the free and peaceful life in the North better. After several days of conversations, he said we could come along. We would first be going up the west coast of Victoria Island to Walker Bay, then south along the east coast of Banks Island and across Amundsen Gulf to Baillie Islands, and on to Tuktoyaktuk. We would leave him at Baillie Islands and hope to get a ride back to Coppermine on the *Fort Ross*. We agreed to pay for half the fuel for the *Fox*, and feed ourselves. With that arranged, Link and I spent much of the next week painstakingly chipping fossil shells out of the local limestone dolomitic bedrock. Later identification of the fossils indicated that this bedrock was of Ordovician age, about 450 million years old.

A high wind prevented our departure, but kept the mosquitoes down and gave us time to explore the little island and its beautiful raised beaches. Lin joined us one day, and we took the jolly boat across the bay to pick up some large fossil spiral cephalopods, but by the time we had them loaded a sudden wind was whipping spray off rushing whitecaps. We pushed the jolly boat into the rough water, and Lin and I, each using an oar, tried to keep it headed into the wind while Link worked with the balky old outboard, which refused to start. The waves broke over the side and carried the boat sideways along the shore in spite of our best efforts to hold it steady. Suddenly, a hard blast swung the boat broadside to the waves. Jumping overboard to keep it from being slammed against the rocky shore, we struggled to beach it on a gravel strand.

Soaking wet, we looked up and were relieved and grateful to see Chitty coming across in the cargo boat to our rescue. He said Ray had worried about the old engine. Since Chitty had to lie to about 75 feet offshore to avoid grounding, we, up to our waists in the freezing cold waves, wrestled the jolly boat out far enough to catch the line he threw to us. Numb, with teeth chattering, we scrambled up over the jolly boat's side and he towed us back across the bay.

Ray had watched the action and had a hot rum ready. The glow from its fire quickly warmed us from the inside out, and nothing ever felt better except getting out of our wet clothes. Later, I successfully kept my first radio schedule with Coppermine. We learned that the *Audrey B.*, an erstwhile rumrunner but now operated by traders Bill Storr, Art Watson, and Slim Purcell, was en route to Read Island. When she arrived we found that they were taking Count Gontran de Poncins to Gjoa Haven on King William Island, where he would study the Inuit for a year. An interesting afternoon and evening were spent with them, the Rosses, and Chitty.

The wind, swinging round to the northeast, continued to blow for 24 hours, driving the ice offshore and on out to the westward. In the morning, already August 4, George said we should leave. After a farewell lunch, Lin and Ray took us and our duffle out to the *Fox*. We hoped we would meet them, Chitty, and our new Inuit friends, Lena and Avarana, again the following summer. By noon we had stowed our belongings in the little forecastle on the *Fox*. As there was just one narrow wooden bunk, Link and I decided we would take "turnabout" sleeping on the floor space. Opposite the bunk were two shelves; the lower one was sheathed with galvanized tin, and held our little single-burner Primus stove on which I would cook our meals. Access to the cabin was either through a tiny sliding door to the hold, where the Inuit families were staying, or through the hatch above the center of the cabin.

On board were ten Inuit: George and Martha Porter with Georgie (seven), Mary (three), and Walter (four months); Luke and Lila Maluksuk with three-month-old Andrew James; Pat Kunellik, Nellie's son from Herschel Island, and Joe Malukshuk from Walker Bay. Luke, Pat, and Joe were crew. There were also eighteen sled dogs tied down on the main hatch and in the jolly boat, which was secured athwart the stern. The cool air was calm as we made our way peacefully along the coast to the west, when a sudden blast of shots made us jump. Luke and Pat had both tried to hit a seal's head that appeared in the water. Good-natured laughter and teasing followed, for both men missed. As the evening waned, the northern sky caught fire and the occasional pan of old ice reflected its borrowed glow in the still sea.

We dropped anchor at 4:00 A.M. close in the lee of an island off Cape Kendall, and after a few hours' sleep we awakened to find our world muffled in a drizzly, light fog. All day we wound our way among small floes of old ice, ghostly in the chilling dampness. We headed across the mouth of

Audrey B. with Bill Storr, Art Watson, and Slim Purcell.

Read Island. Lena Kuptana and children.

Georgie Porter *(left)* and Mary Porter on board *Fox.*

Read Island. George Porter with wife Martha and two children, Mary and Georgie. Also helpers Luke and Joseph.

Prince Albert Sound for Ulukhaktok, a prominent bluff, so called by the Inuit because good stone for making blades for the women's knives, or ulus, was found there.

Suddenly, directly ahead of us, a shadowy blackness rose from the sea. A cliff! George turned hard to port but almost immediately we bumped over an almost flat-topped trap reef and saw another phantom cliff looming ominously close ahead. George threw the *Fox* into reverse, and with a great jerk we bumped back over the reef. At dead slow he crept around a large ice floe into deeper water, soon rounding Holman Island as hundreds of gulls screamed down from the invisible cliffs to drive us away.

George's half brother, David Piktukana, had his cabin in the harbor below the cliffs of Ulukhaktok Bluff, now lost in the fog. George said David was not home. His schooner, the *Sea Otter*, was not there, but we all went ashore in the jolly boat and walked around the ice-filled head of the harbor to his house. There were several kamotiks (sledges) and sacks, a barrel of traps and one of sealskins, and various other items lying about. We noticed that some places along the beach seemed bouncy under foot, and George said they were where seals were buried under the gravel to keep until needed. Link and I collected specimens of all the different kinds of stones along the beach and took a sample of the trap which rose in dark, columnar cliffs above the tundra. We found striae on the cliff tops caused by former glaciation. It was 3:00 A.M. when we returned to the *Fox*, but it was still daylight.

When Link and I awakened, we could see the relatively flat top of Ulukhaktok and decided to climb up for a view of how much ice lay to the north. As far as we could see under the low and threatening gray sky, the sea fog was still pretty thick. Then light rain began to fall and we turned back down the slope. A movement caught our eyes and we found a gyrfalcon with a wing broken by gunshot. He was so starved he had hardly enough strength to spread his good wing in protest. He tried to scream, but could not. We felt the kindest thing was to put him out of his misery, which Link did with a quick rap on the head. When he lifted the poor bird it seemed only feathers.

Back on shore we joined Mary, Pat, and Joe, whose sealing efforts were unsuccessful and who were about to row over to David's to dig up a seal for the dogs. One was found, a rope tied around its neck, and with Link's help they dragged it back along the gravelly beach joking and laughing while I

Ulukhaktok, northwestern Victoria Island. Glacially smoothed and striated trap bedrock.

carried Mary to the jolly boat. Pat said the seal had "lost all its clothes" by the time we got there, and indeed it was a hairless, blubbery mess. The wind, whistling down over the bluffs, churned the water. But Pat was strong, and Mary, warm in her white Arctic hare kuletak, fell asleep on my lap as we returned to the *Fox*.

Fog again wrapped our world the next morning, preventing our departure. George brought me a wonderful pair of long "duffles" Martha had made—"Because," he said, "little Mary likes to be with you." While Pat and Luke went off to hunt ptarmigan or Arctic hare and the women to gather roots, Link and I took off to climb up through a gap in the cliffs where a stream tumbled down. Hidden from below we found a lovely little lake cradled between the dark rock walls. An Arctic loon laughed at us from the sparkling water and a pair of screaming gulls dive-bombed us. They were driven off by a hawk which continued the attack, making us constantly duck our heads, until we turned to follow a smaller stream that had cut its way through the cliff face. Another little lake lay at the next level, and when we finally gained the plateau at the top, we were excited and pleased to see that the bedrock, which rose gently inland to large lakes and more cliffs, had been well smoothed and striated by glaciation.

We had a good run north along the coast on the *Fox* the following day. The Inuit traveled when the weather was right, resting and eating when it was convenient. Little or no attention was paid to clock time. Link and I were beginning to adjust to the 24 hours of daylight and seemed to need less sleep. We wanted to observe the land as we passed, so grabbed a little sleep when we could, then hiked cross-country for 10 or 15 hours while the Inuit anchored to visit friends or to sleep.

Our next stop was Ikey Bolt's place in Minto Inlet. There we found Ikey, Diamond Klengenberg, one of Jorgen's brothers, and Tommy Goose, who, like Ikey, was originally from Point Hope, Alaska. As we approached the shore and the Inuits' encampment, the few canvas tents which replaced the winter snow houses seemed to emphasize the emptiness of the vast stretches of land. I reflected that there was no one between us and the North Pole, nor beyond on the Russian side, some 2,800 miles away. For some odd reason the thought brought a feeling of serenity to me.

After warm greetings, Link and I headed inland to check a low trap out-crop, and I was amazed by the rich tundra vegetation and the bright orange lichen on the cliffs. Upon our return we found that Ikey was breaking camp to continue up the Inlet about 20 miles to where the big Kuujjuua River, "full of fish," entered a good harbor. George decided we should go on ahead to save time, so Link and I boarded the *Fox*. Ikey would join us later. Link and I were impressed by the high cliffs, banded by dark trap flows and creamy limestone along both sides of the inlet. Finally, George wound his way around some floe ice and up into the river's mouth, where he nosed into the bank to tie up .

After brief greetings to the Inuit camped there, Link and I took off to in-vestigate a big hill called Niakoqnajuak that rose above the camp. It, too, was formed of bands of trap and limestone, and as we climbed we were happy to find some fossil corals in the limestone. Bags and pockets bulging with specimens, we headed down, reaching the base at midnight as an enor-mous pale gold moon rose over the dark cliffs across the river. Summer was already waning. We were about two degrees of latitude north of Cambridge Bay and the sun had begun to set. All the tents were silent, but Luke and Joe were fixing the long chain to which George's dogs would be tied, and then Tommy Goose appeared, so we visited for a while. When Link and I re-turned to the *Fox* we found she had grounded when the tide went out, which meant we could not leave for several hours.

July 21–August 30, 1938 ✶ *34*

Minto Inlet, northwestern Victoria Island. Ikey Bolt's camp and schooner *Jane B.*

Walker Bay, northwestern Victoria Island. George Porter's *Fox.*

This gave me time for a shampoo, so I got a bucketful of river water, added shampoo powder, and whipped up some good suds. When I knelt by the bucket, as by magic the women appeared and sat in a row on the ground nearby. We all smiled at one another and with this attentive audience, I ducked my head in the bucket of lather. I could hear the startled combined "Ehhh," as they caught their breath. Perhaps, expecting me to wash my shirt, they thought I was going to drown myself! They obviously had never seen anyone put their head in a bucket of sudsy water. Certainly the two very old ladies, who were beautifully tattooed, had never seen a woman behave in this way. As I found out later from Ikey, I was in fact the first Caucasian woman they had ever seen. They all looked relieved as well as amused when I finished rinsing my hair and left the bucket upside down while I rubbed my head dry.

Ikey appeared and asked us all to come for tea in his tent, where we enjoyed delicious bread his wife Etna Klengenberg had made in a pan on a tiny square stove. Link and I were especially interested to meet Natkusiak, or Billy Bankland, as he was widely known. He was famous among his people because he had traveled with and greatly helped Vilhjalmur Stefansson on the Canadian Arctic Expedition of 1913–18. He was interested to hear that we knew Stefansson well, and asked many questions about him. He also talked about some of the journeys he had made with Stef over the ice and on Banks Island more than twenty years earlier. As though on cue, when cups were empty everyone rose and left the tent, another of the Inuit customs we were learning to follow.

Link and I joined a small group of people near the *Fox* and found Pat's bitch sitting on the beach as stiff as a stone carving, soaking wet, eyes closed, her two tiny pups squealing distractedly nearby. Nobody was paying much attention to her or the pups, and when I asked George how she got wet he said, "She got tangled in her chain and a cloth in the water when she tried to get a drink. Nobody knows how long she was there. It's too bad, but it couldn't be helped. She and the pups will die."

My father had taught me to tackle any problem with conviction, so I tried to get her to stand up, but she could not. I squeezed water from her thick coat and rubbed her hard with my hands for about fifteen minutes, after which, on wobbly legs, she came with me, slowly, struggling to breathe. Link helped me get her across the gangplank onto the *Fox* and down into the forecastle, then he ran back to get the two tiny pups. With the Primus stove roaring, we laid her on the floor and continued to rub her briskly with our towels. We stuffed each squealing puppy into a thick wool sock and held them close to the mother's nose, but at first she did not even open her eyes. When their scent and squeals gradually got through to her, she looked at us with an alarmed expression. We stared hard at each other; we smiling and trying to convey warm caring. Gradually her expression softened and, with a sigh, she closed her eyes. Her milk was like slush ice, but we warmed it with our hands and thawed it with gentle manipulation until we could hold the pups' noses against her teats. They suckled frantically, pushing with their little paws through the wool socks, before falling into satisfied sleep. We then pushed both bitch and pups under the bunk and fell asleep ourselves. When we awakened, the little family was fine.

Meanwhile the twenty-six other dogs belonging to Pat and Luke had been tied on the deck. We left Niakoqnajuak and headed for Fort Collinson, the Hudson's Bay Company post at Walker Bay, named in honor of Captain Richard Collinson, who had wintered there in 1851–52 before sailing to the head of Prince Albert Sound then around the coast to Cambridge Bay. Collinson had been searching for the lost Franklin Expedition, as had Captain McClure, sailing on the *Investigator*. Twice they just missed each other, in Prince of Wales Strait and around the southern and western coasts of Banks Island, Collinson unknowingly following McClure.

Charlie Rowan, who was post manager at Walker Bay, was going to exchange posts with Jock Kilgour, the manager at the Baillie Islands post, for which we were also headed. There, the Hudson's Bay Company supply ship, *Fort Ross*, would pick us up and take us back to Coppermine. After the usual friendly welcome and cup of tea, Link and I went out to collect samples of clay and sand at a number of locations above present sea level. We would later examine them for fossil foraminifera, microscopic marine creatures that could provide dates of former sea levels. With sample bags full, we returned to catch up on sleep with George and the others.

Awake again, Link and I joined Pat and Luke, who were about to cross the harbor to obtain water at a small river. We left them there and climbed up Flagstaff Hill, continuing down across a beautiful valley. The floor of the valley was a large area of nonsorted nets, a form of patterned ground intermediate between a circle and a polygon and lacking a stony border. We then climbed up some rugged cliffs. Two pairs of rough-legged hawks swooped down at us when we neared their aeries, in one of which we could

Walker Bay. George Porter's post.

Walker Bay. Nonsorted nets, a form of patterned ground.

Walker Bay. Rough-legged hawk nestlings.

Banks Island, inland from De Salis Bay on southeastern coast. The author beside mudflow from slumped hillside with buried ancient ice core.

see three young nestlings. We also saw five snowy owls. Ptarmigan and lemmings were the principal food for both birds as well as for Arctic fox. Lemmings breed very rapidly until an area can no longer support the population, which then crashes. This causes a decrease in the number of foxes, owls, and hawks. The tundra vegetation was fairly lush and in some protected spots against south-facing cliffs, where a stream cascaded down into a valley, the willows, rather than the usual six inches to two feet high, were as tall as six feet at the point where the branch ends turned up, having first run along the ground for two or three feet. A veritable jungle, we thought!

At each stream we knelt and drank the delicious cold, clear water, and in the warm sunlight, by a bounding cascade, we enjoyed pilot biscuits and a can of grapefruit. A little Lapland longspur dropped down for a quick drink, eyed us with a surprised "peep," and flew off. Refreshed, we scrambled and climbed up over big broken blocks of columnar trap, piled in a jumble against the cliff face like ruins of an ancient temple. At the top lay a tundra plateau which led us to yet another set of cliffs to scale. Beautiful high country spread out before us inland and southeast towards Minto Inlet, beckoning us to explore its secrets, but there was no time. Finally, happy to have found more glacial striations on polished trap surfaces and many areas of thick tundra, we headed back, wearily reaching the *Fox* at 4:00 A.M. Twenty-four hours of daylight tends to ruin one's sense of time.

As we traveled west then south along the Banks Island coast, Link and I slept, ate, and slept again until we arrived at De Salis Bay on Banks Island, where George anchored. While the others slept, Link and I rowed the jolly boat to a long, low, pebbly spit along which we walked, finally reaching higher tundra-covered ground. There were low hills in the distance, which we decided to investigate. However, they were higher and farther away than they had appeared. Disillusioned after several hours' walking, we had to turn back toward the boat. Making a loop, we came to a place where half a small hill had slipped away, revealing massive blue ice. Mud was still flowing from the base of the break. The top of the ice was about five feet below the surface, and Link decided it might date back to the time of the last major glaciation. How old was it, we wondered, as we thoughtfully chewed some chips of ice. Perhaps ten thousand years?

When we reached the long spit again we were alarmed to see the enormous tracks of a polar bear, which had apparently followed us after we started inland. We looked back somewhat apprehensively and quickened our pace, stooping to give as low a profile as possible lest the bear was still looking for us. A bear ashore with no ice in sight is likely to be a hungry one. It didn't take Link long to row out to the *Fox*.

An hour later George pulled out, heading south across Amundsen Gulf toward Cape Parry on the mainland. From there we would head west to Baillie Island, where George would leave us to wait for the Hudson's Bay Company supply ship *Fort Ross*, while he continued on to Tuktoyaktuk. As we rounded Nelson Head, named by McClure in honor of Lord Nelson, we ran into a hard westerly blow which strengthened rapidly, the sea running higher and higher. Pat's two dogs were tied at the bow, and as the *Fox* slammed down from the crest of a very big wave, Jack's collar broke and he was flung overboard. When George shouted, I yelled, "We can't leave him," and Luke somehow brought the *Fox* about aiming to come alongside the dog's big black head, which appeared and disappeared in the wild waves.

George lay flat on the deck by the bow, Pat amidships, and Link at the stern. The bow rose too high and also the midships, but the stern was down at the critical moment and Link got a hold on the scruff of Jack's neck. One moment hanging alongside, the next submerged, the soaking 150-pound dog was heavier than Link, who, clinging desperately, began to slip over the low gunwale. Pat grabbed Link's legs, I flung myself on Pat's legs, George scrambled over us all and grabbed hold of Jack too, and together he and Link heaved the great dog aboard.

As we had with the bitch, we squeezed water from Jack's rough fur, then dragged the stiffened dog into the wheelhouse. I grabbed our towels and began rubbing while Link started the Primus stove, and when Jack's fur was pretty dry we wrapped him in a kuletak. Gradually his shivering subsided, his breathing sounded more normal, and he opened his eyes for a moment. We kept him bundled up while he slept and when he wakened he seemed none the worse for his terrifying experience. I will never know how Luke was able, in those wild seas, to bring the *Fox* alongside Jack without running over him. A master helmsman!

The storm continued to toss us violently about during the few night hours, while we vainly tried to sleep. How long could the schooner endure the pounding she was taking? Each time she came over a wave crest and crashed down into the trough, her ribs and planks made ominous cracking sounds, unlike the usual creaks and groans when running in rough weather.

At last the storm subsided, but our Brunton compass had been flung over-board at some point and George did not recognize the coast and land that lay ahead. He figured we had been blown many miles east, so he steered west and by evening we came to a little harbor where he remembered riding out a storm some years before. We were in Darnley Bay south of Letty Harbour, about 45 miles east of where we should have been.

Everyone needed a good, quiet sleep, so George anchored. Unobserved while we slept, a thick fog crept in, holding us captive for 36 hours. When the fog thinned somewhat, we ran north along the coast, around Cape Parry to the Booth Islands and on southwest across Franklin Bay to where the mouth of the Horton River cuts through the Smoking Mountains. (These mountains had been smoking for as long as anyone remembered, but no one knows when their bituminous material caught fire.) George dropped anchor near Silas Kangegana's house. Old Kutakok, a respected shaman, was visiting and they welcomed us warmly.

It soon became obvious that they had been enjoying "home brew," the mystery of its creation having been learned, ironically, from the priest's brewing of sacramental wine. The old wife, who had earlier been married to a whaler, mistook me for her older daughter, Margaret, who had gone Outside to become a nurse. Smiling broadly, exposing her even teeth worn down by years of chewing the tough edges of seal and caribou skins to soften them, she beckoned me to sit beside her on the polar-bear skin. She patted my head and spoke to me, repeating the name Margaret over and over as she rolled a cigarette for me from loose tobacco. I tried to explain that I was not Margaret but, not understanding English, she only smiled and patted me again and again. I have always hoped it comforted her to think that Margaret had returned, if only for a brief visit.

Late in the morning George decided we should continue on our way north along the shore in spite of a light fog. Old Kutakok joined us for a visit, planning to walk back the 50 or more miles across the tundra from Baillie Island. There was a lot of ice, which became thicker as we proceeded. George decided to tie up against the beach for a short stop so Link and I could go ashore to examine an area where the bituminous material in the slopes was no longer smoking. Minerals, released by the heat of burning, had stained the burned and crumbled rock and clayey material varying shades of orange and red, and there were also severely contorted yellow and black layers which were very striking. We collected samples of each type

Mainland coast, Franklin Bay. Smoking mountains and Silas Kangegana's place.

West coast of Franklin Bay. On board *Fox*, Link trying to discern land through fog.

while George gathered chunks of the red material, which the women used to stain strips of wolverine and sealskins for decorating kuletaks and kamiks.

As we continued on our way, the ice and fog became thicker until we could no longer see the shore. George chugged along slowly, warily winding in and out around the pans of ice, trying to avoid the small ones which could bend or break the propeller shaft or blades and hoping the big floe would not press in against the shore and crush us. Link climbed up the little mast to get a better view when George thought we must be nearing Cape Bathurst. He did not want to enter the Beaufort Sea, where we might be caught in heavier ice. Suddenly Link called down that he thought he could see a darkness that might be land. Listening intently, we heard the faint howling of dogs. George headed for the sound, and soon we dimly detected the low sand spit of Baillie Island. Again and again he sounded the boat whistle and finally the welcome, if dismal, sound of a foghorn drifted through the icy fog.

Cruising along beside a big floe, we rounded the end of the spit and could just make out the buildings and Charlie Rowan's schooner, the *Adanac*, looming as ghostly forms through the fog. Charlie, Jock Kilgour, a husky Highlands Scot, and his apprentice Art Figgures, a slim young Canadian, came out in the dinghy to welcome us and take us ashore.

The Hudson's Bay Company post house was larger than usual, having an attic room as well as two bedrooms, living room, and spacious kitchen. With a broad smile and a twinkle in his eyes, Jock invited us to occupy the second bedroom as long as we liked. There were also the store, and large warehouse, a small, old warehouse and workshop, plus two deserted RCMP buildings strung out along the spit. Beyond them was the house in which Tunaomik, the post helper, and his family lived.

After tea, I packed up our rock and soil specimens for George to send south from Tuktoyaktuk, while Link and the others loaded the *Adanac* with freight for Walker Bay. That was lucky, because morning dawned, still foggy, but increasingly windy. The schooners began pitching wildly and Jock said they must be taken to the lee of one of the higher islands, where deeper water would prevent their bumping on the shallow bottom. Charlie rowed out to the *Adanac* while Jock rowed George and Link to the *Fox*. Climbing aboard from the jolly boats was a challenge, because the big waves first lifted, then dropped, the little boats. Finally each was made fast

Baillie Island. Hudson's Bay Company post buildings after the big storm.

Baillie Island. Hudson's Bay Company Post Manager Jock Kilgour and Link, after the big storm.

astern but almost immediately George's jolly boat, yanked up and down with the wildly pitching schooner, broke its line and drifted rapidly along the shoreline toward the open sea. Then the other jolly boat snapped its line. Luckily they were blown inshore close enough to the beach for us to splash out to catch and then drag them to the top of the beach. There were also tense moments on the schooners. The *Fox*'s engine faltered, gasped, quit, then fired again. Jock, who was in the rigging, trying to guide the boats to safe anchorage, was nearly knocked off when an outsize wave slammed over the deck.

Tunaomik joined Art and me as the storm gained strength. Two months earlier a storm had pushed the sea right up to the walls of the house, so Jock had told Art to take all precautions. We secured all loose objects around the post, reset the dog line and dogs by the house, and then prepared to haul in the three 100-foot-long fishnets. We worked feverishly as the storm increased in ferocity. The wind-whipped clouds of spray rose from the roaring waves, which broke higher and higher up the beach and beyond, washing across the spit at low places. When we began to pull in a fishnet it was enormously heavy, and we discovered that the storm had driven a school of big herring into the nets, now choked with fish. We held on to the top backing line of the nets to keep from being knocked over by the waves and waded out up to our waists in the frigid water, wrapping our arms around sections of struggling fish and net as we went. Lifting, heaving, dragging, we finally got the three nets, overburdened with more than 400 big fish, to the top of the beach, where we left them beyond the reach, we hoped, of the reclaiming sea. By then it was after midnight. We had been soaking wet and half frozen for hours.

We thanked Tunaomik for his great help and then poured the water from our boots at the door, hung our soaking attigis in the entry, and dripped though the kitchen to the bedrooms to look for dry clothing, suddenly realizing how weary we were. Dry again, we found that a hot cup of tea gave us sufficient energy to attack another problem we had discovered as we came in. Just before our arrival, Art had put bread dough on the range shelf to rise. It had overrisen and oozed over the pan edge to pour down onto the hot range top. During the hours we were battling the raging sea, the dough had quietly burned into mounds with cemented black carbon bottoms and sticky tops. It took a while, but eventually we got the stuff

Captain R. J. "Shorty" Sommers on board Hudson's Bay Company supply ship *Fort Ross*.

Victoria Island, Wollaston Peninsula. Mount Bumpus.

Victoria Island. Link on the summit of Mount Bumpus.

scraped off the range top and at last fell onto our beds. The wild storm subsided; the sea retreated without the fish; and Link, Jock, and the rest returned from their relative shelter behind the higher island to anchor again
near the post. Soon after sandwiches George departed for Tuktoyaktuk.

The *Fort Ross* appeared briefly, but vanished to the east, as the seas were
still running too high to anchor. In silent despair we hoped she would find
shelter behind Cape Bathurst and return to discharge the freight and pick
us up. To our relief she did so the next day, and as soon as the wind abated
that night, the men hustled Link and me, with our few belongings, out to
the *Adanac*. Although it was still rough, Charlie managed to bring the
schooner alongside the *Fort Ross*. As we came over the rail from the Jacob's
ladder, Captain R. J. "Shorty" Sommers welcomed us aboard. He then introduced us to the officers and crew—a fine bunch—several of whom were
from the coastal towns of Newfoundland. The Reverend George Nicholson,
a quiet, pleasant man, was en route to relieve the Reverend Harold Webster
at Coppermine while he was Outside on leave.

July 21–August 30, 1938 ✱ *48*

We returned to the post for the night, and in the morning the *Fort Ross* anchored closer to shore to offload freight and load the post's baled fox skins. When we thanked Jock for his warm hospitality, he said, "Come visit me at the Walker Bay post next year." At noon we steamed east. Soon we encountered the same great ice floe we had met while on the *Fox*. Since it stretched as far as we could see, it forced the captain to make a long loop south around it, then north again to Cape Parry before crossing Amundsen Gulf. We reached Walker Bay again that evening and Link and I took off for the nearer hills.

It was hard to believe that autumn had come during our brief absence, but it was August 26, and snow would fly soon. The tundra was now a blazing carpet of scarlet, deep red, yellow, and orange leaves woven together in breathtaking beauty. We walked in silence, absorbing the deep serenity of that lovely place, and I wished that we might make our base there another year. The continuing search for more signs of ancient glaciation was rewarded by our finding striated bedrock and glacial till. All too soon it was 2:00 A.M. The sudden, strident blast of the ship's whistle shocked us into hurrying back to continue our journey.

Twenty-four hours later we arrived at Read Island. When we went ashore with the cargo scow to see everyone, I was touched to find that Lena Kuptana had made a beautiful pair of short blue and white stroud (tight-woven wool cloth) "visiting" kamiks, with white-tanned sealskin soles for me. Although she had never measured my feet, they fit perfectly, so accurate is an Inuit's eye. We also received a radio message that Wop May and pilot Rudy Huess were bringing Ken Muir, the managing engineer at Camalaeron gold mine near Yellowknife, to Coppermine. It was arranged via radio that they would come to Read Island and fly us inland to examine Mount Bumpus and look at some pingos, large volcano-shaped mounds of soil-covered ice, formed in part by hydrostatic pressure of water.

In the morning Wop, Rudy, and Ken flew in, and after tea and scones we took off for the inland hills, landing on a lake at the foot of Mount Bumpus. It was too shallow for the plane to reach shore, so we doffed boots and socks, rolled up our pants, and waded through the freezing water. We teased one another about our "boiled lobster" legs. Then, with boots on once more, we hiked over swampy stretches of tundra, grateful the mosquitoes were no longer biting. Mount Bumpus has many shoulders, then steeper slopes up to 35 degrees which lead to narrow ridges, and finally the bouldery summit. But this "mountain" is only some 1,500 feet high, a glacial deposit composed primarily of sandy sediments with some cobbles and boulders, but we saw no evidence of till. On the summit we all built a large cairn to commemorate the day, then headed back to the plane.

When we reached Coppermine, Mr. and Mrs. Deacon kindly asked us all to join them for a delicious Arctic char dinner and a pleasant evening of conversation. The Nicholsons took us back to the post for the night and, because Link had decided that we would return in 1939, they suggested that we store our tent, outer garments, extra dehydrated food, and anything else we wished, with them. Weary, we slept well.

Satisfied that Victoria Island had been glaciated, Link was also pleased with the samples of bedrock and erratics that we had collected, hoping to trace the origin of the latter to areas on the mainland. This would strengthen the premise that the continental ice had indeed crossed over onto the islands. In the morning Rudy called all aboard, and we said good-bye until the following year.

Link felt sure that Professor Flint would be interested and pleased with our findings, and we planned to return to Victoria Island in 1939.

3 / Fossil hunting on Read Island
With Ikey Bolt on Jane B. to Minto Inlet
July 20–September 13, 1939

*W*ith the arrival of May 1939, I ordered our dehydrated food, renewed first aid and medical supplies, and readied our woolen clothing. Link checked his instruments and other equipment. We both checked and rechecked everything, to be sure nothing had been forgotten for our new sojourn in the Arctic. The birds would have been long in residence when we reached Coppermine again in July. Link had asked Preston Cloud, a good-natured, stout-hearted, and highly competent fellow graduate student to join us. Pres was interested in all facets of Earth history, but was majoring in invertebrate paleontology and looking forward to joining us in the collection of the fossil remains of the spineless forerunners of modern shell-fish. He rapidly became known coast to coast and abroad, his outstanding work bringing him many honors in the coming years.

Bad weather over the Arctic coast delayed us at Yellowknife and again at Eldorado radium mine, where we met Father Roger Buliard, who was en route to the new Roman Catholic mission at Ulukhaktok. The ceiling lifted at Coppermine in late afternoon, and we reached there in the bright evening. Three busy days later Pres, Link, and I joined Trader Slim Semmler, his wife Agnes, and their two children to accompany another trader, "Chips" Leonard, to Read Island on his 50-foot schooner *Chinook*. The Semmlers and Chips had been trading with the Inuit for many years and we were happy to have the chance to be with them. At Read, Post Manager Ray Ross, Lin, and Buddy, as well as Henry Jensen, who traded for Slim, came out in the jolly boats to meet us, and it really felt like coming home. Pres, Link, and I set up our two tents near the Hudson's Bay Company post house and spent several days happily chipping fossils out of the bedrock for our separate collections.

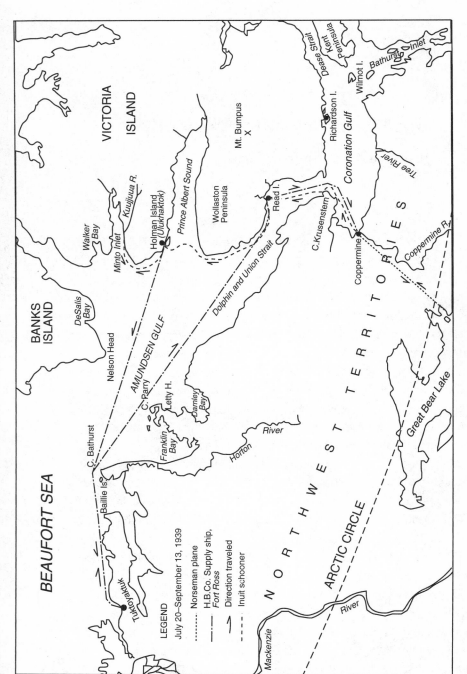

MAP 4. July 20–September 13, 1939

Yellowknife, N.W.T., Canada. Link and Tahoe.

As we were saying goodnight to Lin and Ray one evening, Ray suggested we sleep in the warehouse because a "big blow" was expected. Pres shrugged and retired in his tent anyway. He had experienced plenty of "big blows" as a hand on commercial cargo ships, but Link and I opted to sleep in the warehouse. The gale "made" during the night, hurling a flood of rain before it. Cozy under a roof we slept soundly, blissfully unaware of what was happening. When we stepped out in the morning we were amazed to see our tent lying in a puddled, lumpy heap. Its pole had snapped. Pres's tent stood in a pool of water. We quickly pulled open the drawstring entry and found him, just rousing, afloat on his air mattress, all his possessions lying soggily around him.

Ray and Lin came out and we soon had all of Pres's possessions spread on the stony gravel to dry in the sun. He had brought hundreds of sheets of special paper to wrap fragile fossil specimens. We placed a small stone on top of each piece to keep them from blowing away, and the area looked as though the storm had blown through a paper mill.

Avarana, Lena Kuptana, and several other Inuit had arrived with Ikey Bolt on the *Jane B.* about five in the morning. They were still in a state of shock from almost being swamped during the storm. Ikey planned to return to Ulukhaktok in about a week and said we could accompany him, to work in that area. That gave us extra time at Read to collect more fossils from the bedrock and gather further geological data on Read and several other small islands, before heading north. The intermittent fog withdrew, giving us three perfect days with long, still, peaceful evenings. Then we were off to the north at last and made good time along the coast.

When still a long way from the tiny Nunaqiak Islands, Ikey said, "There is something whitish on the dark rocks ahead. I think it's a polar bear." Though I strained my eyes, it was all I could do to see the islands. Once again I was impressed by an Inuk's eyesight, which always seemed phenomenal to me, especially considering that I am farsighted. As we drew closer, the white spot proved to be a mother polar bear and cub. Obligingly they took to the water between the two tiny islands, and we circled around them so Link could take photographs. The mother, roaring, tried to make her cub follow her instead of floating motionless, staring at this strange apparition pursuing them. Finally, she swung around and gave him a hard cuff on the head. Instantly he grabbed her stubby tail in his mouth and, hanging on, paddled furiously behind as she sped off with great, powerful strokes. A big male bear was also on the island, but he had wisely kept his distance from mother and cub lest she attack him. Occasionally, a male will kill a cub.

Later, with no ice or land anywhere near, we came upon a bear with a seal in its mouth. This surprised us, but polar bears do catch seals in open water. Ikey said they float quietly until a curious seal comes close enough for them to grab it. As we neared the Albert Islands just east of Ulukhaktok, we saw another bear. We were all so busy looking at it nobody noticed the reef until we were on it! Fortunately, it was fairly smooth and, like the *Fox* the previous year, the *Jane B.* just bounced over it, loosening a few seams so that she leaked a little more than before. It was 11:00 P.M. when we reached Ulukhaktok harbor to find the *Fox* at the beach with our friends Jock Kilgour, Owen Hanson (Jock's new apprentice), George Porter and his family, Father Lucien Delalonde, OMI, and Father Raymond de Coccola, OMI (known as Father Raymond), a boy named Moses, and another boy. We all

Read Island. Ikey Bolt's schooner *Jane B.*

On board *Jane B.*, Ikey Bolt and the author. (Preston Cloud photograph.)

Polar bear and cub swimming between the very small Nunagiak Islands off the western coast of Wollaston Peninsula, Victoria Island.

had a good time trying to catch up on each other's experiences since our meeting the previous year. It was four in the morning when we turned in.

Taking advantage of the endless sunlight during the next week, Pres, Link, and I covered a fair bit of the beautiful area, collecting fossil seashells up to 250 feet above present sea level. This again was evidence of rebound of the land after retreat of an ice sheet.

Pres was also busy collecting small marine invertebrates. One day he brought me an enamel basin filled with water and said, "Please draw whatever you see in the water." I could see nothing, and asked what the joke was. "No, please," he said, shaking his head earnestly, "there *is* something in the water. I *want* it to be a certain thing so much that I don't trust my own eyes. Please, just draw the shadow." Pres handed me a notebook and pencil. Looking harder, I saw the very pale shadow of what appeared to be the anatomy of something, so I drew that, having no idea what it might be. When Pres looked at my sketch he was jubilant. It was a tiny ctenophore, a sea animal with an oval, transparent body, which he had hoped to find.

The Hudson's Bay Company had decided to move its Walker Bay Post south to Ulukhaktok, thus saving time and fuel for the *Fort Ross*. It would also be more convenient for the Inuit who lived along Minto Inlet and trapped mostly on the land between there and Prince Albert Sound. Accordingly, Jock Kilgour and his new apprentice, Owen Hanson, had closed the Walker Bay post and moved to Ulukhaktok. They had chosen an east cove site as the best location for the new post and awaited the arrival of the *Fort Ross*. She appeared August 16.

Where had the week flown? This was her first visit to Ulukhaktok and everyone was worried because the Inuit said there was a reef somewhere, but no one seemed sure just where. We went out to the ship with Ikey on the *Jane B.* and it was really good to see Skipper "Shorty" Sommers and the others again. Post Manager E. J. "Scotty" Gall was returning with his bride Isabel, from Scotland. Scotty was a wiry, warm, and exuberant Scot, who had first come north as a lad in 1923 and had worked for the Hudson's Bay Company in the western Arctic ever since, except for one year when he was with the northern Aerial Mineral Exploration Company. He was widely traveled, a real northerner who knew the country and could handle just about any situation that arose in that land, where self-reliance and swift reactions are essential. Isabel was a lovely, warm Scottish lady and was looking forward to learning all about "life in the North." I did not know until later that she had been a folk song concert singer. They were on their way to Cambridge Bay to relieve the Milnes at the post. Also on board was young Phyllis McKinnon, en route to the post at Perry River to visit her fiancée, Angus Gavin, who was post manager there. She was a vivacious person, full of fun.

After discussion with Captain Sommers it was decided the new Post should be established where Jock and Owen had camped, as it was a good shore for unloading supplies. Later it was christened King's Bay by Father Buliard. Suddenly the unaccustomed roar of an aircraft was heard. The twin-motored Beechcraft flown by our friendly pilot Harry Winnie and mechanic Dunc McLaren brought the Hudson's Bay Company fur trade manager, Mr. R. C. Cheshire, and several others to look over the area and approve a site for the new post. They all agreed to the suggested one, and took off again an hour later.

Jock had come out from the west harbor in the *Fox* to transfer the Company's baled fox skins from Walker Bay to the *Fort Ross*. When that was

Ulukhaktok-Holman area, Victoria Island. Hudson's Bay Company supply ship *Fort Ross*.

Ulukhaktok-Holman area, Victoria Island. Fellow graduate student Preston Cloud, Tahoe, Link, and Ikey Bolt on *Jane B*.

completed, we joined him to go ashore at about 2:00 A.M. and had just pulled away from the side of the ship when the *Fox*'s old engine died. Jock tried frantically to get it started as a strong wind blasted down from the eastern bluffs. Helpless, we drifted rapidly toward the rocky shore. The bow anchor was thrown out but did not hold, and in a few moments the *Fox* was pounding broadside on the big rocks. Moses grabbed the gangplank and I a long boat hook and leaning on these we strained against the rocks trying to keep the *Fox* from pounding too hard. Link jumped into the dinghy and, dragging our stern line, rowed out to the *Fort Ross*, struggling against the wind-whipped waves. When he made it, he, Shorty, the mate, Chitty, and Mr. Copland hauled on the line, finally dragging the *Fox* off the rocks then slowly, slowly, until we were alongside and safely tied by 5:00 A.M. It was a close call, and after a hot cup of coffee we all thankfully found our sleeping bags.

The *Fox*'s engine finally responded the following morning. The *Fort Ross* pulled away, leaving a Scottish master carpenter and all the material for the new post house. Link, Pres, and I looked at the mass of materials and offered our services to assist in whatever way possible. We all knew how to handle tools. The carpenter looked at us and the stacks of lumber and put us to work. We learned a lot—about digging postholes in permafrost; setting posts, joists, and beams; laying underflooring; putting on outside and interior siding; as well as insulating the walls. There were many layers of wood and insulating materials in the floors, walls, ceilings, and roof, and the windows were triple-glazed, all to keep the house warm while conserving coal.

The big, iron coal range would be both stove and central heating. We learned how to place shingles properly and to lay hardwood, tongue-and-groove flooring, placing each nail at the correct angle and point. The carpenter always knew if we were about to make a mistake, though I don't know how he did his own job and kept track of us too. Some of it was hard work, but we enjoyed it all, especially the opportunity to help those who were always so helpful to us. I was grateful that my father had taught me how to use hand tools. I also became "cook's helper," in Jock's nearby cook tent.

When things were far enough along so the carpenter could handle the rest, Link, Pres, and I resumed the scientific work. We hiked inland to the north around Ukpilik Lake, then climbed up through a break in the rugged,

Ulukhaktok-Holman area, Victoria Island. George Porter's *Fox* at beach. Lumber and materials for completing the new Hudson's Bay Company post house and other buildings, plus the food supply for well over a year and trade goods.

dark cliffs. Link and I took samples of the bedrock, and we all looked for the elusive fossils, erratics, and glacially scoured bedrock. Pres confessed that he felt humbled by the limitless space and beauty surrounding us. We knew the feeling. The lakes, holding patches of intensely blue sky, and the gentle slopes, painted with the deep red, scarlet, yellow, and gold of early autumn in the Arctic, were backed by other massive battlements of trap splashed with orange lichens. It was already mid-August.

That evening, although the fog had rolled in, George and Ikey decided they would head north along the coast together as far as Minto Inlet. George, with two other Inuit, Tommy Goose and Jimmy, would continue in the *Fox* to Walker Bay to take down the warehouse, which was to be rebuilt at the new post, and they would also transport the remaining coal. We would go up Minto Inlet with Ikey to his place at Sikosuilak to pick up some sleds and sheet iron he had been keeping for the new Catholic mission at King's Bay. One of our interests in visiting "Sikosuilak" was to take photographs of Natkusiak, explorer Stefansson's helper, and his family.

Stef had been greatly interested when we had told him the previous winter that Natkusiak was fine. Stef had great admiration for him and appreciation for all his assistance during the Canadian Arctic Expedition.

Even though it was 3:30 A.M. when we arrived, Link, Pres, and I hiked out to hunt for fossils in nearby limestone outcrops, but they were barren. When we returned, we found Andrew and Bob Klengenberg, who had heard the boats and walked over from their camp to visit. Later that day after supper we visited Natkusiak, who talked about his travels with Stefansson and was happy to hear that Stef was still living. Still later we continued up the Inlet on the *Jane B.* to the camp at Kuujjuua River by "Niakoknajuak," where, among others, we met several elders—Onayak, Annie Ottoayuk, and her husband old Jack Nukatlak. He told us that his older brother had remembered Collinson's Expedition, which had wintered in Walker Bay (1851–52) when searching for Sir John Franklin's Expedition, which disappeared after 1845. Ikey lined up Etna's brothers and their families, other relatives, and family connections for a photograph.

We hiked to locations Link and I had not visited the previous year, searching, as always, for traces of glaciation and fossils. The river valley was a riot of autumn color against the dark brown and cream of the cliffs, and we were sorry to leave when Ikey said it was time to return to Ulukhaktok, but grateful to have visited with Natkusiak and the others in that lovely place. As we pushed off in the jolly boat, we suddenly realized with alarm that the *Jane B.* was moving slowly out toward the inlet, away from us. The tide was running out, and she had pulled her anchor. Ikey bent to his oars, laughing, and we soon overtook her.

"How far would she have gone alone, if we had waited another hour," he wondered aloud, laughing again. We were learning that when an unfortunate incident befell him, an Inuk simply said, *ayorama* or *momiyana*—too bad, it can't be helped—and carried on, often with laughter. A wise approach to problems, we thought.

Upon our return to Ulukhaktok we happily went back to work on the house, which had progressed during our absence, and continued to work during the following week before our departure. Father Delalonde and Father Raymond from Coppermine were helping Father Buliard and Brother Tesnière build the new Catholic mission church-house and warehouse. We were glad to see that they were making good progress, for light snow flurries had already begun. When we climbed the cliffs to the top of the plateau

Minto Inlet, Victoria Island. Link with Natkusiak, well known as Billy Banksland, who assisted explorer Vilhjalmur Stefansson during part of the 1913–18 Canadian Arctic Expedition.

Minto Inlet, Victoria Island. Natkusiak (Billy Banksland), his young daughter Lila, his wife Topsy Ekeuna with baby George Tapkarluk, and Molly Goose, wife of Tommy Goose, with baby Simone.

Minto Inlet, Victoria Island. Preston Cloud and Link discussing a geological problem.

Minto Inlet, Victoria Island. Onayak.

Minto Inlet, Victoria Island. Sketch of Annie Ottoayuk, wife of Nukatlak.

Minto Inlet, Victoria Island. (Left to right) Ikey Bolt; Henry Aolatuk, wife Eva Mapauk; Joan Okalik, daughter of Henry Aolatuk and wife of Andrew Klengenberg, with adopted daughter, Martha or Martina Aviligak, who was Diamond Klengenberg's daughter; Andrew Klengenberg with William Kaklon, son of Henry Aolatuk; Elsie Alekamik with baby Evakluk, and her husband Malgokok with son Appiana; Bob Klengenberg, his wife Lily Akanasiak with baby Akepgak; young Margaret Tagik Malgokok and little Roy Ennuktalik Malgokok; Diamond Klengenberg.

Ulukhaktok-Holman, Victoria Island. Work progressing on the new Hudson's Bay Company post house.

the country was glistening—an enchanting sight with all the bright yellow, red, and orange leaves of willow and other tundra vegetation fairly glowing through the sparkling coverlet of snow. Later in the evening, when much of the snow had melted, the moon slipped out through scudding, dark clouds spilling silver over the wet rocks, then vanished. What a sternly beautiful corner of the world it is.

Autumn had indeed arrived. The fish had begun to run and the seals were coming near. The hunters had been busy and lucky. We were all enjoying fine dinners of delicious fried seal liver, boiled seal meat, and fried or boiled Arctic char, surely the finest of all fish. Pres, Link, and I were grateful to share in this bounty. Far superior to our own usual dehydrated meals!

Suddenly it was September and the *Fort Ross* was again pulling into the bay. Everyone rushed about, then out on the *Jane B.* to welcome her. As I climbed up the Jacob's ladder over the side of the *Fort Ross* to greet Captain Shorty Sommers, he took my hand and said, "I should put you in irons!" He was noted for his straight-faced teasing, so I laughed and said, "That's a fine greeting!"

"Canada is at war," he continued somberly, "and you have given aid to the enemy by breaking radio silence." I was horrified. Not knowing that war had been declared, I had repeatedly tried to keep my "sked" with Coppermine. Everyone could hear my call, even though it supposedly could carry only 500 miles at most. But there had been no interference in the silent air. Years later I learned that I had been heard "loud and clear" in both Alaska and Greenland! "Germany is attacking Poland," Shorty continued, "and both England and France are standing by their word, and Canada, together with them, has declared war on Germany."

We were aghast. It seemed incomprehensible that mankind was once again to indulge in a horrible bloodbath.

The offloading of freight was a somber affair, the usual banter and laughter missing as we were wrapped in our own thoughts. Who would enlist? Who would be called? That night we heard on the ship's wireless that Australia and New Zealand were also standing beside England. An English steamship with 1,200 passengers had been sunk. The United States had not yet declared war, but we felt sure that unless it came to an immediate end, we too would be involved. My heart sank. I looked at Link. Poor Owen, Jock's apprentice, had to leave with the *Fort Ross,* for as a reserve officer he would be among the first to be called. He was. Owen told us his brother was with the Air Force and his father had been shell-shocked and gassed in World War I—"The War to End Wars."

Rain shrouded the land as we pulled away, reflecting the sadness in our hearts—sadness for the horror that had been let loose and sadness at leaving dear friends we might never see again. The *Jane B.* followed us out to the mouth of the harbor before turning back to the new Hudson's Bay Company post. As we steamed slowly away, the little new house and white tent came into view again between the two high points, and as we watched a rainbow grew up from the bay, arching over the new post for a few moments. A good omen, we hoped, as the air suddenly was filled with snowflakes.

The *Fort Ross* steamed steadily, reaching Tuktoyaktuk a day and a half later. There she loaded cargo for Read Island and Coppermine. While that was in progress, Owen introduced me to the art of fur baling. It was quite a process. The baler was a contraption about seven feet high, three feet long, and two and a half feet wide. It had a solid floor, the ends of vertical two-by-fours spaced a few inches apart, a top of three horizontal two-by-fours with the center one reinforced, and sides of two removable four-and-a-half-foot gates. Two thicknesses of hessian, a closely woven tough burlap—full width and about six feet long—were stretched along the bottom and up the ends and sides, and tacked at the folded corners, forming an oblong receptacle. We laid the fox skins in, three across, tails over backs, and two deep until they filled the hessian. The gates were put in place and the rest of the skins laid in on top of the others. Two more pieces of hessian were placed over the furs and tucked down at the ends and sides between the gates. A solid cover of wood was laid on top. Several large blocks of wood and a very heavy jack were then put on, and the pressure applied by winding up the jack.

It required considerable "push" to get the skins squashed down to form a tight, solid bale. When that was accomplished, the gates were removed and the top and bottom pieces of hessian were sewn tightly together with waxed twine, using a special lockstitch, a process rough on the fingers. Three pieces of half-inch rope were then slipped around the stitched bale and drawn as tight as possible. After that, the pressure was removed, the bale taken out, the ends tightly sewn, and another rope drawn fast around the bale lengthwise. All the twine ends were fastened with special metal seals. The job was finished by sewing a red label with the London destination on one end of the bale, and by painting on both ends in black paint: the Outfit number (270 = 1939), Post number, "Hudson's Bay Company," number of foxes (about 100), and weight. The Company's Outfit number 1 was 1670. My hands were sore, but I was pleased to have learned the art of baling fur and to have been able to help Owen.

Together we managed to make three and a half bales before sitting down to a delicious caribou meat supper. Starting at seven the next morning we finally finished making eight bales of 814 skins by midafternoon, in time for Owen's departure for Aklavik aboard the *Saucy Jane*.

Since Chief Engineer John Piercey was busy helping with the freight, I had a great time putting a high polish on the engine room brass for him. We sailed for Read Island about 4:00 A.M. The second day, I developed a severe case of what I thought was ptomaine poisoning. Four awful days later I longed to hurry up and die. Although he was worried he might lead me astray, Shorty opened the opium pills in the ship's first aid box. They knocked me out—and tightened me up. Pres and Bill Starks suffered from milder cases. "It might have been caused by flies walking on the caribou hindquarters while they were hanging in the open air at Tuktoyaktuk," the cook suggested. I guess I ate the outside piece. It *tasted* delicious!

During this time, the radio brought only bad news. France was fighting the Germans and England was making plans for at least three years of war. The Germans were already at the outskirts of Warsaw.

The *Fort Ross* anchored off the post at Read Island. Ray, Lin, and Buddy Ross, as well as Henry Jensen and some Inuit, came out to the ship. Ray was being transferred to the Coppermine post, and the unloading of freight and loading of their belongings proceeded in dismal rain. When we reached Coppermine, the *Fort Ross* had to anchor some distance northwest of the settlement due to shallow water and several sandbars. Unloading freight onto the scow, which was tied alongside for lighterage, began at once and was well under way by the time Bill Storr, Johnny Norberg (two traders), and Post Manager Ralph Jardine came out in the whaleboat to pick up the Rosses.

The Rosses and all of their belongings, including three of their carefully bred great black and white sled dogs, were quickly loaded. I joined them, leaving Link and Pres to come later on the scow they were helping to load. Pres, who had once been an able-bodied seaman, thoughtfully offered to stand watch so that all the crew could go ashore with the last load. When Link arrived with them, the Reverend Harold Webster's wife, Edie, came over to the post to invite us to join them for supper. It was good to have time to hear all the news of our friends along the coast and enjoy the delicious home-cooked Arctic char.

When we returned to the post after supper we found that the local citizens with Shorty and the crew were enjoying the annual "celebration." Each year the Caucasian residents were permitted to order just one case of "spirits," and each person contributed one bottle, to celebrate the occasion. The spirits were already well shared and we happily, but cautiously, joined the festivities. The captain and crew were, of course, on "short rations," and at 9:30 Shorty said, "Well, lads—I'm sorry to break up the party, but I plan to start loading at five in the morning and figure we'd best all get a bit of sleep." When he stood up, Link and I joined him and the crew and walked down to the beach where the power launch, with the big scow full of fur bales in tow, was tied.

It was a cold night, bright and clear, with a stiff wind blowing out of the

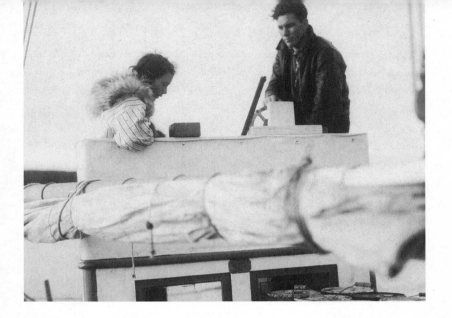

Mainland coast, Coppermine. Inuit trader Johnny Norberg and his wife, Bessie.

southwest. Piercey had a little trouble getting the engine started, but it finally caught. We chugged along past the first sandbars a few hundred yards from the post before it gasped and died. As Piercey and Len Adey, the mate, fussed with it we drifted before the wind toward yet another sandbar, but in the nick of time the engine caught and we were off. We had gone beyond the last sandbars when again it coughed and died. That time we drifted out some distance before they got it running again, to everyone's relief.

The little light of the *Fort Ross* slowly grew brighter. We could make out the dark bulk of the ship against the night sky and could see Pres's flashlight as he came aft to throw us the line Len stood ready to catch. The sulky engine, however, having brought us almost within reach, seemed to chuckle and then stopped. Pres threw out the line, but we had already drifted back beyond reach. The light on the ship grew dimmer and dimmer as wind and tide carried us out toward Seven Mile Island in Coronation Gulf. No amount of persuasion, coaxing, or underbreath epithets had any effect on the engine, although all the men worked on it, physically or verbally, for well over an hour.

Finally Shorty said, "We'd best put up a flare." There were none. A rag wrapped around the end of a boat hook, dipped in gasoline and ignited, made a brief but beautiful light. We looked expectantly toward the diminishing lights on shore hoping for an answering signal. Nothing. A sack was found and burned, to no avail. The sky, as if to mock us, or perhaps in response to our feeble efforts, now became a whirlwind of auroral light, great shafts and swirls and mounting pillars of colored light, weaving, shooting, climbing, and waving across the dark arch of heaven.

Link remembered the long flashlight in his rucksack. He handed it to me as the darker darkness which was Seven Mile Island loomed off our port bow. With quiet desperation, I pressed out SOS over and over and over again until my fingers were almost too cold and tired to work. An interminable time passed. Someone must see our little light. We all knew that beyond Seven Mile Island lay the open waters of Coronation Gulf!

But on shore an Inuit woman did see the blinking SOS. After consulting with others who also watched it, she decided to tell Jardine, the post manager, that a boat was coming in from the Gulf. The celebration was still in full swing, and it was some time before Howey, the radio assistant, went out with the woman to look at the light. He read my SOS, realized that someone was in trouble, and blinked an "OK" in response. What a relief! We had been seen at last. We were cold, but hunched up together to wait, while the wind had her way and the sky blazed with cold, eerie light. An extraordinary display of the aurora.

Howey ran back to the post and said, "There's a boat out by Seven Mile Island sending SOS!" Wondering what boat it could possibly be, everyone jumped up and rushed down to Bill Storr's whaleboat. At last, we could hear an engine and the wonderful sound of singing and shouting voices. Then the whaleboat became visible, loaded down almost to the gunwales with people. Everyone was aboard and feeling no pain. A line was passed over and fastened to our bow and off they all chugged with us in tow, into the frustrated wind toward the *Fort Ross.*

All this time Pres had been beside himself with desperation. He realized our plight and set about to notify the people on shore. But how? He ransacked the ship for flares. None. He discovered a gun, but no shells. He tried to blow the ship's whistle, but found he would have to get up steam to do so and was afraid he might accidentally start the ship. He discovered a small foghorn and blew it, but the wind whisked the sound out over the gulf. He was frantic. He had seen our faint SOS and was helpless.

Mainland coast, Coppermine. Oliver Howey, Canadian government radio operator with whom I had a weekly schedule.

Pres finally found a red lantern, which we could see as he swung it to and fro, but which was not recognized as alarming by anyone on shore. When he at last saw moving lights on the shore and knew that someone was going to our rescue, he hurried to the galley and made coffee, knowing how cold we must be. He was right. We were cold, but once we were aboard, the coffee, laced with firewater, had us glowing in no time. Shorty related the saga of our recalcitrant engine and said we might as well get what sleep we could. Our rescuers soon went ashore cheering, and we gratefully fell onto our bunks.

It was nearly noon before we took our things ashore in case the plane arrived from Great Bear Lake. Bad weather, which had blown in with the wind during the early hours, held until the following afternoon, giving us a welcome breathing spell for farewell visiting before Jack Crosby flew in. Once airborne we discovered that winter had come to the higher country between Coppermine and Great Bear Lake. The smaller, shallow lakes were frozen and the higher rocky ground was already wrapped in a snowy blanket.

Two days later our feelings were mixed when we saw the lights of Edmonton ahead. We looked forward to meeting Wop and Vi May and other friends there, but the shadow of the war lay over us. Would we be heading north again? For now, we would return to Yale, hoping that the war might end soon.

4 / Cambridge Bay area
Snow house living
March 26–April 18, 1940

*B*y winter of 1939, the United States had not yet declared war
on Germany. Link had discussed his thesis problems with Professor Flint,
and it was decided that we should be at Cambridge Bay in early spring. We
could then travel by dog team along the coasts, and perhaps inland. That
would enable us to study areas we could not otherwise reach easily. Link
also wanted to witness the spring thaw, occurring there during May and
June. Our plans fell into place, and early March 1940 found us in Edmonton ready to board a twin-engine Barkley-Grow for the flight north. Just
before takeoff we were joined by thirty-two baby chicks, destined for our
friends Ray and Lin Ross. It was –20°F and snowing lightly, but Sila, the
Inuit Spirit of Weather, smiled, and the snowstorm ceased. Link and I
squeezed hands. We were headed north again.

At Yellowknife, Alf Caywood and his copilot, Pat Cameron, were waiting by the dock and helped us quickly transfer our gear to the now ski-
equipped Norseman "BDG." Then we and the chicks were off for Great
Bear Lake and an overnight at Eldorado radium mine. Below us spread a
slowly changing kaleidoscope of frozen lakes, snowy, rounded rock outcrops, dark forests, and great, irregular burned-over areas that looked bleak
and desolate. Stark, gray skeletons of the dead trees stuck up through the
snow.

We enjoyed a most pleasant evening at the mine and in the morning
headed for Coppermine. The thin, snowy forests below us gradually gave
way to an endless and undulating mother-of-pearl world. Finally, we circled several times over the bleak snowbound buildings of the tiny hamlet.
Landing on the frozen sea we taxied up to the beach, where our good
friends were excitedly waiting despite the subzero temperature.

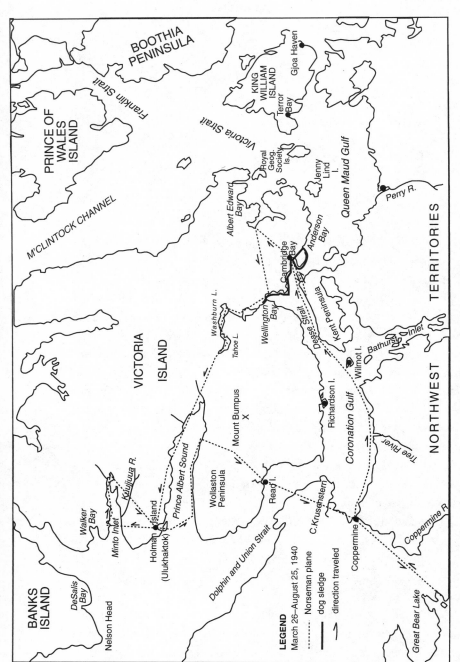

MAP 5. March 26–August 25, 1940

Early spring. Great Bear Lake, N.W.T., Eldorado Mine. Pilot Alf Caywood with Bob Seksmith and Mine Manager Ed Bolger.

Early spring. Coppermine, on Coronation Gulf, N.W.T. In winter the frozen land and sea become one snowbound expanse.

Ray and Lin, delighted by the still madly peeping chicks, quickly bundled them in an attigi and rushed to the house. There was so much news to exchange, but no time to visit. We had to collect the gear we had left the previous September and the new deerskin garments that Billy Joss, the Hudson's Bay Company post manager at Gjoa Haven, had arranged to be made for us. Then, after quick hugs, everything, including ourselves, was stuffed into the little Norseman. Not even enough room was left for a lemming, should one have tried to stow away. We lifted off the ice and headed east, the sparkling frozen expanse of Coronation Gulf below blending imperceptibly into the generally low-lying coastline to the south and the indistinguishable horizon to the north. It was almost impossible at times to tell whether we were flying over frozen sea or land, and it was always comforting to be able to check one's position on the map by recognizing the occasional dark cliffs of a particular island or headland.

There were seven Caucasians and eight or ten Inuit awaiting our arrival in the early afternoon sunlight at Cambridge Bay. The cleared runway, marked by coal sacks, was on the bay ice below the bank in front of the Hudson's Bay post buildings. Snow blocks completely enclosed the post house, roof and all. (Scotty Gall said he burned less coal than any other post, because of the good insulation provided by the snow blocks.) As soon as greetings were over we all quickly helped unload the mail sacks, parcels, and cases for the local inhabitants, plus all our gear, because Alf and Pat wanted to return to Eldorado before dark. Without landing aids, there was no night flying. If, for unavoidable reasons, darkness or foul weather was about to overtake him, a pilot would usually try to find a suitable place to "sit down" and wait for morning light or better weather conditions.

We all had a quick cup of tea with Scotty and Isabel, and then the Norseman took off and Kopun, one of the older local Inuit, helped us pack our gear on his big kamotik (sledge). My heart sang as we rode on the load for a quarter mile up the bay, the dogs' harness bells jingling merrily, like sleigh bells of old. Kopun had traded fox skins for them at the post. We later found other Inuit who had three or four bells on their teams. Kopun called directions to the lead dog, keeping him headed for Captain Pedersen's old Canalaska Trading Company buildings. I had to pinch myself to believe we were really there, in the snow. A grin as big as the Cheshire Cat's spread over my face and I wanted to shout for joy.

Early spring. Cambridge Bay, Victoria Island. Hudson's Bay Company Post Manager E. J. "Scotty" Gall and his wife Isabel, by their snow-block insulated house, which conserved coal.

Early spring. Cambridge Bay, Victoria Island. Buildings built for his trading post by Captain C. T. Pedersen. Father Raymond de Coccola, OMI, occupied them intermittently when he visited Cambridge Bay. Our snow house is near the "Interpreter's" house at left, and the Royal Canadian Mounted Police post and Anglican church in the background on the right, with Mount Pelly on the horizon.

We had been given permission to use the old "Interpreter's" house, to store our gear and to live in later when the weather was warmer, if we wished. Since no coal was available to heat it, we were instead going to live in a cozy snow house, to be built nearby. Father Raymond, whom we had met at Ulukhaktok the previous summer, occupied the larger two-room "house-chapel," a couple of hundred feet distant. A slight, earnest young man, he had been sent from Corsica in 1937 to carry the Word to the Inuit in the eastern Coronation Gulf and Bathurst Inlet areas, a far cry from the warm waters and lush shores of the Mediterranean Sea.

As a missionary priest, Father Raymond was expected to adjust to whatever circumstances might confront him in the Arctic and to learn to speak Inuktitut as fluently as possible. Like all the priests, Anglican missionaries, and Royal Canadian Mounted Police officers in the Canadian Arctic at that time, he made winter kamotik journeys often totaling 2,000 miles or more a year, visiting all the Inuit camps in his wide-flung area. He had just come up from his home mission at Burnside, near the bottom of Bathurst Inlet, roughly 200 miles southwest of Cambridge Bay.

Scotty and Isabel, thoughtful as always, asked us to stay with them that first night. When we had stored our gear, we walked over the ice to the post for supper and to hear the local news: what kind of winter it had been for trapping, how many skins were traded, who brought in the most, was everyone well. After his evening radio "schedule" to exchange local news and messages with the government station at Coppermine, Scotty contacted Angus Gavin at Perry River to check up on Company Inspector Copland's plane. It had left Cambridge Bay for there the previous day, but had not returned. Angus told us that the plane had made an emergency landing on the ice by the Finlayson Islands near Wellington Bay.

With thick fog blanketing the land, it was impossible for the pilot to follow the coastline. An Inuk at a nearby sealing camp heard the plane come down, and quickly hitched up his dog team to investigate the strange happening. When he materialized out of the fog near the plane, the stranded men told him they could not find their way through the fog and would have to wait for it to clear. He grinned and built a comfortable snow house for them. He also boiled some seal meat on his Primus stove for them and provided caribou skins to put under their sleeping bags. By morning the fog lifted and they continued on to Perry River.

Early spring. Cambridge Bay, Victoria Island. Royal Canadian Mounted Police Constables Louis Kaglik and Reginald Goodey with Corporal Scott Alexander.

Fortified by Scottish oatmeal, we accompanied Scotty to the Interpreter's house near which Father Raymond, Kopun, and Amos Cockney, Ole Andreasen's stepson-in-law, had located a suitable drift of hard, wind-packed snow where our first snow "home" could be built. Ole had accompained Stefansson on his long explorations over the ice during the Canadian Arctic Expedition of 1913–18. Einar Farvolden, Slim Semmler's associate, came across the bay to see what was happening. Of Finnish ancestry, he was a thoughtful and friendly but somewhat somber person.

To cut the snow blocks, the men used their snow knives. These are longer than a butcher's knife and have a straight, broad blade. Each man outlined a rectangular block with the long blade, then stuck it straight down into the snow in several places along the outline. He then made a quick slice with the knife under the bottom of the block and lifted it out. Each block was about three feet long by two feet high, and one and a half feet thick. The top edge was slightly angled by a quick slash, and the blocks placed on edge lengthwise, end to end, in a mounting spiral around the inner space, each block being shaped and tilted slightly toward the center. Two men worked inside the circle, the others outside.

Inside the snow house, about half of the original snow was cut out for building blocks. The remaining snow served as a sitting and sleeping bench, while the snow floor was partly occupied by a kudlik or Primus stove and cooking utensils. An opening about 30 inches high was cut in the center of the wall, and a trench, sloping up and outwards, was cut out of the snow as blocks to make the entry passage. This was then enclosed with snow blocks forming an entry tunnel. Each block was trimmed to interlock with the two on which it rested and the one immediately before it. Link learned the technique and helped to cut blocks while I learned how to chink any spaces with snow to prevent wind erosion. This was generally the wife's job after she had unharnessed the dogs, fastened them to the dog line, and fed them.

With the spiral dome finished by setting in the key block, we crouched to go along the low tunnel and three-foot-high entry into our snow house. When we stood up inside, we were stunned by its beauty. Ten feet in diameter and eight feet high at the key block of the perfect dome, it glowed like candle-lit alabaster in the sunshine. The history of each block was delineated in the varying layers of snow that had been wind driven from first one direction and then another, their patterns now radiant with the sun's glow. What a fabulous space to live in, I thought.

Quickly we began to set up house. Having neither willow mats nor polar-bear skin to lay hair side down on the snow bench, as a good Inuit wife would have had, we spread out three dried, raw caribou skins, thick hair side down. On these we laid several more skins, hair side up, and on top of them one open, heavy eiderdown sleeping bag, then our caribou-skin sleeping bags, which had the hair side inside, and finally the second eiderdown on top. Although the temperature in the snow house slowly became equal to that outside, about −25°F, a warmer, more sensuously enveloping bed has not been invented! Our personal ditty bags lay at hand, one at each end of the snow bench.

On the floor to one side of the entry we placed a block of snow, which we would thaw over the Primus stove for water in the morning. The two wooden boxes that held a few weeks' supply of dried and canned food, the Primus stoves, kerosene lantern, and tin washbasin were also on that side.

Early spring. Cambridge Bay, Victoria Island. Our remarkably comfortable snow house.

On the other side, we kept a five-gallon tin of coal oil for lantern and stoves, and also a block of snow to close the entry at night. On the floor against the sleeping bench, in lieu of china chamber pots, we placed two large, covered coffee cans for emergency night use; a thoughtful contribution by Isabel. Life was reduced to basics.

Father Raymond was also more than kind and helpful. He made a little wooden door frame with stretched sacking to place across our snow house entry during the day. He was afraid his big, furry, three-month-old pup Napoleon or his bitch Minerva, both being loose, might raid our supplies or tear up our sleeping skins. Napoleon was at that stage where everything needed thorough investigation.

During our second day in the snow house we decided to have a "snow house warming" party. Each of our friends declared it was a wonderful idea and said they would bring a dish of food to go with whatever we provided, plus their own plates, cups, and flatware. Scotty and Isabel brought canned peaches, Constable Reg Goodey contributed roast caribou, and Father Raymond brought a loaf of his freshly baked bread. Reverend George Nicholson brought compressed Tabloid Tea tablets, while Einar and Kopun brought themselves.

IGLOO-WARMING
Cambridge Bay   March 30, 1940

Julienne Printemps

Goodey Tuktuk à la Gall

Maize   Turnips
Americaine   Isle Victoria

Pain Raymond

Peaches Isabelle

                    Apples Canadienne

Demitasse Cambridge Bay

                    Tea Tabloid.

Early spring. Cambridge Bay, Victoria Island. Our "Snow house warming" menu.

We all squeezed together along the edge of the snow bench, the deer-skins making a warm cushion. Great good humor reigned. Thanks to our friends, the dinner was delicious and everyone enjoyed the novelty of a "formal" dinner party in the glistening dome. Kopun, who, as an Inuit, had done this all his life, was not impressed by eating in a snow house, but he was impressed by the fact that both Father Raymond and the Reverend Nicholson were with us. The ecumenical idea had not really reached the western Arctic in 1940, and competition for the Inuit souls was keen. It was not often that leaders of the two churches dined together. Later that night as I lay in the warm fur bag, I remembered the first "snow house" I had seen in the museum so long before. Lying snug beside Link I felt completely content and at home as though I had returned to a well-known and dearly loved place.

The weather remained clear and cold during the following couple of weeks, and we spent a good deal of time studying maps and deciding on places to visit by dog team. Link set up an observatory in front of the Interpreter's house which held his thermometers and barograph. Some evenings we visited at the post with Isabel and Scotty while he kept his radio "sked" with Coppermine. We learned much from him about what to expect when we set out by dog team with one of the Inuit, and we also heard news of the European war, which became steadily worse. At other times we visited with Father Raymond or spent the evening at the RCMP detachment.

Corporal Scott Alexander, who was in charge of the detachment, returned from his King William Island dog team patrol. As he did not know of our arrival, I walked across the frozen bay to alert him. When I knocked on the outer entry door a somewhat muffled voice sang out, "Come in." Just inside the inner door a wall mirror reflected a pair of incredulous, bright-blue eyes above a half-shaven, half-foamy face under a tousled mop of bright red hair. Smiling, I said "hello." Slowly Scott turned from the mirror to look directly at me, razor still held by his face. Finally, he asked slowly, "Who *are* you? Where on earth did you come from?" I explained briefly, telling where we were situated, then left him to finish removing his fine red beard.

No general geologic study had been made of Victoria Island and little was known of the interior. In talking with Scotty and some of the Inuit, we learned that in earlier times, when crossing the Island to or from Prince Albert Sound and Minto Inlet on the west coast, the Inuit had traveled beside two very large lakes in the interior. They had known of a special place where they could find native copper for their knives and spear points. Scotty said Sam Carter was a good traveler, so Link asked him if he would like to attempt to locate the lakes and possibly continue on to the west coast. None of the local Inuit had made the crossing, but Sam said he was pretty sure he could locate the old route, given good visibility. Of course I wanted to go along, but Link had other plans for me.

Before either of us could travel anywhere by kamotik we needed caribou-skin overpants as well as kamiks (boots), duffles, and mitts. We asked Mary Kaglik, an excellent seamstress, if she would make these. She was glad to do so and also refitted the kuletaks (outer caribou-skin parka), which Billy Joss had had made for us. Like most Inuit women Mary had only to look at a person for a few minutes, after which she was able to cut and sew skins into garments, boots, or whatever, that almost always fit perfectly. Patterns were never needed. She also made us each a pair of wolf's-head overmitts. These were attached to a multicolored, braided-wool harness to keep them from being lost in a blizzard.

Link gathered together all the items he would need for a couple of months. With rifles and fishing lines, Sam figured they could feed themselves and the dogs if they were away longer. He knew some fish could be obtained at an Inuit fish camp and a cache at the head of Wellington Bay. With all gear lashed securely on the kamotik, the harnessed team, sensing the approaching departure, lifted their heads howling, and all the tied dogs joined the uproar. What a spine-tingling sound! Link just had time for a quick kiss before jumping on the kamotik and they were off. With a sinking feeling, I wondered when I would see them again.

During his absence, Link wanted me to go east along the coast to Anderson Bay to collect rock samples from the upper section of the cliffs. By climbing to the top of the snowdrift banked against them, I could get specimens that would be out of reach in summer. Scott and Scotty finally agreed to my going, but insisted that I be in charge of this "expedition." I was to take Mary Kaglik and little Eva, her four-year-old daughter, as well as Kopun and two young lads, Joe and Sam's son Georgie.

At that time, no Caucasian woman had led even a short trip out of Cambridge Bay, and it was not considered proper for me to go out alone with Kopun. Scotty and Scott were afraid that he would not understand that the custom of cohabitation, accepted by the Inuit when a man and woman

Early spring. Cambridge Bay, Victoria Island. Sam Carter, Scotty Gall, Link, Louis Kaglik, and other Inuit checking the load lashings on the sledge before Sam and Link left for an attempt to find the ancient Inuit crossing to the northwestern coast of Victoria Island.

Early spring. West of Cambridge Bay. Sam Carter fishing through a pressure ridge in Coronation Gulf ice.

Early spring. Wellington Bay, Victoria Island. Kayak cached out of reach of Arctic foxes at the site of an Inuit summer camp.

were on the trail together, would not apply in our case, while I felt sure he would accept our customs without question. Scott and Scotty impressed upon him that I was to say when and where we were to camp or travel, something an Inuit woman was not likely to do, and which troubled me greatly, especially because I knew next to nothing about sledge travel.

After Link's departure with Sam, I got together what I would need. Scott and Scotty decided we should take tents, as it was then the middle of April and the snow was no longer good for snow house building. I moved everything, except what I was taking with me, into the Interpreter's house, where it would be safe if our snow house dome collapsed. The top of the dome had already started to drip when the Primus stove was burning. The snow blocks had gradually become iced on the inside, because they had been heated and refrozen and glazed by steam too many times since we moved in. However, I had learned a remedy for "ceiling-drip" that was both easy and efficient: a chunk of fresh, hard snow, when pushed against the offending area, adhered to the wet spot, acting like a sponge and effectively stopping the drip. If you forgot to change the "snow sponge" before it became supersaturated, it would splash down freezingly on your head.

Although it had snowed lightly and intermittently each day for a week, Scotty had heard the call of a snow bunting, so we knew spring would not be long in coming. It is amazing that the little birds survived so early in the season, for there were few bare spots of ground and the night-time temperatures were −20°F or lower. Also, there were frequent "blows," when the high wind sent hard, dry snow crystals zinging through the air with stinging force. Such storms often lasted a week or more. Of course, the temperature at ground level was several degrees warmer than that above, but still cold.

5 / Investigations around Cambridge Bay
area by dog sledge
April 14–May 29, 1940

*F*or the Inuit, "time" was not measured in seconds, or minutes, or even days or weeks. The passage of wild fowl in spring and autumn and the run of fish in the rivers; the times when seals, walrus, and whales came into bays or passed along certain shorelines; the movement of caribou, musk ox, and polar bears; the periods of freeze-up and break-up of the waters; the need to be at a Hudson's Bay Company post for Christmas and Easter and again for "ship time" for trading their fox, wolf, and other skins—these were the "moments" that governed the thoughts and movements of the People. Our concept of time is still a problem for many of them.

The morning of April 19 had been set for the departure of my trip to Anderson Bay. At dawn I was ready to load my gear on Georgie's kamotik, but my travel companions had slept in, and it was nearly noon before everybody was on hand. Scott had loaned Kopun the RCMP detachment's "puppy team" of nine eager young dogs, together with a basket sled instead of a kamotik. With Mary very pregnant and having to carry Eva on her back snug inside her kuletak, Scott thought she might be more comfortable in the basket sled than perched on the load of a kamotik.

Two two-by-twelve-inch planks eight to sixteen feet long placed on edge formed a kamotik's runners. They were held two feet or more apart by crosspieces two or three inches wide lashed to the top edge of the runners with ugyuk-skin thongs laced through holes near the top of the runners. The front ends of the planks were cut to curve up from the bottom with an additional curved piece added so that the kamotik could ride up over rough ice. This curved front area had no crosspieces. To load the kamotik, a big square of canvas was laid over it, the two long ends lying folded on the snow on each side.

All heavy articles were loaded first, with the frozen seals, fish, and blubber at the rear, away from the dogs. Duffle bags and other softer items were placed on top of any boxes, and the sleeping skins were arranged on top of all. This assured a comfortable seat when the going was good and one rode briefly on the load. The two sides and ends of the canvas were then lifted and folded over the whole load, which was lashed on from side to side with a long ugyuk-skin line that was passed under a fixed side line which ran around the kamotik and the ends of the crosspieces. A long line was made by cutting a narrow strip of skin in a spiral around and around the whole skin of an ugyuk, which is specially strong and tough.

Georgie had his nine-dog team and kamotik and Joe and I traveled with him, while Mary and Eva accompanied Kopun, who drove the puppy team. With a sense of some reserve on my part and surely on Kopun's as well, the "expedition" headed out the bay for quite some distance before turning east up over the higher land to take a shortcut to the head of Anderson Bay. The going was good until early afternoon, when we came to a deep stream gorge that was partly filled with big snowdrifts forming high ridges down the sides and across the gorge. The banks had a sheer drop of 50 feet or more, with overhanging snow cornices curling over the top. Since this formed an impassable barrier, we traveled upstream above the gorge until we finally saw a steep, sloping bank that Kopun thought we could descend.

With our arms flung over the loads, we broke our speed as much as possible by sliding feet first. Enveloped in clouds of flying snow with shouts, shrieks, and laughter, we flew down. We arrived at the foot somewhat breathless but grateful that neither the kamotik nor sled had overturned. After a few moments we started up the valley, hoping for a way out on its far side. Too soon, we came to one of the high, knife-edge cross-drifts. Shouting encouragement to the dogs, pushing, pulling, slipping, and struggling we inched our way up, but not without having to right both sled and kamotik several times.

The dogs, of course, were already on the downslope when the kamotik and sled reached the knife-edge top so we instantly started another precipitous descent. Again we hung onto the kamotik and sled and flew down feet first. By jamming the anchors into the snow at the bottom the teams were stopped, and, panting and laughing, we decided it was time for a "mug-up." The thermos provided us each a cup of hot, sweet tea which we enjoyed with hardtack while the dogs curled up thankfully in the snow. Mary was smiling, seeming no worse for the rough going, and the boys were in high spirits. Refreshed, we continued up the gently sloping valley floor without major problems and eventually came out onto high, rolling country that vanished into infinity.

As we jogged along beside the kamotik, Georgie spotted a ptarmigan. He stopped the team, and was about to shoot, when his dogs started a free-for-all fight. He whacked them with the rifle, but that broke apart, so he grabbed the dog whip and quelled the riot by hitting them with the hardwood handle. With the dogs quiet, he untangled the traces by lifting the dogs over one another.

The first time I saw someone beating fighting dogs on their heads with a stout hardwood stick I was horrified, but the dogs often severely injure and sometimes kill a teammate unless quickly stopped. The surest way to stop a fight was to hit the fighters hard on the head while shouting as loudly and fiercely as possible to gain their attention. Nine big dogs all snarling hideously and biting and slashing at everything moving, piling up into an incredible melee of teeth and fur, is a fearsome sight and disastrous if prompt and strenuous action is not taken. One's life depended on maintaining a healthy team. During the confusion, the ptarmigan, wise bird, had vanished, and with everything under control again, we jogged on, avoiding rocks, bare ground, and too-thin snow patches as much as possible.

I found the early Arctic spring more exhilarating than any I had experienced in temperate climates. The exquisitely sculptured, long, sleek, wind-carved sastrugi, the fantastically shaped ridges, and the turrets and minarets of rough ice were dazzling white, blue, lavender, and pale pink in the clear sunlight. Their cobalt shadows reached across glistening stretches of ice, while the sky, a deep and unbelievably intense blue, arched over all from horizon to horizon. When we stopped to rest, there was sometimes nothing to be heard save the light hiss of the breeze over the frozen world, and the beat of one's own heart. Traveling by sledge over sea ice often created a veritable tone poem, with the song of one's Inuk companion being accompanied by the high, lilting melody of the gliding kamotik runners, their deep-toned echo rising from the bottom of the ice, while the harness bells rang a rhythm of the trotting dogs.

April 14–May 29, 1940 ✶ *90*

When we came to a little hill I asked Kopun to stop so I could investigate some large boulders on top, to check them for striae and perhaps to take hand specimens. While I was thus engaged Kopun unloaded the basket sled, turning it upside down so that he could re-ice the runners for better sliding. In the autumn, to prepare the sled or kamotik runners for the winter, the Inuit took dark brown, peaty mud and froze it onto the narrow, sometimes metal-shod runners, forming it to curve out into a broad, rounded runner about four inches wide on the sliding surface. When the mud had hardened and frozen, it was coated with layers of ice. This was done by squirting mouthfuls of water on the frozen mud or wetting a piece of polar-bear skin with urine or water, and wiping it quickly and lightly down the runner from front to back, much as one applies wax to a ski for better sliding. This was repeated several times to give a hard, durable surface. In late spring, the icing wore off more quickly than in winter, and sometimes, when traveling over rough ice or thin snow on land, chunks of the mud were knocked out. When this happened, the chunks had to be thawed, replaced, and re-iced, or if lost, the gap had to be filled by some other material as soon as noticed, or the remaining mud would break out quickly.

Finally we followed a little draw or gully down onto Anderson Bay, and by 7:00 P.M. we had made camp on a point a mile from the head of the bay. I pitched my little tent a few yards from the Inuits' big canvas one, then joined them for the evening meal; we laughed again about the fast runs down the steep slopes and the broken gun. Kopun and the boys decided they would chop a hole through the ice next day and try their luck at fishing, while I worked on the cliffs. Later, snug in my sleeping bag and looking out through the open tent entry at the dark, exposed rock of the cliffs, I wondered where Link and Sam were. What experiences were they having? Had they found the fish cache at the head of Wellington Bay? In the utter silence surrounding me, my thoughts sounded loud, as though spoken. I smiled and wondered if they had leapt the miles between us, to echo in Link's ear.

In the morning the crisp, clear calls of a snow bunting cheered us as we ate breakfast. With a bowl of hot oatmeal, a piece of frozen fish, and a cup of sweet tea to hold me until lunch, I set out to investigate the cliffs rising above the bay about a mile away. They were 80 to 90 feet high, and the windblown snow lay up against them more than halfway to the top, in very

Early spring. Anderson Bay, Victoria Island. Looking southeast at the cliffs.

steep, hard-packed drifts with frequent small, horizontal, sharp-edged cross-ridges.

Using my geology hammer, I slowly chopped toeholds up the frozen surface and finally reached the crest of the drift. There it sloped down a few feet toward the rock face, forming a trough along which I happily worked, knocking off hand specimens of the different rock types as high as I could reach, putting each into its own marked sample bag. When I came to the end of the trough, my Bergen rucksack was almost full and must have weighed a good 60 pounds or more. I was pleased to have collected so many samples. Before descending, I looked out over the frozen bay and thought again how lucky I was to be realizing my childhood dream of traveling with the People under Polaris.

As I cautiously began the steep descent, the soft moosehide sole of my caribou skin kamik slipped out of a toehold and both feet shot from under me, the heavy rucksack holding me on my back. As I slid, I tried frantically to dig the point of my geology hammer into the frozen surface. It was not sharp enough, so my coccyx took the full blow of each small, hard, cross-ridge. When I finally slipped out onto the bay ice below, I was in such total pain that I could neither move nor think. After a while the cold crept up from the ice, seeping through my heavy clothing, alerting my brain. I realized I would have to get up or freeze. I did not dare turn my head, but out of the corner of my eye I could see the tiny figures of Kopun and the boys where they were fishing through the ice nearly a mile away, too far to hear me if I tried to call. I then attempted to figure out where I hurt most and what to do.

I decided that if my neck was broken, I would not be able to turn my head. Very gingerly, I tried. It worked. Carefully I checked my fingers, hands, and arms and found they worked without extra pain. That left my lower back. If it was broken, I would not be able to move my legs. Again, starting with my toes, I found that they, and then my ankles, moved easily. But when I tried to draw up my knee, I knew at once that I must have broken my coccyx. Unfastening my pack I managed, slowly, although the pain was excruciating, to regain my feet and then get the pack up on my back again. This accomplished, I started very carefully across the bay toward the men. As I watched, Mary and Eva walked out from camp to see what luck the men were having at the fishing hole. When I joined them, I found they had caught several tomcod. I said nothing about my fall.

Back at camp Mary melted snow over the Primus stove in a big pot to get water and then slowly boiled the fish for our lunch. The pungent aroma drifting out of the tent set the dogs moaning and growling in hopeless anticipation. I was sorry for them, but knowing they would eat later I joined the others around the bubbling pot. As I carefully sat down on the bed skins I discovered that not only was it painful to walk, it was too painful to sit properly. I had to perch on one buttock or the other, moving with the greatest caution. Mary turned the Primus stove low and as soon as possible we took turns lifting chunks of fish from the hot soup with our fingers, and there were many contented sounds as we ate. When the fish was gone, Mary poured the cooking water soup into our cups so that we would get all the nutrients available as well as the fluid.

Realizing I would not be able to do much in the way of work for a few days, I decided, in my ignorance, that we might as well pack up and move

Early spring. Anderson Bay, Victoria Island. Kopun, Mary Kaglik with Eva, and Georgie Carter fishing through the ice.

on to look at some cliffs that Scotty had told us about. The cliffs were on the coast a little west of Anderson Bay, and Kopun said it should take us a couple of hours to reach them, giving us time to get back to Cambridge Bay late the same night.

We packed up and started off, but the ice was rough and hummocky and there were endless small, snow-covered tide cracks, marked only by a hairline crack or slightly different color in the snow. Our progress was very slow and our route became well marked by too frequent, messed-up snow patches where we stumbled and fell or the sled or kamotik overturned. For me, every step was painful and each fall excruciating. After five hours, we decided to make camp although we could see the cliffs in the distance. Kopun discovered that his rifle had fallen off the sled unnoticed somewhere along the way, but as soon as we finished supper we all crawled into our sleeping bags. I eased into mine as gently as possible.

The following morning was very foggy, but Georgie took several dogs and the empty kamotik and retraced our route to look for Kopun's rifle. I spent the morning looking up at the few small areas of exposed rock near the cliff top. The sun had dissipated the fog, the air temperature was about 40°F, and large chunks of frozen snow were breaking off the snow cornice, landing with loud "whumpfs." It was too dangerous to approach the bottom of the cliffs. There was nothing I could do about it, so I resigned myself. On the small spots of exposed beach I found chunks of an interesting fossiliferous, sandy limestone.

Georgie returned proudly bearing the rifle, and I decided we should pack up and start back to Cambridge Bay after a light lunch. Unfortunately I didn't think about the runners. Maybe it was a subconscious desire to hurry home, where I could lie down and not move. Poor Kopun. He said nothing. He had promised Scott and Scotty to do whatever I said. The rough ice and sun worked quickly and we had not been traveling more than 20 minutes when the mud of Georgie's kamotik began to break and fall off so fast that Georgie and Kopun decided to knock it all off. There was no way they could thaw and reapply it. Since wood slides very poorly on snow and ice, our progress was even slower than on the previous day. Once again we were falling over the endless small invisible tide cracks and righting the dumped kamotik or sled. I worried about Mary, pregnant as she was, being dumped so often.

Every step continued to be a small agony for me, but an occasional attempt to perch on the load was even worse. The sun became so hot we moved along in our shirt sleeves, and between the sun and the reflected glare from the frozen sea our faces and hands turned deep red. At a snail's pace we traveled on, finally reaching a sealing camp at Cape Colborne about six in the evening. It had taken three long hours to go ten miles. There were four couples and a baby girl at the camp, and Mary, Eva, and I were invited into one of the snow houses for a mug of tea, while Kopun and the boys talked with the men about borrowing a kamotik, for there was nothing available with which to "re-mud" the runners of Georgie's.

It was always interesting to see the combination of old and new in the snow houses. Sometimes the Inuit used Primus stoves for cooking, but these really created too much heat, causing the dome icing I had encountered in our own snow house. Also, the coal oil was very expensive. Many

Inuit at that time still used the carved soapstone kudliks, which burned seal oil. The wick was made from either willow fuzz or Arctic cotton, the latter being the silky white fiber of the fruiting heads of cotton grass (*Eriophorum*), which grows in wet meadows, glistening in the summer sunshine. In earlier times the cooking pots were also made of heavy soapstone. Whalers, missionaries, and traders brought iron kettles and pots to the North, and later aluminum cookware, which delighted the Inuit.

As I sat with Mary and the women on the skin-covered snow bench, I watched two women laughingly playing a game called aiyakok. Usually the playing piece is made from a seal-flipper bone, but this one was made from two and a half inches of a musk-ox horn tip. One hole had been drilled in the very tip and many small holes in the broader end. A fine "string" of plaited sinew about 14 inches long was attached to it through a small hole drilled in the middle of one side, and a sharp-pointed sliver of horn was tied to the other end of the sinew. The idea was to hold the sliver, swing and flip the horn end up in the air, then impale it on the sliver. It is much more difficult to develop the knack of this than it would seem at first glance.

I coveted the aiyakok. Wondering what I had that I could spare that would be useful to the owner, I remembered the small aluminum cough-drop box in which I kept my sinew sewing threads, needles, and moosehide thimble. When the owner saw my box, she smiled broadly and raised her eyebrows while inhaling, making a soft, sibilant "iyeh" sound, all of which indicated that she wanted the box at least as much as I wanted the game. We happily traded items, each, I feel sure, believing she had made the better bargain. I longed to be able to talk with her and the others. Another wonderful opportunity to learn so much was lost because we could not communicate.

One of the young men at the camp and his girl planned to be married by Reverend Nicholson and to trade for supplies, so it was decided that Georgie's dogs would be hitched behind his, and we would all ride on his big kamotik. Georgie would return to get his sledge. Half an hour later the gear was loaded, the dogs howling, and we were off with a rush. The night was perfect—clear and cold. The shadows cast by the endless pinnacles and fabulous shapes of the rough ice grew longer and longer and deeper blue as the sun sank into the frozen sea. Then, imperceptibly, the colors changed to violet, pink, and soft blue, and an improbable rose-hued moon lifted over the rim of the silent world behind us. I was deeply content in spite of my aching tailbone, but I wondered where Link and Sam were.

Everyone was in a cheerful mood and the Inuit's proverbial delight in practical jokes knew no bounds. As I balanced carefully on one buttock, facing sideways on the load, legs hanging over the side, I was bewitched by the beauty of the night and the swinging rhythm of the kamotik-runners' song. Suddenly and unaccountably I did a back-flip onto the snowy ice. Painfully struggling to my feet, I saw the bride-to-be leap off and race ahead urging the dogs to a headlong dash! Somewhat perplexed, but figuring it was all in the spirit of fun, I walked along in the tracks wondering how far they would go before stopping. About a quarter of a mile later they did stop and I was greeted by gales of laughter as, with an answering laugh, I climbed up on the load—this time *behind* the little bride. I had decided that one good joke deserved another and I would try to tip her off in the same manner, by suddenly lifting her feet with mine.

I waited. Half an hour later I suddenly jerked my feet up under hers. It hurt me, but it worked perfectly. Off she toppled with a little shriek of surprise. Her husband looked, laughed, and shouted the dogs into a gallop. At length he stopped to wait for her and everyone was bent double with laughter.

The Inuit did not suffer from any Victorian social taboos, and all bodily functions provided numerous sources for their humor. Any time someone had to urinate and stepped aside, the dogs were invariably put into a short run and the unlucky person had to trot behind like a puppy until the sledge was stopped. If a dog needed to stop it lifted its hind feet off the snow, and running on forefeet, partly supported by the traces, it satisfied its need. This frequently gave rise to ribald comments and laughter.

Scotty and Isabel, glad to see us safely back at half past ten, invited me to spend the night with them. I most happily accepted then continued on to dump my gear. That accomplished I started over to let Scott know we were back, but he had seen us and met me halfway. We walked back to the post together over the frozen bay.

Unexpectedly, and to my delight, Link and Sam returned the next night. They'd had very bad weather, with heavy fog virtually obliterating the landscape. That made travel especially difficult because Sam was in unfamiliar, gently undulating snow-covered terrain with no distinguishing features.

Early spring. Cambridge Bay, Victoria Island. Scotty Gall, Tahoe, Scott Alexander, Isabel Gall with "Napoleon," and Father Raymond de Coccola before Father Raymond left for his mission at Burnside, near the bottom of Bathurst Inlet on the mainland.

We were all sorry that the weather had dashed their hopes, but I was nevertheless happy they were back. Link was pleased with all my rock specimens and upset about my mishap, but I had been brought up to make light of injuries and was determined to be as stoic as the Inuit, who seldom admitted pain or discomfort. It was, however, a few weeks before I could sit properly.

We found that our neighbor, Father Raymond, was busy preparing for his annual spring sledge trip to visit the widely scattered Inuit families of his flock on the mainland, east, south, and west of Bathurst Inlet, a round-trip of some 800 miles. Because our snow house had become unsafe, we decided to use the Interpreter's house to work in. Though it had not been occupied for some time, it was occasionally used as a warehouse. After washing down the walls and floor and cleaning the small coal stove for use as our rubbish burner, we unpacked our few possessions. The house was cozy, warm, and much more convenient to work in than the snow house or our eight-by-eight-foot mountain tent. However, we still preferred to sleep in the tent.

While the house had definite advantages, it also entailed an astonishing amount of "housework." The coal stove seemed to exude old coal dust through numerous invisible cracks, and soot from the Primus stove settled on everything. The caribou hairs from our deerskin clothing were every-where—in our coffee, tea, porridge, and stew, and in little drifts on the floor, no matter how often I used the well-worn remains of an ancient broom. Isabel said that winter was a constant war against caribou hairs, and summer against sand. She was right!

The process of washing our long-sleeved and long-legged woolen under-wear, shirts, and socks in the small enamel hand basin seemed endless. I was able to fit only one arm, one leg, or similar-sized section in the basin at a time, while the bunched-up remainder of the wet garment quietly but steadily created a pool on the floor. The end result, of course, was that the floor also got washed. The offending items of clothing became hoar-frosted, stiff facsimiles, swinging hard-frozen, like dried fish, from an im-provised clothesline strung outside against the south-facing wall. If we were blessed by sunny skies a day or two later, the clothes would be fluttering as they dried. It is amazing how much softer and fresher freeze-dried gar-ments are than those we roast in our overheated electric dryers.

During the last week of April and first week of May we spent much time working on maps and aerial photographs of the southern coast of Victoria Island. I was drawing an enlargement of the 30-mile-per-inch Northwest Territories map, to continue a partial two-inch-per-mile government map that had been made from aerial photos. It was exacting work, but interest-ing. We also resacked and marked some of the rock specimens we had collected.

We frequently passed the evenings visiting with Father Raymond or at the Royal Canadian Mounted Police detachment or Hudson's Bay Com-pany post. With the radio blackout lifted, we also listened to the weekly radio "skeds" with Coppermine or to the ham skeds with the other post managers. There were only nine Hudson's Bay Company posts across the western Canadian Arctic at that time. Most posts were 100 to 400 miles apart; travel between them was by boat in summer and dog team in spring or winter. Scotty said the ham skeds provided him and the other post managers with an opportunity to drop in for a visit, so to speak, and catch up on the gossip and general news of people's movements. Along with the subconscious knowledge that there was always someone out there ready to listen and break the sense of isolation, this was an important morale factor.

By the first week in May the temperature on some days was as high as 40°F, but that could change abruptly. The snow had begun to disappear, and it was astonishing to see the surface accumulation of dropped and blown debris. Soot from the coal ranges, house sweepings, bits of caribou hair and skin, dry waterfowl wings and tail feathers, matted tufts of shed dog hair, dog droppings, urine, bits of bone and sealskin, along with all manner of undefinable objects, combined to make the snow near the buildings unsightly and certainly no longer clean enough to use for a water supply.

During the long, dark, sunless days of winter it was impossible to keep track of objects. Everything dropped was immediately covered by falling or drifting snow and lost until the spring thaw. Waste from the snow houses of visiting Inuit and their teams, especially at Christmas and Easter, of course contributed greatly to the debris. Since we could no longer use the snow, each time Link and I needed water we walked about an eighth of a mile over a little rise to a small lake where we chopped clean ice with an ice chisel. After filling a big duffle bag, we each grasped an end and lugged the awkward, lumpy thing back home, where it lay by the door.

With the arrival of May the period of endless daylight had come. The sun traveled but briefly below the horizon, the rose and blue of sunset merging into the paler gold and turquoise blue of dawn. We seldom turned in before midnight, our bodies easily adjusting to fewer hours of sleep. The Inuit, having no fixed schedules to follow, slept when they felt like it, day or night, and children were often playing at midnight and sleeping at noon.

Food was eaten pretty much whenever someone felt hungry. With the snow cover lessening and small bare patches of ground appearing on higher areas, wolf spiders could be seen dashing over the snow from one exposed patch of tundra to another. I wondered what they ate, for there were no visible flying insects. Had I examined the snow-free patches closely, I could have found the answer. Numerous minuscule insects inhabit the eight-inch high "forest" of the tundra—tiny beetles, mites, and others, a fascinating, miniature ecosystem.

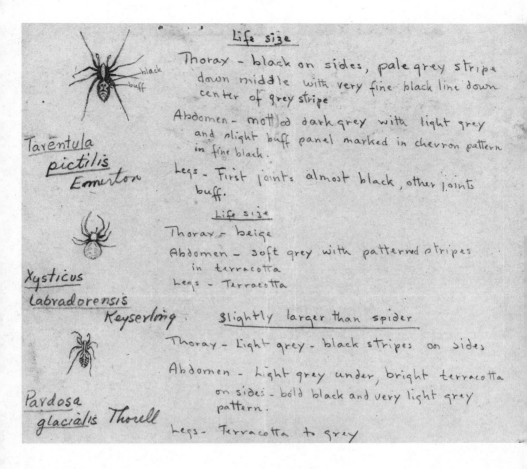

Life size

Thorax - black on sides, pale grey stripe down middle with very fine black line down center of grey stripe

Abdomen - mottled dark grey with light grey and slight buff panel marked in chevron pattern in fine black.

Legs - First joints almost black, other joints buff.

Tarentula
pictilis
Emerton

Life size

Thorax - beige
Abdomen - soft grey with patterned stripes in terracotta
Legs - Terracotta

Xysticus
Labradorensis
Keyserling · Slightly larger than spider

Thorax - Light grey - black stripes on sides

Abdomen - Light grey under, bright terracotta on sides - bold black and very light grey pattern.

Legs - Terracotta to grey

Pardosa
glacialis Thorell

Sketches of spiders.

The snow would soon be gone and travel by dog team would be over. Link had decided that we needed to make a week's trip west along the coast as far as Wellington Bay to look for evidence of former glaciation and to collect samples of bedrock and erratic stones. We would also search for marine shells at elevations that would provide further information about former high sea levels.

Sam Carter agreed to guide us, and Scott loaned us their big, steel-shod kamotik. With the temperature a pleasant 16°F, the going was fairly slow because the mud runners had been broken off earlier. We asked Sam to stop from time to time, leaving him with the team while we examined snow-free riverbanks and hilltops, collected bedrock and erratic specimens, and looked for glacial striae that could give us the direction of the former glaciation.

On one such foray we were circling around a hill when we came upon an enormous flock of at least 150 ptarmigan. Not knowing they flock in winter, we were amazed to see so many. Link continued around the slope out of sight of the fowl, and I hurried back to tell Sam, then remained with the team while he ran toward the hill, hoping to get enough birds for dinner. That evening when we reached Starvation Cove, we belied its name with a most delicious and welcome feast. Not being residents, Link and I were not permitted to shoot wildlife, but the Inuit could take what they needed, and the fresh fowl were certainly a welcome change from our usual fare of bully beef and dehydrated meat.

After supper, Sam taught us how to toss my aiyakok. One is supposed to successfully spear the piece ten times in succession to win. If you miss, you pass the aiyakok to the next player. Hardly moving his arm, Sam flicked the little horn tip around with quick wrist movements, spearing the piece time after time. His eyes were full of warm amusement as he watched our frowning efforts, but before we slept both Link and I had succeeded in spearing the single hole in the point, and on subsequent evenings we were occasionally able to do it ten times in a row.

The following morning, after wrapping and marking the shell and rock specimens collected the previous day and writing up the field notes, we set out from camp on foot in a light snowfall. We left the dogs curled up with snowdrifts piled against their backs, grateful for a day of rest. Sam hoped to track an Arctic hare or more ptarmigan, while Link and I were sure of discovering more pieces of our geologic puzzle.

We found several rock exposures near camp, and about two miles up the coast came to a river valley drifted almost full of snow. When we climbed up the bank we saw many inukshuks, the stone "men" made by former Inuit hunters who built rows of them along the tops of ridges to aid in pursuing caribou. The inukshuks stood out like men against the skyline to frighten the caribou into the narrow valleys. One or two hunters would chase the animals toward the valley, while other hunters hid at the ends. The frightened animals, seeing the inukshuks, could only rush into the valley, where they fell to the arrows of the hiding hunters. Bows and arrows later yielded to guns brought north by the traders.

We decided to go out to the nearby Finlayson Islands, where we trudged around in intermittent snow squalls with our chins tucked gratefully into our furry hoods. As we knelt to collect an erratic, we were startled by a harsh, raspy croak. A big raven, landing on a nearby boulder, cocked his shiny black eye at us and croaked again, as though inquiring if we had found something edible. Later, we jumped when a great snowy owl materialized out of the drifting flakes just in front of us, only to vanish as abruptly and silently as a puff of steam.

When we broke camp the next morning we headed inland to gain a height of land about two miles to the east. It was a long, hard pull through the soft snow and we occasionally helped the dogs by pushing the kamotik. By intermittently checking his Paulin altimeter, Link determined when we had finally reached the 300-foot elevation. There we left Sam with the team and climbed to the wind-exposed areas of the ridge. We found a few fossil seashells, which would help us in determining the date of the former sea level. There were no striae at that place. When satisfied, we turned back. Just as Sam came in sight, we saw him grab his rifle, shoot one ptarmigan, wound another, and then aim at a third as a ghostly white owl, appearing through the falling snow, snatched the wounded bird in its talons before evaporating into the snow-filled air.

When Link felt he had sufficient data, the team was turned toward home, the dogs immediately picking up their pace and pulling with a will, despite a stiff headwind. Near a point where we had camped on the way out, I noticed something dark on the ice. It was the first seal I had seen that spring. Excited, I watched with interest as it raised its head for the briefest of moments to look for danger, then lowered it to snatch an almost equally short nap. Sam said seals, Arctic hare, and ptarmigan are always more wary on cold or windy days. Gradually a chilling fog enveloped us, drawing our horizon ever closer until we and our team seemed the only occupants in cool, mysterious space.

Quietly content as we trotted beside the kamotik, I thought of some friends who might envy me, and others who would be at a loss to understand why I would wish to undergo what to them would be extreme hardship. I could not have explained my feelings to them then, nor can I do so now almost sixty years and many Arctic field seasons later. One is very close to the earth and one's companions, but at the same time quite detached—an odd feeling of being free, yet an integral part of the nature of things. The Inuit know they belong to the Arctic. They *are* an integral part of the natural world around them, while sadly many of us have lost touch with it.

It was already mid-May and the days were passing too quickly. We reached home about 10:30, unloaded our gear, and walked over to the RCMP Detachment to let them know we were back, and to listen to the news. When we entered, everyone was there and all began to speak at once. The Germans had invaded Holland and Belgium and had breached the Maginot Line at one point; the Allies had their backs against the wall; President Roosevelt was telling Italy to keep out of the war; 100,000 Dutch were killed in four days; once again in Flanders' Fields the crimson poppies grew!

How *could* it be? Bishop Flemming wired Reverend Nicholson that all Anglican churches would hold special war services on Sunday, so we planned to join in prayers for peace. Surrounded as we were by the vast, peaceful, snowy tundra and frozen sea, with people of several nations living in friendship, it was hard to comprehend the strife that seared Europe and Britain. We all wondered how soon the United States would become involved. Several of the young Hudson's Bay Company apprentices and at least one Royal Canadian Mounted Police constable along the coast planned to volunteer.

The next few days the weather was as bad and unpredictable as the news. It blew, snowed, rained, and froze, at times almost simultaneously; or fog enveloped the world. The late spring thaw made walking more difficult because any moment a step could plunge one hip deep in snow, and it was sometimes a struggle to get out. Nevertheless, the days could not be wasted. For a beginning of soil movement research, Link selected a snow-free slope a few hundred yards behind the house. We drove stakes into the partly thawed ground and stretched twine around them to designate the area, hoping people would not walk across it. We set up a wire grid over a patterned-ground feature called a sorted circle and placed a painted pebble under each six-inch square of crossed wires so that we could tell if the pebble moved during the thawing or freezing of the ground.

On still other features, we placed painted pebbles in a large cross for the same reason. These were pretty rudimentary scientific methods, but they were a beginning for us. Intermittently since then, we have spent parts of many years in further investigations of patterned ground, which is widespread in areas underlain by permafrost and subject to intense frost action.

Late spring. Cambridge Bay area, Victoria Island. Link setting up his transit.

Cambridge Bay area, Victoria Island. Marked stones, precisely placed so that any movement, over time, could be noted.

In these areas, the slow movement of water-saturated soil and stones on slopes forms gelifluction lobes, sheets, and stripes, while circles, polygons, and nets form in nearby horizontal areas. These have now been studied by many people for many years, and while some definitive answers to questions regarding processes have been found, many are still under active study.

One day, while Scotty and Link were out in the warehouse, Isabel told me a bit about her life in Scotland before she and Scotty were married. She had been a concert singer specializing in the old Scottish and Irish ballads and songs. I wanted to learn the words and melody of "The Road to the Isles," so she agreed to sing it for me. We sat on the floor of the little living room, a pile of sheet music between us, I, spellbound, while Isabel, lost in her own world, sang song after song. It brought a constriction to my throat, "gooseflesh," and a tingling to my spine. Of all the lyric soprano voices I have ever heard, hers was the fullest, purest, and truest. It is the world's great loss that she never recorded these songs.

Spring seemed determined to rout the winter, for in spite of more wind-driven snow, a lovely little Arctic horned lark came to feed on bread crumbs frozen onto the snowbank outside our window. The wind was so strong it blew him over backwards or sideways, and almost turned him over headfirst, while he struggled to keep his foothold on the frozen snow. Heedless, he defiantly and joyfully sang his lilting song between pecks, staking claim to the area. Many snow buntings were already in residence, and Lapland longspurs were also singing and chirping. Four Canada geese and a group of big gulls flew by, and the southerly wind bore the definite earthy smell of spring. How far removed we were from the World Conflict! Quoting from my journal:

May 28th: King Leopold of the Belgians surrendered to Germany last night!——What a frightful slaughter is going on! It now seems likely that Italy and possibly Spain will join Germany's effort to subdue England. It also seems probable that before very long the states will be involved, too. Roosevelt is asking for billions of dollars for re-armament programs!

6 / Mount Pelly
Local investigations
June–July 1940

*L*ater that night we packed our gear and enough provisions for three weeks. Link wanted to investigate the raised beaches on Mount Pelly, and an Inuk who had come up from Perry River agreed to take us out with his team. Despite a high wind, we set off at 11:00 P.M. Our course took us directly into the gale, which felt as though it had teeth, since the driven snow, scurrying like wraiths along the ridges, took on a very real character when it came in contact with our faces. The tiny, sharp crystals bit in no matter which way we turned our heads. The sun traveled but briefly below the horizon in late May and it was always daylight. By 4:00 A.M. we had located our cache, set up the tent, stored gear and provisions, and enjoyed a cup of tea with our friendly companion, who then departed on his return trip to Cambridge Bay.

We had been working several days on Mount Pelly, weather permitting between frequent snow and sleet storms, when Kopun, his nephew David, and several other family members arrived with two teams. One of the elders was beautifully tattooed. They intended to summer at Wellington Bay, but wanted to lay in a supply of fish first. In the late spring the enormous lake trout, large and fat as seals, were caught through holes chipped through the five or six feet of lake ice. An Inuk would either spear a fish as it passed under the hole or sit on a piece of polar-bear skin on a snow block and jig for fish with a line and *very* large hook. I tried the latter method and it really takes the patience of a cat at a mouse hole, or polar bear at a seal hole. Peering down the hole while huddled against the cold, I watched more than one fish pass by, first looking at, then apparently "blowing" at my hook as I tried in vain to snag him. What frustration!

Late spring. Cambridge Bay area, Victoria Island. Our work camp at Mount Pelly.

Cambridge Bay area, Victoria Island. Sketch of the tattoo on face and hands of an Inuit elder.

is tattooed, as are all the older women. The crow's feet at the corner of each eye >>> , two long Vs on the forehead - the points of hers reaching part way down her nose between her eyes \/ ; three bars on each cheek, hers at quite an angle, rather than almost straight and seven lines on her chin - ////. Her hands are also heavily tattooed - I can't tell how far up the arm it goes but would guess the full forearm from this part of the She is Island -

David came to our tent for a visit and told us that Scotty was really ill with a badly infected tooth. Worried, we asked if he would make a quick trip back to the post with us to see if we could help in any way. On arrival, we found Scotty with swollen face and in terrible pain. Frequently, an offending tooth was pulled with a handy pair of pliers. The sufferer was first "anesthetized" by a very heavy dose of commiseration and "strong spirits," then helped to sit on the floor with arms and legs wound around a stout table leg, while a friend yanked the tooth. Link offered to undertake the task, but, with a wry smile, Scotty declined the treatment, to Isabel's relief, for sometimes a tooth broke in the process. Eventually the pain subsided.

We also stopped to see Father Raymond briefly before heading back to camp, and were astonished, when we opened the door, to behold a nearly finished small rowboat. He needed one to go sealing for dog food, since it was not always possible to catch enough fish. Having no way to acquire such a boat before mid or late summer, when the Catholic supply ship *Our Lady of Lourdes* would arrive, he decided to find some wood and build one. With lumber scarce, he took down some long shelves and created *The Santa Maria*. She had a very pointed bow and a stern squared to hold an outboard motor. Her bottom was virtually flat with a little keel. We admired his resourcefulness and determination, but worried a bit about the boat's seaworthiness. Still shaking our heads we headed back to camp where, at 1:30 A.M., Kopun greeted us, and after a cup of tea we all turned in. We need not have worried about Father's boat. He used her frequently, pulling the dead seals over the sides. No one understood how he managed.

Summer kept trying to arrive. Every few days the temperature would creep up to above the freezing point and we would be treated to blowing rain instead of blowing snow. Winter was loath to relinquish its hold. Frequent snow squalls and an occasional blizzard would envelop our world again, the high wind lashing the snow horizontally, obscuring the landscape completely, while the tent walls bulged in or flapped in and out, greatly restricting our movements in the little seven-by-seven-foot tent. We had to move one at a time to avoid touching the slanting walls, because to do so would cause leaks.

Despite the weather, we saw numerous ptarmigan. And early one morning, breaking slowly free from sleep, I thought there must be "a fox in the hen yard," such a bedlam of quacking, squawking, honking, peeping, and singing was taking place. Thousands of wild fowl and birds had arrived during the night. There were black-bellied plovers, golden plovers, sand-pipers, phalaropes, and ruddy turnstones; snow buntings, Lapland long-spurs, and Arctic larks; Canada geese, blue geese, eider ducks, old squaws, and whistling swans; loons, terns, gulls, and more—all frantically singing, displaying, pairing, and staking their territories and nesting sites. The air was alive with birds. The love songs of the red-throated loons so closely re-sembled choking screams that we wondered if we should jump out of our sleeping bags to save someone.

After an early breakfast, Kopun and his family left on their summer journey, and Link and I continued our work on Mount Pelly. While I held the stadia rod, Link set up the Gurley mountain transit on its tripod to measure altitude differences along the old raised beaches. The steeper rises between the beach levels were still buried under deep snowdrifts, into which we frequently sank to our hips and floundered, laughing.

The deeper part of the snow was transformed into large cup crystals rest-ing loosely against each other, which caused it to suddenly collapse with a swoosh under our weight. The more gently sloping beaches and gelifluction lobes were kept mostly snow-free by the wind and we collected more shells at different levels. When the sun occasionally broke through the clouds, we would say, "Hey, look at that!" and push our hoods back to bask in its warmth as we worked. It also thawed the ice around the shores and on the surface of the lakes, making waterproof sealskin kamiks essential. I had learned to keep kamiks supple and waterproof by frequent rubbing with seal oil, a jar of which I kept for this purpose.

By the third week in June the first flowers had burst into bloom. Mats of the bright fuchsia-colored flowers of *Saxifraga oppositifolia* were suddenly everywhere, and big bumble bees, hungry after their underground hiberna-tion, were zooming from patch to patch. Arctic hare and ptarmigan were well into the process of changing their coats from winter white to summer brown to maintain their protective camouflage, but a little ermine, who raided our small food cache in the snow beside the tent opening one evening, was still white.

I knew that the ermine, or weasel, had a reputation for being fearless to the point of foolhardiness, but was nevertheless astonished when this tiny creature, "skreeking" furiously, flung himself at me over and over again. Leaping waist high, he caused me to step back, thinking he might be rabid, at which moment he grabbed hold of the ptarmigan which Kopun had

Cambridge Bay area, Victoria Island. Raised beaches on Mount Pelly.

Cambridge Bay area, Victoria Island. The author with stadia rod, used with the transit when leveling the raised beaches.

given us. I had planned to boil it for dinner, and as he started to drag it off, still uttering muffled "skreeks" through his teeth, I grabbed hold of the bird and jerked it away. But he held tight, tearing off one leg. I was going to try to retrieve that, but on second thought figured the weasel might have little ones to feed, so let him keep it.

On the official first day of summer the low, ominous, gray clouds, which had gradually darkened the sky the evening before, opened and, whipped by the wind, the rain was driven against our little tent unceasingly. Finally, it began to leak along the back seam. Link and I hurriedly moved the sleeping bags up onto the Primus stove box and tried to keep our rucksacks and duffle bags dry, but the water slowly spread on the canvas floor and we had to punch a small hole to let the flooding water drain away into the gravel. We joked about being marooned in our seven-by-seven-foot tent as we sat huddled on top of our possessions close to the center pole, while trying to write notes without bumping elbows.

The previous day we had heard some shooting and wondered who might be hunting. Penuktuk, his brother Taipana, and their father, together with their families, had been out on the land for some weeks, fishing and shooting ducks and geese. After setting up their camp on a small island in the big lake near us, the three men came up for a visit and cup of tea, and we all laughed a lot trying to make conversation although we could not speak much of each other's language. They had caught a seal-sized lake trout, which must have weighed some 75 to 100 pounds.

The next day one of the wives, Hadlelah, and her friend came to visit and, while Link went out to take photographs, the women and I enjoyed tea and pilot biscuits mixed with smiles and giggles. Since we could not converse, I tried to think of things that might interest or amuse them. Link's small ten-power hand lens did both when they looked through it at the creases on their palms and small hairs on their arms. They giggled and exclaimed and could not believe what they saw. They were delighted with my little sewing bag, which they examined item by item, and a pair of magnets amazed them when they jumped together. This startled and puzzled them, and they tried again and again to bring the magnets together without a "jump."

I decided that soap bubbles would probably be something they had not seen, so I made suds in a cup and blew bubbles with Link's pipe. The pipe probably tasted terrible the next time he smoked, but it totally mystified them when the beautiful, gently floating bubbles simply vanished as their outstretched hands tried to grasp them. The women questioned me with their eyes and I tried to explain. I then decided to see if I could tune in anything on my little shortwave radio-transceiver. Even I was astonished when a magnificent operatic baritone voice suddenly filled our tent. The women looked at me intently, then at the small metal box. They were familiar with the Christmas and Easter radio programs at the post, but they did not seem to equate that with the little aluminum box. They spoke together softly and wonderingly and first one then the other went out and walked carefully around the tent, pausing at the corner nearest the transceiver, apparently looking for the man. Each returned with a questioning, disbelieving expression.

After another cup of tea, the women decided to return to their camp. I walked with them to the lakeshore, where, to our dismay, we discovered that almost a foot of water covered the lake ice. The sun and warm air were doing their work, melting the ice. The women looked down at their beautifully decorated, low caribou-skin "visiting" kamiks, then at the sparkling water. They could not wade across to the small island upon which their camp lay, perhaps a hundred feet distant. Laughing, we looked at each other. Like most Inuit women, they were smaller than I. Since I had on my high, waterproof sealskin kamiks I could ferry them over piggyback. It took me some time to make them understand my proposition, and when they did they went into gales of laughter, pushing each other toward me to take the first ride.

Finally, Hadlelah stood on a big rock from which I took her on my back, immediately realizing that she weighed at least as much as a 100-pound sack of coal. She was short but solid. Starting across I found the underwater ice incredibly slippery, and wondered moment by moment if the next step would see us both freezing wet. Slowly, very carefully, with encouraging cheers from the shore, we reached the island safely. With Hadlelah shrieking excitedly from the island and my second passenger shaking with suspense and laughter, we finally made it across.

A jolly boat was lashed on a big kamotik beside the tents. With much laughter and gentle shoving they persuaded me to climb up into the bow seat of the boat. While I sat, amused and wondering, the two young women hugged each other and were practically convulsed with laughter. Maybe they were teasingly trying to tell me I needed a boat, but I never did figure out what was so funny and longed to be able to really converse with these wonderfully warm, strong, and fun-loving—but also philosophical—people.

When the men returned to camp that evening, we asked Penuktuk if he would take us to Cambridge Bay for a short visit, returning the same night. We'd had no news from Scotty and wondered how he was and what the European situation might be. The summer thaw of lake and river ice was progressing rapidly, and there was up to a foot of meltwater on top of the ice where the water could not yet drain down through cracks. When we got right out on the big lake, the ice was pretty dry; it was beginning to candle and the meltwater could drain through. Because the ice crystals were very sharp on top, the Inuit tied little sealskin boots on the dogs' paws to protect them.

Link and I found walking in sealskin boots over candled ice odd, for we could feel it wriggle under the soles of our feet. As the thaw continues, travel becomes dangerous, particularly on lake ice, where the melting crystals no longer interlock firmly, causing even quite thick ice to suddenly collapse under one's weight.

When we reached the outlet river, we occasionally had to go up over dry land because the river had broken through the rotting ice. I enjoyed watching the behavior of the dogs. The leader, wise with years of travel, ears pricked forward, nose down, tail up, carefully sensed the uncertain places where we had to cross through water on the ice or leap over a deep channel cut through the ice by the swift current. Penuktuk never urged him at such times, knowing that he would go only if the ice would support the kamotik.

At one place Penuktuk wanted to cross a narrow, swift channel to avoid going along a steep bank under a small cliff. The leader tried, but two of the following dogs became fearful and pulled back, so we had to flounder along the steep bank up to our waists in wet snow, the dogs sinking to their necks at each lunge. The old leader, knowing he must keep high enough up the bank to prevent the kamotik from sliding sideways into the water, tried to scramble right up the cliff, but Penuktuk called him back to keep the kamotik from rolling over.

As we approached Cambridge Bay, Reg Goodey walked out to greet us and invited us to join him for supper with Isabel and Scotty. It was a real treat after our dehydrated or canned camp fare, but the war news was grim.

Late spring. Cambridge Bay, Victoria Island. Penuktuk with team wading through spring thaw-water on lake ice en route to Cambridge Bay.

Italy, entering the war on Germany's side, had occupied Corsica, where Father Raymond's family lived, and had also invaded France. Southeastern England, where Reverend Nicholson's family lived, was under sustained bombing by the German Luftwaffe. Both men were deeply worried. And we wondered how long it would be before President Roosevelt would commit U.S. troops. Sobered by the world news, we rejoined Penuktuk for the return trip. He asked, "What are the white men fighting for?" How could I explain?

The going was even wetter after the intervening hours of bright sunshine, and at one place our hearts skipped a beat when the rotting ice began to give way under the weight of the kamotik, but the team leapt forward and pulled us to firmer ice just in time. Penuktuk looked back at us with a smile, which we returned. Back at camp, Taipana joined us for a mug-up before we all turned in for a good sleep.

The following morning after breaking camp, our Inuit friends came to bid us a smiling farewell, and as the teams pulled away I watched them wistfully. They were still nomadic, free as their earliest forebears to come and go as they felt inclined, traveling from one location to another according to the season, to take advantage of the availability of seals, fish, fowl, caribou, musk-ox, hares, and white fox. They still used dog teams and snow houses when snow and ice permitted, traveling from place to place along the coasts in autumn or spring or crossing the frozen seas to other islands or the mainland. A few Inuit had open whaleboats with inboard engines, and a few had schooners for summer travel. However, most moved camp by land walking and using the dogs as pack animals. Tubers, berries, and the leaves and flowers of several plants were still an important part of their diet, and they also collected the fuzz from willow catkins to make the wicks for their kudliks, and willow branches to make into mats to lay under the sleeping skins.

There were perhaps a dozen really top Inuit trapper-traders who had selected prime trapping and hunting areas where they built little cabins for themselves and their families. The homesites were generally far removed from any competition from either Inuit or Caucasian traders, and they succeeded by using their native skills as well as those learned from Caucasians. Since they frequently trapped many white foxes and some wolves, and shot a few polar bears, they earned enough in trade to buy schooners on credit, giving them mobility in summer, but sometimes keeping them in debt to the Company. A handful of Inuit families were retained by the Royal Canadian Mounted Police, the Anglican and Catholic missions, and the Hudson's Bay Company, who provided them with small, generally one- or two-room houses next to the official establishment. The husband acted as interpreter and travel companion, while the wife made the caribou-skin clothing.

During the last week of June and the first week of July, we continued working with the transit, to establish placement of white cloth crosses along two originally horizontal raised beaches on Mount Pelly. Link wanted to know if the beaches had been tilted during the rise to their present altitudes. However, the level line of crosses did not appear to change their position with regard to the raised beaches, as also checked by aerial photography. Nevertheless, with the instrumentation and procedures used, a tilt of some two to three feet over the area surveyed could have escaped detection.

When the leveling was finally completed, we had a great time laying out the cloth crosses on these beaches. It sounds simple enough, but the first time we untied one of the accordion-folded bolts of cloth, the wind snatched the end, and with the snap of a sail when a boat comes about in a stiff breeze, it zipped out, vibrating like the 50-foot tail of a great Japanese kite. Trying to get it under control, we both fell upon it and got to laughing so hard as we struggled that we were as happy as two kittens with a ball of wool.

Each arm of a cross was 20 feet long, which meant that we had to cut these lengths from the bolt and then stretch them out on the ground. The best method we devised was to start by placing the exact center of the cloth over the surveyed stone marking the center of the cross, securing the cloth with large stones. Then, with each of us kneeling on an end of the tightly stretched material, we would reach forward and place sizable stones along the edges, gradually becoming prone in the process. Kneeling again and again, we moved forward like inchworms until we finally met. It took 40 minutes to an hour to complete each cross, depending on the strength of the wind. The crosses were to be photographed from the air later.

We were particularly impressed by the patterned ground forms and by the widespread process of gelifluction, discussed earlier (page 110). Link and I used the transit and leveling rod to sight in and place a row of small stakes across a gelifluction lobe near our camp at Mount Pelly, so that he could measure the amount of downslope movement occurring during one season and, hopefully, over a period of years.

All across the land there were still bright, white snowbanks to be seen where the drifts had been deepest, and most of the myriad ponds and lakes were still largely covered with glistening ice. But sun, wind, and rain were gradually wearing it away, and widening bands of ice-free water around their shores reflected the dazzling blue sky. The warm air was alive with melody, 24 hours a day. In the rotting edges of the ice, candled crystals broke free gently bumping each other, tinkling like multi-toned wind chimes and blending with the constant chorus of the jubilant birds. I don't know when the birds slept. Maybe when we did.

The tundra itself was gradually coming to life. The little prone willow "trees," their "trunks" and branches spread horizontally, from two inches

Cambridge Bay, Victoria Island. Nonsorted polygons, a type of patterned ground, probably associated with frost cracking.

Cambridge Bay area, Victoria Island. Gelifluction lobe on Mount Pelly. Marked with stakes for measurement of any movement over time.

to two feet above the ground, were a palette of pale green and silver set off by the tiny red blossoms, with the new leaves being almost as fuzzy as the blooming catkins. Patches of Cassaiope, and many grasses and sedges, were greening. Numerous wee plants were beginning to bloom—bright yellow and white Drabas, creamy yellow, purple, and white Saxifraga, golden Ranunculus, and white Cerastium, as well as drifts of dancing pale yellow Papavers, to name a few.

Each evening I got out the little plant press that our friend Dr. Hugh Raup of Harvard University, a botanist, had made for me. It grew fatter and fatter as I pressed each newly blooming flower for him. I also collected lichens for his wife Lucy, who was a lichenologist. Surprised to find so many different ones, I became more closely observant. The very air was vibrant with an intense exuberance and a sense of urgency, reflecting summer's brevity and winter's imminence.

Link decided we should send a wire to Wop May informing him that the lakes were breaking up late. Also, we had not heard from Scotty for two weeks and again wondered if something was wrong. With a lunch, a change of socks and boots, and a couple of small instruments, we started off for the post. We had some misgivings about the route we had taken two years earlier, where we'd had to wade through an icy stream and pond, and our misgivings were strengthened when we came to a wide stream running through marshlands. Before, we had crossed it at the same place with no difficulty, but this time we had to follow it back upstream about a mile.

All the birds had settled down to the business of nesting. Only geese, swans, jaegers, gulls, and terns would fly off before we reached them. The small birds, ducks, and ptarmigan lay flat and invisible on their nests until our next step was about to crush them. On numerous occasions, when walking on the two-foot-wide natural dikes dividing small ponds, Link or I would nearly fall in when a duck flew up squawking from under a raised foot. The eider nests of beautiful, warm, interlocking brown-and-gray down held from one to five olive-green eggs, some of the nests being up on the hillsides quite a distance from water. Several times one or the other of us leaned forward to gently stroke an eider's back as she lay eyeing us. The nests of larks and Lapland longspurs held three to five blind, open-beaked baby birds.

I saw a female ptarmigan glide to a landing on a patch of tundra nearby.

Cambridge Bay area, Victoria Island. Female eider duck "hiding" on her nest, which is lined with soft, warm down, plucked from her breast.

Without looking directly at her, I wandered slowly along to see how close I might be able to approach. When I knelt and gently stroked her back she remained motionless, just observing me with one bright black eye as though understanding that I intended no harm. Link and I leaned over and picked up a fuzzy little baby Arctic hare, two of which were fending for themselves on the slopes. We were greatly tempted to adopt them, they seemed so very small and defenseless, but realized they were far better off free. There is something enormously rewarding in experiencing acceptance by a wild creature.

As we walked along the low hilltops, we saw off to one side two odd stony bumps that did not resemble any geologic feature we could think of. Perplexed, we climbed up the rocks of the nearer of the two humps and were surprised by a slim Arctic fox, not much bigger than a large cat, with a brownish summer coat. She bounded away at high speed, her bushy brush flying behind. It was the first one we had seen that year. In the lee of the rocks were the remains of three circular sod houses probably dating back to the Thule Inuit culture. The sods were placed upon each other like the snow blocks in a snow house, although the sods were much smaller, about one to one-and-a-half feet long and eight to twelve inches high. The walls were not much over two feet high, because many sods had fallen, and the floor was not more than five feet in diameter. The fox had dug a snug den into the side of one, and we wondered if she had kits.

When we reached the outlet river from the big lake to Cambridge Bay, our fears were realized. There was no way we could ford the wide, deep, and swift-flowing icy stream. All the other streams and lakes were deeper and wider, so after an hour we sat down, disappointed, to munch on pilot biscuits and malted milk tablets before returning to Mount Pelly, disgruntled to have wasted part of one of our few beautiful days.

As we neared camp, I remembered that Scott had told us we should eat a couple of duck eggs from time to time to give us fresh protein. I therefore took two eggs when I stepped over a nest, wondering how they might differ from chicken eggs in flavor. I boiled them for breakfast, and with great anticipation we cracked them open. To our horror, they contained baby ducklings! Scrambling out of the tent, I dug a little pit and buried them. We did not try eggs again. Later, when we told Sam, he laughed and said the Inuit find the small ducks very tender and delicious. I expect he was right, but the shock was too great.

The following week we spent completing our planned work, including a day's circuit of the lower slopes of Mount Pelly. That day was a perfect one, with just enough breeze to keep the omnipresent mosquitoes down. All the little flowering plants were in bloom, and bird songs filled the air. The night before, a wild wind-and-rain storm had cleared most of the ice from the lakes, and when we had lunch on the shore of one of them, we were overwhelmed by the infinite beauty and serenity of the Arctic summer.

July 17 was another warm, breezy day and we decided to once again try to walk to Cambridge Bay. On our previous try Link had lost his Brunton compass, so we attempted to follow the same route in case we might spot it. Given the sameness of the endless low hills and lakes, we were not too sanguine. But quite improbably, when I stopped for a moment, I saw it snuggled in a tuft of grass at my feet. Amazed and jubilant, I presented it to Link, to his astonished relief.

Continuing beside the lakes and streams we had no problems with high water, and reached Cambridge Bay at 7:30 P.M. We stopped at the RCMP detachment to say hello to Reg and Scott and gratefully accepted their invitation to supper. Warm bread, fresh from the oven, and fish fresh from the

Cambridge Bay, Victoria Island. View toward Cambridge Bay. Almost more water than land?

river. Wonderful! After supper, Scott decided to sweep the inlet cove of the middle stream with the big fishnet, so we joined the others to pull on the ropes. While we all pulled, Scott paddled back and forth along the net trying to free the bottom when it became snagged on stones, which happened too often. It took eight of us from 8:00 until 11:30 P.M. to bring it in, and unfortunately many of the fish escaped because, in spite of Scott's efforts, the lead line had become caught and torn from the bottom of the net in two places, each about 12 feet wide. This allowed those sections of the net to float up enough for fish to escape.

Final melting and break-up of the ice brought an end to peaceful isolation and put Cambridge Bay back in contact with the outside world. The Hudson's Bay Company ship *Fort Ross* was due August 7. In preparation there was a flurry of activity during the last two weeks of July and the first week of August. Finishing touches of fresh paint were applied to buildings; vestiges of winter debris disposed of; unfinished reports hastily completed; and the fox skins baled. Link and I took time off from our work to give a hand in the clean up, painting, or wherever we could. The *Fort Ross* arrived on schedule, the fur bales were loaded for shipment, and the winter supplies put ashore.

It was good to see Captain Shorty Sommers, Len Adey, and the other crew members again. Phyllis, now Angus Gavin's wife, was en route to join him at Perry River. The dory we'd had built in Shelburne, Nova Scotia, was a beauty, rigged to hold an extra-long-shafted outboard motor. Everyone helped carry the HBC freight—boxes, crates, sacks, and bales of goods and food—up the bank to the Company warehouse or store. I watched the Inuit women to see how they got the 100-pound sacks of flour, coal, and sugar up on their backs, then copied their method. With everything stowed away, Scotty and Isabel asked us all to come for coffee and sandwiches after supper, and we had a great evening. Phyllis taught us how to do the latest dance step called the "Bumps-a-Daisy," which required partners to turn part way around with the rhythm, bumping bottoms. Well, everyone wanted to learn and the little house shook with music, stomping, bumping, and laughter.

Ship-time also brought changes among the population. Reverend Nicholson, deeply upset by the war and worried about his family, departed on the *Fort Ross* to begin his return to England. Father Raymond was to be aboard as far as Ellice River on the mainland east of Kent Peninsula, and Alec Eccles, who ran a trading post for Patsy Klengenberg on Wilmot Island, was leaving for Aklavik with his furs.

7 / Flying to the west coast of Victoria Island

August 4–25, 1940

$\mathcal{A}$ telegram arrived from Wop May saying he was sending someone north to join us and share expenses on flights we had arranged. We were bewildered and wondered who it might be. The following day, Alf Caywood and Pat Cameron flew in, bringing Charles Godefroy, a vacationing cosmetics manufacturer from Cincinnati. I think he must have been the first real tourist to visit Victoria Island. He had been to Aklavik several years earlier and, although recently hospitalized with severe bursitis, had decided he wanted to see more of the Arctic. Slight and frail, dressed in a thin summer suit and silk socks, Charles seemed a most unlikely soul to be flying around the Arctic, and we looked at him with some concern. One never knew what emergency might arise on a flight. At Coppermine, Constable "Frenchie" Chartrand had put his own great RCMP winter overcoat on Charles, which made him appear pathetically small and thin.

Link and I consulted Scotty about Charles's inadequate clothing and decided to propose that he should get some suitable items. He agreed, so we took him to the Hudson's Bay Company store and helped him select heavy wool long johns, pants, shirts, socks, and mitts, plus an attigi and boots. Because it had been hot in Aklavik when he was there, he had assumed that all the Arctic was hot in summer. As it turned out, he proved to be an excellent traveling companion. Interested in everything, never complaining about anything, he helped in every way possible and was enthralled with the country. One day, handing Link his movie camera, he rolled up his pant legs, took off boots and socks, and stepped into the icy water, asking Link to photograph him wading in the Arctic Ocean!

We made a flight south to Kent Peninsula, to try to find the coal that Tommy Goose had told us about, and collect some bedrock samples Link needed to check against specific erratics we had found. We searched the area where the coal was said to be, without success, but returned to Cambridge Bay burdened by numerous rock specimens. We had made plans to fly north, then west across Victoria Island to Ulukhaktok to the Hudson's Bay Company's Holman Island post. Excited by the prospect of seeing our old friends there and at the Catholic mission, in that lovely place again, we were anxious to be off.

The weather was not very cooperative, but on August 8 we loaded our gear and ourselves into the plane and taxied down Cambridge Bay. It was dead calm, the glassy surface of the water reflecting the many-hued grays of the overcast sky. Alf gunned the motor, getting the plane up on the step of the floats, but with not a riffle on the water, the heavily loaded aircraft would not lift off. He tried again and again with the same result. Somewhat crestfallen but resigned, we said *momiyana*—too bad—and returned to the dock to wait for a breeze.

In the morning, Link and I awakened to find the cool, pale dampness of thick fog pressed against the windowpane. Alf, who had spread his sleeping bag on the floor beside ours, was still sleeping soundly. We prepared breakfast quietly, and when he awoke we served his to him in his sleeping bag. He was flabbergasted, and said it was the first time he had ever had breakfast in bed. The better we knew Alf the more we appreciated his calm approach to life and his quiet sense of humor, and we had complete confidence in his judgment and flying.

The morning radio sked with Coppermine told of heavy rain and a low ceiling there, but sunshine at Holman Island. To our delight a vagrant breeze gathered up the fog and by 10:30 A.M. we had lifted off to fly over Mount Pelly. After taking aerial photos of our crosses of white cloth on the raised beaches, we headed west toward the head of Wellington Bay to locate the river that was supposed to flow from the two big lakes Sam and Link had hoped to locate on their spring trip.

We flew above the river, the end of a small lake, and then a second river, to reach the first big lake, which amazed us by its size. We decided to land at its western end. Taxiing slowly in the shallow water, Alf brought the plane close enough for us to wade ashore. The heavily vegetated, low-lying land was very wet, and we walked into impossible masses of mosquitoes. They swarmed up around us in clouds so thick they plastered our faces, actually flying into our eyes and noses and into our mouths when we spoke. It was incredible and so was the shrill, ear-piercing crescendo of their ravenous singing. As we had neither headnets nor mosquito dope, it was impossible to remain for long. Madly swatting ourselves and spitting out mosquitoes, we rushed back to the plane as soon as Link had collected his rock samples. Airborne, we could see black, evil-looking clouds to the south almost lying on the land. However, to the northwest the sky was bright as we flew over the second big lake and along the north coast of Prince Albert Sound, reaching Ulukhaktok-Holman by midafternoon.

The Hudson's Bay Company house we had helped to build the previous summer looked beautiful, newly painted bright white with red roof and green trim. We were warmly greeted by our old friend Jock Kilgour, who was going out on furlough, and the incoming manager, Bill Calder. Father Buliard and many Inuit friends were also on hand, including Ikey and Etna Bolt, Natkusiak, and one of the very old women from Minto Inlet.

Later, when we were visiting, Ikey came up and said, "I hear white men are fighting. . . . Is that true?" "Yes," I replied, "That is true, Ikey." After a minute or two he said, "I hear they have very big guns. Can shoot people they can't see." Another pause. "Is that true?" he asked. "Yes, Ikey, it's crazy, but it is true." He stood silently gazing out the harbor, finally saying, "That's too bad. He might kill his best friend." With a sad, uncomprehending and reproachful glance, he walked slowly away. He was so right, and there was no way that I could explain such apparently irrational behavior to him.

After tea, Jock joined us for a flight to Minto Inlet, where Alf followed the northern shore eastward to its head. The sparkling air was so clear we could see, farther north, both Walker Bay and Collinson Inlet, the latter still choked with ice, while the land below us was beautiful with its dark, rugged trap bluffs and cliffs rising abruptly from amid a landscape of surprisingly verdant lowlands, rushing streams, waterfalls, small sapphire lakes reflecting the brilliant blue of the sky, and larger lakes still imprisoned under gleaming white ice. Landing on the clear waters at the head of Minto Inlet we waded ashore. The vegetation was so lush, I yearned for my plant press and time to collect specimens of the flowers and grasses; unfortunately the pace of geologists is not the same as that of botanists, and geology had priority.

By the time we returned to Holman Island, the sun was dipping toward the horizon and Bill had a fine supper ready for us all. Later Link and I visited Tommy Goose, who had said he would tell us more about the coal on

Ulukhaktok-Holman area, Victoria Island. View south.

Ulukhaktok-Holman, Victoria Island. Hudson's Bay Company post house which we helped build in 1939.

Ulukhaktok-Holman, Victoria Island. Hudson's Bay Company post manager, Bill Calder.

Ulukhaktok-Holman, Victoria Island. Catholic missionary, Father Roger Buliard, OMI, and Link.

Kent Peninsula. After that we stopped to see George Porter and David Pik-tukana to discuss the possibility of traveling east with them on David's schooner, *Sea Otter*, from Coppermine to Cambridge Bay via the mainland coast.

"That would be OK," they said, "if you don't mind being crowded." We certainly did not mind, so we agreed to join company when we all reached Coppermine. Etna Bolt had made sealskin waterboots for us, so we went over to her tent to pick them up. She and daughter Jane had also refitted the hoods of our shikshik (ground squirrel) attigis. Mine had a backing fringe of long-furred, black-tipped white wolf, which stood up behind the wolver-ine around my face, in the custom of the Mackenzie River Delta region.

Arms full, we left their tent and were silenced by the serene beauty of the evening—air cool and still, dark cliffs rising above us, high mesa etched against a flaming sky. We felt embraced by the very spirit of the place. Pen-sive, we returned to the post house, where we joined Bill, Jock, Charles, Alf, and Pat over a cup of tea before spreading our sleeping bags on the polar-bear skin beside Jock's big dog, Vickie, a husky.

Two hours of sleep later, at 4:00 A.M., the alarm clock wrenched us all awake for the weather sked with Coppermine. It was still bad there, so we enjoyed the beauty of dark cliffs standing stark against the pale turquoise, canary, and peach tints of the sunrise sky, while eating good Scottish oat-meal, bacon, and eggs. What a rare treat! After breakfast Link and I walked out toward the entrance of the bay for a last look around the area. Molly Goose was scraping a sealskin, another was stretched out to dry, and there were two whole sealskins with openings sewed up—one filled with blubber and one with seal oil. A small kamotik and kudlik were nearby. It was al-most mid-August, and the early autumn carpets of dark red, scarlet, and ocher formed by small prostrate willow trees and berry bushes were high-lighted by bright patches of orange, white, pale yellow, pink, and fuchsia flowers. No weaving by human hands could ever match such perfection. Returning to the post, we found that the weather had cleared at Copper-mine and the moment of departure had come.

When all our gear was stowed, we climbed into the Norseman and waved farewell. With prop roaring, Alf raced over the water, lifting the plane on the slight breeze, and headed east up Prince Albert Sound. Link needed to get some soil and erratic stone samples from near the base of Mount Bumpus. Later he would check the soil for foraminifera that might

Ulukhaktok-Holman, Victoria Island. The author holding Gutsie and wearing western-style attigi with wolfskin hood trim.

Ulukhaktok-Holman, Victoria Island. Molly Goose scraping a sealskin.

Ulukhaktok-Hølman, Victoria Island. Sealskin stretched to dry.

Ulukhaktok-Holman, Victoria Island. Sewn sealskin filled with blubber.

Ulukhaktok-Holman, Victoria Island. Sewn sealskin filled with seal oil.

Ulukhaktok-Holman, Victoria Island. Small kamotik with a large, carved soapstone kudlik (stove-lamp).

relate to former sea levels, and study the erratic stones to see if they were brought from the mainland by the continental glaciation. We landed on a convenient lake as a sudden squall struck. I jumped out, gathered the required specimens, scrambled back into the plane, and we roared off, bouncing along the waves. En route to Coppermine, we circled over Read Island, landed for a brief good-bye to Chitty, then headed across Coronation Gulf.

Life in the Arctic seemed to shift abruptly from peaceful stretches to periods when there was no time to sleep. When Sila, the Weather Spirit, smiled, you traveled, no matter the hour, day or night. The weather was reported good all the way to Edmonton, and Alf was anxious to leave Coppermine at the earliest possible moment. Lin Ross, expecting a second baby, was packing last-minute items for the trip south. Ray Ross was packing things, to return to Read Island. Hudson's Bay Company Inspector Paddy Gibson was going to Gjoa Haven. Charles Godefroy, ecstatic about his Arctic experiences, was rearranging his belongings for the flight south with Alf. Jock Livingston, who had been trading from Wilmot Island, was picking up loose ends, as he was leaving the Arctic and also going out with Alf.

Pretty sure that we were going to overwinter on Victoria Island, we bought Jock's dog team and small kamotik sight unseen. He had left them at Wilmot Island. We planned to pick them up after we joined David Piktukana. It was suddenly after midnight, and breakfast was to be at 3:30 A.M. for an early takeoff. Alf, Charles, Link, and I found out-of-the-way corners and slipped into our bags for a brief nap. Minutes later it seemed, breakfast was ready, and at 4:00 A.M. we waved good-bye to our friends as the little Norseman roared off. We were sorry to see Alf and his engineer Pat leave, for we had all had a really great time together. Climbing wearily back up the bank to the post, Link and I once again crept into our sleeping bags for a few hours of solid sleep.

As expected, the *Fort Ross* arrived later in the day, and the hamlet hummed with activity as fur bales were loaded into the ship's hold. Little Donald Kaglik, who was perhaps seven years old, leaning too far over the edge to watch the operation, lost his balance and fell into the hold. He dislocated his shoulder and injured his groin. The men picked him up carefully and carried him to the Anglican mission, and while I assisted Reverend Nicholson with administering ether, Reverend Harold Webster examined Donald's shoulder and slipped it back into place. When Donald came to he said, "I feel fine," but it was decided he should go to the hospital in Aklavik to be checked out. A stretcher was contrived and he was carried aboard.

During the entire episode Donald maintained a solemn calm. Except for a somewhat anxious expression in his eyes, one would never have realized he was undergoing a most frightening and painful experience. His ability to control his emotions in the face of shock and pain was typical of the Inuit. Late that evening Harold came to tell us that it was feared that pains his wife, Edie, had been suffering might be appendicitis. They had decided she should also go to the hospital at Aklavik with the *Fort Ross*. Edie, in considerable pain, was worried and upset by the turn of events, so I helped her get packed and settled in her little stateroom. She said she would keep an eye on Donald.

While we waited for George and David to arrive from Holman Island, Link and I spent the time investigating the local geology and making short exploratory boat trips to some of the numerous small islands, hoping to find fossils, but without notable success. We joined Harold on two trips up the Coppermine River to Bloody Falls to get fish from the Inuit, where, as they had for centuries, they were netting fish to dry and add to the winter food supply. Again, Hearne's grisly experience of the Inuits' massacre there came to mind, as I watched the local Inuit draw in a net full of fish. Later, Link and I talked at some length about what our future might hold and he came to the conclusion that if the United States entered the war, which seemed more and more likely, he would sign up. He also wanted very much to complete his doctoral dissertation at Yale, but felt he needed more information about the geology of the region, so we definitely decided to overwinter in order to examine areas we had not yet seen.

Since Jock Livingston's team consisted of only five dogs, we thought we should try to add at least two more if possible. We spoke to several people and found that Harold had one dog he was willing to sell, named Tuk because he was the color of a tuktu (caribou), and shaped somewhat like one as well. Father Lucien Delalonde, the fine, soft-spoken Oblate priest we had met at Holman, said he really did not need Nero and would be happy to sell him to us. Nero was one of the offspring of the husky bitches bred to the Saint Bernards that the Fathers had brought from the French Alps, believing that five big dogs could pull as heavy a load as seven to nine regular huskies. It did not work out. They ate more and had far less stamina than a husky, so they were crossbred with huskies. Nero was big, but we bought him anyway; there was no choice. He had lived a checkered life, having belonged to two different Fathers and to the RCMP at Cambridge Bay. While there he had apparently missed his teammates back at Coppermine. One night he broke his chain and headed home, making his way back along some 300 or more miles of frozen coast and gulf to rejoin them. Gaunt, starved, and exhausted, but happy, he made it. I wondered if he would try to leave us later.

Among the Inuit, the man drove the team. His wife hitched, unhitched, fed, and cared for the dogs. As wife, that was to be one of my pleasant duties, so I went to see first Nero and then Tuk. Their greetings were anything but reassuring! Nero stood tall, tail up but not wagging, head lowered with lips drawn up, while a lion-sized rumble welled up and his baleful yellow eyes glared at me, daring me to come one step closer. Mustering my most soothing voice, I repeatedly intoned, *"Good* Nero, *good* boy, *good* dog," over and over, meanwhile wondering how I could ever hope to get a dog harness on him.

When I approached Tuk he slunk to the end of his chain and lay there in a shaking frenzy of snarling, choking growls, his eyes filled with fear and hatred. Again speaking as reassuringly as possible, I repeated over and over the same refrain I had used with Nero. Later that day, and whenever I could find a few spare moments, I went out to them, each time filling their water dishes, bringing some small tidbit as a peace offering, and speaking with encouraging warmth. Gradually their growling lessened and the expression in their eyes changed. Nero no longer lowered his head, but met me eye to eye and finally waved his big plume and allowed me to pat him. After that he welcomed me with arpeggios while lunging at the end of his chain, forefeet pawing the air and his big, wet tongue lolling out to slobber my face. The same gradual change took place in my relationship with Tuk, although he was not as demonstrative as Nero. Later both dogs turned out to be good pullers, but Tuk really outdid himself, straining to pull the whole kamotik whenever Link called out to him. We decided that kindness and encouragement got the best results, although there were a few times when force was required. One had to maintain a position as "Top Dog," as well as best friend!

One night we went to the weather station for dinner and to send a message to Captain Henry Larsen on the *St. Roch.* Lin Ross had asked us to please take her young cockerel, the sole survivor of the baby chicks, over to

Isabel at Cambridge Bay. Since we could not take it on the overcrowded *Sea Otter,* if we traveled east with David and George, we asked Henry if he would be willing to give it a lift. Kind friend that he was, he said he would be happy to do so and also offered to pick us up at Wilmot Island while en route to Cambridge Bay. Surprised and pleased, we gratefully accepted.

That evening an Inuit dance was held in the RCMP warehouse. It was fascinating to watch both the dancers and those who were sitting around on piles of fishnets, rope, or dried fish, holding little limp forms of sleeping infants across their laps. They danced or sat almost expressionless, their faces lighted only by occasional, momentary smiles or laughter, yet all were enjoying themselves hugely.

8 / With Sea Otter to Wilmot Island

On to Cambridge Bay

August 26–September 10, 1940

*D*avid Piktukana and George Porter arrived at Coppermine August 26 on *Sea Otter,* with their families and two young Inuks, Norman and Harry, also with their families. Link asked David if we might still be able to join them as planned at Holman, if we helped to pay for the fuel. "That would be fine," he replied. "You can sleep on the shelf in front of the wheel in the wheelhouse. I most times sit on the edge of the open hatch above, and steer with my feet. I can see over the deck load better that way. You can tie your two dogs on the deck with the forty-three other dogs." We said, "Great," and then Link told him that we needed to stop at Wilmot Island to pick up the small kamotik and five more dogs we had just purchased. David smiled, the imperturbable Inuk, and said again, "That would be fine."

The following day, when we put our possessions on board the 45-foot *Sea Otter,* it looked as if a furry blanket covered the deck. David was moving and had taken down his one-room house at Holman and stowed the lumber in the schooner's hold. Twelve members of the families were camped on top of all this. There wasn't much headroom or space to move about, nor any privacy, but everybody was happy and excited by the prospect of traveling to a different area where they would meet new people as well as see some old friends. Through the millennia the Inuit had learned to find something funny in all hardships and to make the best of any situation, laughing and joking about problems instead of wasting time and energy grousing, one of their many wise ways which I try to keep remembering.

On deck, besides the dogs, were sacks of dried Arctic char for dog food, three basket sleds, one jolly boat, one canoe, and all the drums of fuel oil,

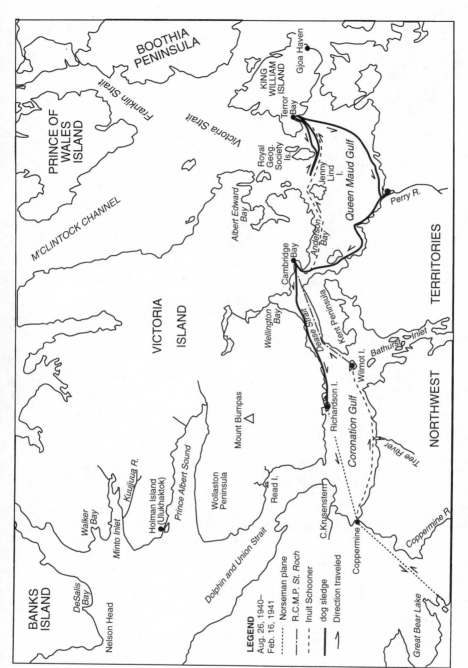

MAP 6. August 26, 1940–February 16, 1941

coal oil for lamps and Primus stoves, and cases of supplies for the winter. By squeezing some of the dogs together, impossible as that seemed, we had managed to open some huddling space for our two dogs, bringing the total to forty-five dogs on the deck. It was tricky to try to walk forward, for there was no deck visible between dog bodies, and we were never sure whether we would be bitten or not. One timid dog was driven by his neighbors to climb up on a winch. He sat on the main part with his front paws on a crossbar, but when he fell asleep, exhausted, and sagged down between, the dog under him would snarl and bite his stomach. We finally asked George to squeeze a couple of dogs over, to give the poor beast enough deck space to lie down. No dogs were tied on the narrow aft deck.

The waters of the mainland coast east of Coppermine are dotted with numerous small islands, and for some distance the coastal land rises gently to the south. Thick, white fog obscured the world, and since no one on board had sailed along this coast, we proceeded with caution. At sundown, the fog behind us became tinged with red and we dropped anchor in the lee of an island, hoping for better visibility the following day. The "red sky at night" proved to be our delight as the morning dawned clear. Weighing anchor at 7:00 A.M. we resumed our journey and passed *Our Lady of Lourdes,* which we discovered at anchor around the point from where we had spent the night. She overtook us about two hours later as we were turning into the inlet where the Tree River empties into Coronation Gulf.

David found a place where we could anchor beside the beach, and as soon as we made fast, Norman and Harry jumped ashore and started out over the land hoping to find caribou, not only for meat but also for skins, which their wives would tan to make winter clothing, the hair being long and thick by the end of August. The poor dogs were finally led off the boat, taken to the river for a drink, and given a little piece of dry fish and an opportunity to relieve themselves before being tied up again. When traveling by boat, the dogs were given food and water only every two or three days so that they would not defecate on the deck or each other.

The women and children, laughing, chattering, and glad to be able to stretch, took sealskin bags and went off to pick blueberries, dig roots, and collect cotton grass and willow fuzz for wicks in the kudlik stove-lamps. The countryside was beautiful. On both sides of the river, high trap cliffs, strikingly decorated by patterns of bright orange, black, and white lichens,

Coppermine, mainland coast of Coronation Gulf. David Piktukana's schooner, *Sea Otter*, loaded except for dogs.

On board David Piktukana's schooner, *Sea Otter*. David, Link, dogs, and David's wife and son.

framed the view to the south. Verdant valleys near the river mouth rose to rugged hills and a distant low mountain.

Link and I spent the day happily exploring the area, photographing and collecting hand specimens of bedrock to check against erratics on Victoria Island and soil samples to check for foraminifera. Later, Norman and Harry returned laden with the meat and skin of a big bull caribou, one of a small herd they had found. We congratulated them on their success and they told us they had seen a herd of fourteen musk-oxen, which we regretted having missed. That night we squeezed onto our three-foot shelf in front of the ship's wheel, lulled to sleep by the continuous, low, singsong snarling and growling of the cramped dogs next to our ears, on the other side of the glass window. From time to time during the night we were awakened by short-lived frenzies of teeth-clashing hysteria. These subsided again after high-pitched tirades from either David or George.

David weighed anchor before dawn, although a cold, clammy mist obscured the world and the chill seeped through our clothing. Later the skies cleared and we marveled at the seemingly numberless, rugged islands and islets among which we slowly wound our way. We made good time crossing Bathurst Inlet to Wilmot Island, where Alec Eccles came out from the little post in a jolly boat to pilot us around the reef to a safe harbor. We spent an enjoyable evening with him, and the next morning rowed his jolly boat to the adjacent islet where our five dogs were tied. The bitch had broken loose and had apparently been catching lemmings to feed her brother and two old teammates, but not the fourth, a young newcomer who was so thin we had to shoot him. The dogs were overjoyed to come with us, and we tied them up near the *Sea Otter*. They drank feverishly and gulped down the dried fish without chewing. When I asked where we would put them, David replied matter-of-factly, a smile behind his eyes, "There's only forty-five dogs on deck. Plenty of room for four more." We could not see where they would fit, but fit they did when the time came.

The wind was too high for David to start for Cambridge Bay, so he said we might as well look for the material that Tommy Goose called coal. Amid an earsplitting uproar of snarling, howling, fighting dogs and shouting people, we loaded up after breakfast and set off on the *Sea Otter* to search for that substance on some of the small sheltered islands. We all looked carefully and found some pitchy material in the dolomitic rock which would

Wilmot Island, off west point of Kent Peninsula. Patsy Klengenberg's trading post and beautifully preserved raised beach ridges.

Cambridge Bay, Victoria Island. Royal Canadian Mounted Police *St. Roch*.

burn, but no real coal. Back on Wilmot Island, Link asked Alec if he had a deerskin tent we might purchase for our base camp, wherever that might be. Luckily, he did. It had been much used, the hair was short, and there were many small .22 caliber rifle holes to be patched, but we figured it would serve our needs.

Wondering when the *St. Roch* would arrive to pick us up as Henry Larsen had offered to do, Link and I went up to Alec's to wait out the windy weather and to listen to the Coppermine 5:00 P.M. broadcast. While we all visited, I sewed pairs of tartan drapes for the two small windows in his tiny house. At five o'clock, Coppermine came on the air and said that the *St. Roch* expected to reach Wilmot that evening. We looked forward to being with Henry Larsen for the trip to Cambridge, and when he failed to arrive we wondered what had happened. The *St. Roch* was built in 1928 as the supply ship for the RCMP's Arctic detachments, and had spent most of the time since then in the Canadian Arctic, under the very able guiding hand of Captain Larsen. About 100 feet overall, she was a stout little ship with an armor of iron-bark to help her withstand the grinding ice as she plied her way through Arctic seas, or when frozen in during the long winters.

As soon as the wind died down David and the others departed for Cambridge Bay to get winter supplies, visit, and leave off our dogs. Link and I set off to examine the geology of Wilmot and adjacent islands in some detail while pondering our situation and thinking about alternative plans if the *St. Roch* failed to pick us up. Alec was delighted by the possibility of having our company until after freeze-up, when we would be able to cross over to Cambridge Bay with his team. He said it was a lonely time until Christmas, when the people came to trade. However, to remain there would have radically changed our plans.

In the Arctic, because of the weather, the easiest thing to break is a schedule. The *St. Roch* anchored at Wilmot on the third morning, having been delayed by the wind. Captain Larsen said they would pull out the following morning, weather permitting, so Link and I went on board. But Sila, controller of the weather, was not in a cooperative mood, and we had to wait two more days before weighing anchor. To my delight, the cockerel was safely on board, albeit complaining bitterly about being cooped up in a small box. Corporal Duncan Martin, a pleasant, soft-spoken fellow, the relief for Scott Alexander, who was going Outside, was also on board. Link

Cambridge Bay, Victoria Island. Royal Canadian Mounted Police detachment.

and I were happy to have the opportunity to become acquainted with him, as we expected to keep in frequent touch with him by radio during our winter travels. Our time on board passed too quickly as we listened to Captain Larsen's tales of his Arctic voyages and discussed his plan to winter at Walker Bay on Victoria Island and make the Northwest Passage, sailing east, the following summer. As we thrust steadily through the seas, I tried to visualize that voyage, and wished that I might be an invisible stowaway. How wonderful it would be to overwinter at beautiful Walker Bay and to experience the attempt to make the Northwest Passage, sailing east and north!

The following autumn, the *St. Roch* made it up the west coast of Boothia Peninsula as far as Pasley Bay, where it was frozen in for the winter, close to the beach. As the pack ice began to thaw and move, the *St. Roch* was freed and on August 4, 1942, began to work her way through terrible rough ice, finally reaching the Hudson's Bay Company post at Fort Ross, at the east end of Bellot Strait, on August 29. From there she went around the northern end of Baffin Island and south to Halifax, where she wintered, having completed during 1941–42 the first Northwest Passage from west to east. In 1944, she returned to Vancouver, British Columbia, by way of Lancaster Sound and Prince of Wales Strait, becoming the first ship to make the Passage from both west and east.

It was dark by the time we reached the outer bay at Cambridge. We anchored off Simpson Rock for the night and went into the inner bay early the next morning. George and David were there, and Captain Larsen asked George if he would like to join him for the winter and their planned attempt to make the Northwest Passage the following year. George accepted at once, so David continued on his journey east.

While Link helped to unload the winter supplies at the RCMP detachment, I took the cockerel to Isabel. She was enchanted by him and he was overjoyed when let out of his small box. As he strutted on the counter, carefully lifting his feet, his red-mahogany feathers gleamed in the light. Scotty made a larger box equipped with convenient pull-out tray, and Isabel stitched a black cloth to cover it when the young rooster's constant monologue became exhausting. I suspect the local Inuit, who had never seen such a bird, wondered if he would taste as good as a ptarmigan!

9 / With Patsy Klengenberg on Aklavik
To Terror Bay, King William Island
September 14–19, 1940

*I*t was good to be home again in our little house at Cambridge Bay, this time with our own dogs tied on a nearby dog line where we could keep an eye on them. Our team! Every time I looked at them I fairly glowed inside. It was already September 10 and I wondered where we would go with them during the imminent winter. They were certainly happy to be on land again, and they appeared to be content with us. Had Nero recognized his one-time home area? He seemed pretty relaxed. We figured the team would take some time to become used to one another, and it would certainly take us a while to get the hang of driving them once the snow came. We anticipated our first run with them and began to get ourselves and our belongings organized for a series of kamotik trips inland on Victoria Island during the winter.

When we looked out the window a few mornings later, an unfamiliar boat was at anchor in front of the Company Post. It was *Aklavik*, owned by Patsy Klengenberg, son of whaling captain Christian Klengenberg and older brother of Jorgen. In 1937, Patsy and Scotty had navigated the Northwest Passage, going east to meet the Hudson's Bay Company's eastern Arctic supply ship *Nascopie* at Fort Ross, the first commercial contact between two vessels using the Northwest Passage.

Interested to meet Patsy, we went over to the post later in the morning. Link began to think about the possibility of accompanying him to Terror Bay on King William Island, where Patsy lived with his brother, Jorgen, and their families. The bay had been named in honor of Sir John Franklin's ship *Terror*, which was lost with *Erebus* off the northwestern coast of King William Island in 1848. That would give us an opportunity to check on any

King William Island-Terror Bay. Jorgen Klengenberg's schooner *Polar Bear* up on the beach for winter. The *Aklavik* waiting its turn. Our dory in foreground on the beach.

King William Island-Terror Bay. Patsy and Jorgen Klengenberg's home.

evidence of glaciation there and would extend the coverage of Link's dissertation. He suggested the possibility to Patsy, who, after considerable discussion of the pros and cons and questioning the local Inuit about us, agreed to take us under certain conditions. We would have to be entirely self-supporting, and we could make no demands on his time, for he would be busy running his trap line. Nevertheless, he agreed to accompany us back to Cambridge Bay for Christmas. We would pay half the cost of the boat fuel and would compensate Patsy for the time he lost on his trap line during the trip to Cambridge.

That all sounded logical and acceptable, but it entailed our being able to shoot enough seals and catch enough fish to feed our dogs, and also ourselves if we ran out of canned and dried foods. It meant Link would have to learn, by watching the men, how to prepare a 100-foot fishnet, chop holes through six or seven feet of lake ice and string the net under it, then with his bare hands haul out the net and remove the fish at −40°F. It meant that he would also have to learn how to make harnesses for our dogs and how to hitch them to our little kamotik. By observing Iglikshik and Mikigiak, Patsy and Jorgen's wives, I would have to learn how to "tan" caribou hides and cut and sew them for our winter clothing. It was a challenge. We discussed all possibilities, good and bad, and in the end decided that if Patsy was willing to risk taking us, and if the RCMP corporal could give us permission to shoot seals, we were ready to accompany him. My excitement rose to fever point. Terror Bay, King William Island!

It was already September 11, and Patsy was in a hurry to return to Terror Bay. Freeze-up was not far off, and both his and his brother Jorgen's schooners had to be hauled up the beach beyond the reach of winter ice shove. The next two days Link and I worked in a frenzy, stuffing clothes and personal needs into our duffle bags, and notebooks, maps, and other fieldwork items into our Bergen rucksacks. We bought some extra staple foods from Scotty at the post to add to those brought in by the *Fort Ross* for us, and boxed them all. We put our two-man cookset in the wooden grub box and made sure the two Primus stoves and lantern were in top shape with enough emergency parts and enough coal oil for fuel. We purchased candles, flashlight bulbs, and batteries. Mary Kaglik helped me select enough caribou skins from which I would make our winter clothing. As the stack grew higher, I wondered how I was ever going to get them all "tanned," let alone sewn. We obtained netting and backing line for the 100-

foot fishnet, ammunition, materials to make dog harnesses and a kamotik cover, and gas and oil for the dory's outboard motor. What we forgot or undersupplied, we would have to do without. We bought a dog from Kopun to take the place of the one on Wilmot we'd had to shoot.

Three days later on September 14, our fifth wedding anniversary, we hugged Scotty and Isabel, and with everybody and everything on board Patsy pulled anchor and headed out the bay. We towed Sam Carter in his boat to conserve his fuel and were escorted by Reg, Dunc, Scotty, Einar, and Louis Kaglik in the RCMP whaleboat. Sam had promised to show Patsy a tiny hidden harbor at Cape Colborne, and we anchored there safely for the night.

Although it was breezy, we started out early the following morning, but soon had to return, for it was blowing too hard beyond the shelter of the cape. Link and I went ashore in the jolly boat and spent the day investigating the vicinity, where we saw several ancient, weathered bone artifacts, probably relics of the earlier Thule inhabitants. These we left in place, hoping that some archaeologist would one day collect them. We returned to the *Aklavik* and retired early, for in order not to miss seeing anything, we wanted to be up when Patsy started.

Iglikshik and Patsy's nine-year-old son Ayalik, as well as his widowed daughter Ikilik and her two babies, three-year-old Iviguak and seven-month-old Ohokok, remained in the hold for most of the trip. It was cold and windy, or foggy, much of the time and warm in the hold. Iglikshik came on deck occasionally but Ayalik, an active and curious youngster, was on deck frequently. Patsy had three two-month-old puppies in a box on deck, and Ayalik had great fun with them.

As soon as the tide was in, we started off in a rough sea against a high headwind—bucking, diving, and weaving in a most unseemly manner. Luckily we were not seasick. We wove around many small ice pans and thick, old ice floes, passing great chunks of rafted ice that had grounded along the shore. The blow increased late in the afternoon, and Patsy decided to turn back a short distance. "We can get shelter for the night," he said, "between the land and that heavy ice we saw grounded off that little hook we passed."

We had agreed with Patsy earlier that Link would take turnabout with him at the wheel, and I would stand watch at night while they slept. When we anchored, I went on deck and took what shelter there was behind the wheelhouse. From this vantage point I could see any ice pans that might bear down on our bow. Luckily for us, the grounded ice stayed where it was, and I had only a few pans to ease off the bow with the long boat hook.

The night was one of strange exhilaration for me. The wind-flung rain, almost freezing, stung my face, and the shrouds sang, strummed, and slapped softly against the mast as the ice pans slipped by like whispering ghosts. By morning the wind had died down somewhat but not enough for us to leave; during the day it regained strength and began to swing round toward the southwest. That was bad, since there was no shelter from a southwestern gale. After our evening meal that night I again went on deck when Link and Patsy headed for their bunks. Soon all was quiet below except for the sounds of regular breathing and the lapping of waves against the hull.

As the hours passed, the wind intermittently rose and died. During the quiescent times I was wrapped in a mysterious sense of unity with the night, the mists, the stealthy, relentless ice. But when the wind gathered force and more and more ice bore down on us, I grabbed the long-handled boat hook, jumped to action stumbling over the dogs or dory on the deck, scrambling first to one side then the other trying to be on both sides of the bow at once to keep the ice at bay by shoving it slowly away from the boat with the boat hook. It was exciting, and I wanted to scream back at the wind which shrieked in the shrouds around the mast. At still other times when the clouds broke and there was a lull in the wind, a light, white, icy fog would materialize, with the full moon gleaming through it, forming a softly iridescent moonbow. It was not difficult to understand how such a mysterious light could beckon a life-weary, weakened grandparent to walk out on the ice to go through its arc into the happy land of the forefathers, a practice among Inuit that died out not so many years ago.

Shortly after midnight, the wind rose from the southwest and drove much more ice around the point. I called Patsy. He took a quick look and said, "We had better get out into open water before the ice jams us against the land." As we headed east, the moon laid a quicksilver path across the turbulent water. It enticed us into the nothingness of a light, low fog, while a pale moonbow arched over our sparkling, phosphorescent wake. Occasionally, some old rafted ice would loom ominously ahead, glistening for a moment in the moonpath as we pitched and rolled before the wind. By 2:30 A.M. my eyes would no longer remain open and I went below.

September 14–19, 1940 ✶ *150*

Six hours later I climbed on deck, just as we were passing Jenny Lind Island, some 13 miles east of Victoria Island, in Victoria Strait. Sadly, two of the puppies had climbed out of the box and disappeared, probably overboard. Early that afternoon Patsy reached the Royal Geographical Society Islands 25 miles farther east, and we dropped anchor in a sheltered area provided by several of the small, low-lying, bedrock islands just off the south coast of the large islands.

As we slowly stopped, an Inuk paddled out from the shore in a sealskin kayak, the first we had seen in use in the central Arctic. It was Utuitoq, who with his wife and two children and a friend, Aylikomiq, with his wife and child, had been camping on the islands since early spring. They came by kamotik from Pelly Bay on Simpson Peninsula, some 400 miles to the east, intending to return home before spring break-up. But a severe late spring storm had roared down Victoria Strait out of the north, breaking up the ice and stranding them on the islands. They planned to return to Pelly Bay as soon as the ice was safe.

Although Father Henry, a widely respected and beloved Oblate priest, had his mission at Pelly Bay, this region was the least exposed to outside influence. The Inuit there, including Utuitoq and Aylikomiq, used bows and arrows as well as rifles, and they still practiced most of their traditional ways. Besides shooting seals, Utuitoq and his group had also survived by snaring ducks, ptarmigan, hare, and small birds for food for themselves and their dogs, and by using the skins for clothing and a tent. The latter was an amazing patchwork of bird skins, caribou skins, and sealskins. Utuitoq joined us on board for a cup of tea, after which we all went ashore for a visit in his remarkable tent, Patsy interpreting for us. Afterward, Link and I went a short distance to investigate bedrock exposures, which we were happy to find well striated.

Through Patsy, Utuitoq had told us that there were many ruins of ancient stone houses on the islands across the harbor. The following day we went over in our dory to see them. The stone blocks had been laid up just as the snow blocks are for a snow house, the diameter being about six feet. Of course the roofs had long since fallen in, and all was overgrown with grasses, willow, and lichens. At one side there was a curved row of blocks built out from the wall, which may have been part of an entry shelter similar to those built out from snow houses. We wondered if they had been made by the earlier Thule People. Although it was a great temptation to investigate them, we knew that one day archaeologists would do it properly. In the spring we reported them to Dr. Diamond Jenness at the National Museum in Ottawa.

Patsy in his jolly boat and we in our dory searched for seals for our dog teams, without success. Aylikomiq returned from his hunt on the big island with one caribou and said another got away. He came over in the little round coracle he and his wife had put together from sealskins, stretched around a form of braided willow branches, made for crossing from island to island. He brought us some of the precious meat, which we were loath to accept, realizing that they were perilously short of food. But it was their custom to share what was available, although with only ten rounds of ammunition left they knew they might well be hungry before freeze-up made it possible for them to return home.

They had only enough coal oil for one more filling of their little tin stove and a Primus. With no available wood or coal and no coal oil, they would have to rely on seal oil in the soapstone kudlik for cooking, heat, and light, as their forefathers had done. The shadow of starvation had always been just ahead for the Inuit people, and food was always shared. We gave them some of our ammunition, hoping the seals would come into the nearby waters, and also kerosene and Primus stove needles to clear out their burner, which was becoming clogged.

The blustery wind continued for two days, enabling Link and me to collect shells and rocks and to investigate the nearby islands. We tried our luck at sealing again, but without success. During this time Aylikomiq invited us to his camp, where we met his wife, who was blind. He told Patsy that five years earlier she had given birth to twins and had lost her eyesight at that time. Because it was impossible for a mother to carry more than one baby on her back, she had given one baby to a mother who had just lost hers. We had never heard of a woman going blind in childbirth, but there must have been unusual strain.

In spite of her blindness, she was able to "tan" the skins, and as long as someone threaded the needle with sinew she could, with one exception, sew the needed garments for herself and her family. Only the sealskin water-boots, which require intricate folding and stitching of the skins, were beyond her skills. This saddened her greatly, for she was an accomplished seamstress. I wondered if I would really be able to learn how to "tan" and sew the skins!

September 14–19, 1940 ★ *152*

She had prepared a fine kettle of boiled caribou. Following the general procedure, we carefully picked a chunk of meat out of the kettle with our fingers and took hold of an edge with our teeth. Then, using a pocketknife in lieu of an ulu or a sheath knife as our hosts did, we were supposed to cut off a piece small enough to eat without cutting off the end of our noses at the same time. This presented no problem for those who had learned the art as babies. But those of us with longer noses, and therefore shaky nerves, inevitably ended with a piece really too big to manage gracefully. Our chipmunk-like stuffed cheeks provided great amusement for our hosts, who tried to conceal their smiles and who undoubtedly thought it odd that we had grown up without learning how to eat properly.

When we awoke on the third day, we found that a north wind had sprung up during the night, lowering the temperature and covering the land with a thin coat of snow which soon vanished under the meager warmth of the low sun. However, the bottoms of the dark gray clouds in the northern sky, now white from ice blink, told us that the ice pack was approaching. Patsy knew that the early autumn storms might begin at any time, as it was already September 21. Accordingly, we bade our new friends good-bye and once more headed east.

The run to King William Island took about five hours. Cape Crozier appeared on the horizon within a couple of hours of our departure. The rest of the low-lying coast gradually rose above the rim of stormy, steel-gray, white-capped waters in which many ice pans rose and bowed with the swells. Under the brooding lenticular clouds, the distant land was not inviting, and I wondered about the months to come.

As we drew near the head of Terror Bay, Patsy and Jorgen's little house and Jorgen's schooner, *Polar Bear*, became discernible, and soon we saw him coming to meet us in the jolly boat. We joked and laughed together with Patsy and Iglikshik, wondering what Jorgen's expression would be when he saw Link and me. There had been no way to let him know that we were with Patsy. We had not met since a brief encounter on Herschel Island in 1936, but we need not have worried. His face was full of amusement and good nature as he climbed on board to welcome us. Towing his jolly boat, we continued to the shore where the beach shelved steeply, and anchored beside *Polar Bear*.

When the *Aklavik* had been made secure, we went up to the one-room house to meet Jorgen's wife, Mikigiak, his eleven-year-old adopted son,

Maneratsiak, and little daughter, Mary. Another Inuk, Tulemaq, was living with Ikilik, her two babies, and the two boys, Ayalik and Maneratsiak, in a tent nearby. Since only Patsy and Jorgen could speak English, our contact with the others was through smiles, with much soft giggling by the ladies. The atmosphere was one of warm welcome spiced by amused curiosity, which made us feel happy. The ladies produced a great supper of fresh-boiled char, potatoes, and real home-baked bread made in the coal range oven. By the time we finished, it was too late to set up camp, so Link and I slept once more in our bunk on the *Aklavik*.

Patsy and Jorgen built their snug little house sometime in the thirties, when they decided to make Terror Bay their home base for trapping. The roomy entry had many shelves and hooks where outer clothing, dog harnesses, fox traps, raw deerskins, and a sealskin poke filled with seal oil for the kudlik, which was used in the camp at the fish lake, were kept. Weathered driftwood boards, perhaps from Sir John Franklin's *Erebus* or *Terror*, which were probably crushed by the ice off the northwestern coast of King William Island in 1848, stood against the wall. Precious bits and pieces of all sorts were kept for some unknown future need. In the main room were the coal range, a table and kitchen cabinet, and long racks hanging from the ceiling holding everything that required drying, from wet clothing to caribou skins.

Personal privacy cannot be realized in a tent or snow house, so it had never been thought of as essential, but one wall of the room was divided into two alcoves by a floor-to-ceiling partition. Across each alcove lay a high, built-in platform that served as a living area and bed for each family. All manner of personal possessions were stored under each platform, while on the rear wall above it were shelves for books and smaller items—an excellent arrangement for limited space.

The following morning was beautiful, bright, and clear. I pitched our two small tents on a rise behind the house, at some distance from the one occupied by Tulemaq and the boys, while Link helped unload the supplies brought by Patsy. As our things were unloaded we packed them away. Bed skins and sleeping bags, rucksacks and duffle bags, Primus box, lantern, grub box with cooking and eating utensils, and some food supplies were all put in our six-foot-square tent. Into the eight-foot-square tent went: a crate each of potatoes, oranges, and eggs (I wondered what would happen when they froze); the raw caribou skins, netting, tapes, and line; dog harness collars, webbing, and sewing materials; rolls of heavy duck cloth; boxes and bags for rock specimens; a broad steel chisel for chopping holes through the ice; and a long-handled scoop for removing the ice debris.

As the hours fled by, the temperature dropped and a strong north wind wove low-flying clouds into a tapestry of grays. We had just put a pot on the Primus to heat water for tea when wet snow began slapping against the tent.

As I walked away from the tent the next morning, a bright sun shone, but the biting wind was still blowing. A vision of warm, tiled rooms with plumbing flitted across my mind. There was no privy. After breakfast, Patsy sewed a skin patch over one of the bullet holes in our old caribou skin tent to demonstrate how it should be mended. I was as a child to Patsy, and he expected me to learn quickly by watching. When he finished the patch, he handed me the sinew-threaded needle and moved on to other chores. I sat on part of the tent, which was too big to take indoors, and sewed and sewed until my fingers could no longer grasp the needle, numbed as they were by the icy wind.

The next afternoon Patsy and Jorgen in their jolly boats, and Link and I in our dory, tried our luck sealing in the bay. Neither Link nor I enjoyed the killing, yet we had to have food for our dogs and ourselves, so we were pleased to shoot three seals the first day. The dory lay over on her side beautifully, making it easy to pull the fat, floating seals into it. Another day as the dory moved slowly over the still water, a large, round head suddenly appeared. Link fired the .22 Special he had been using. We were both sure that the seal had been hit, but it sank instead of floating, as would normally happen in the autumn. We waited about ten minutes to see if it would rise, then gave up and started to look for other heads to pop up.

We had gone perhaps a hundred yards when, looking back, we saw a commotion in the water. Hurrying to the spot we discovered an ugyuk, or bearded seal, which can weigh from 600 to 800 pounds. The .22 lead which hit him in the nose would have killed a smaller seal, but the poor beast looked like some sea monster of old, with his great square head and long whiskers covered with bloody foam. If a young hippo had come to the surface, we could not have been more perturbed. Nonplused, we were unable to get a hold on him. The boat gaff was not sharp enough to pierce his thick

King William Island-Terror Bay. Link in dory.

hide, and we knew he would sink the minute we killed him. Yet we had to try to get him, since he would feed our seven dogs for a week or more and his hide would be of use for heavy lines and boot soles.

By dint of rapid maneuvering, Link was able to grab one of the ugyuk's huge flippers just as he went into shock, standing upright, as it seemed, in the water beside the stern of the boat. Our .30-30 rifle was in the bow, and, as I scrambled aft with it, I stumbled over a dead seal, then slipped on the bloody boat bottom, doing a split and joggling the boat and Link. The ugyuk, reviving, struggled to free himself, but Link held on as the dory tipped precariously.

Making a last great effort, the big seal wrenched himself free of Link's grasp and I handed Link the .30-30. He put a shot into the ugyuk's skull while I grabbed the gaff and once more tried desperately to hook it into his nose, mouth, under a flipper, or almost anywhere, except his eyes, to keep from losing him. But it was to no avail. With great round eyes staring up at us through the clear water, he sank slowly down, down, and out of sight. I shall never forget my feeling of guilt and sorrow at our having killed him for nothing. We looked for more seals but, seeing none, headed for home, retracing our route in the hope that the ugyuk might have come to the surface again. Alas, there was no sign of him.

That evening after supper in our tent we went over to the house to see what luck, if any, Patsy and Jorgen had had, and to tell them of our success with the three seals and sad loss of the ugyuk. Jorgen smiled and said, "I lost half of my ugyuk!" When I asked how he could lose half, he explained, "It was too big to drag into the jolly boat and too heavy to drag aft, so I tied it to the side of the boat and cut it in half. I got one half into the boat and tried to drag the other half astern, but it pulled loose and sank."

He said that I should have jabbed the gaff into the ugyuk's eye to hold him. I suppose he was right, but I do not think I could have done that even if starving. He thought the one we had killed would probably float up later, and might be washed ashore where it could be retrieved. But we never saw it again.

The next morning we were up by half past five and out on the fog-shrouded water by seven. Our whole world seemed to be an opal in which we floated. Water and sky merged indistinguishably except when a seal's black head appeared in the center of silvery, ever-widening, concentric circles. It was impossible to tell if the seal was a small one near the boat or a large one farther away. There was a total sense of unreality. Occasionally we drew near enough to see Patsy's or Jorgen's boat, seemingly suspended, a phantom in an opalescent dream world.

Hundreds of eider ducks and old squaws, gathering for their long flights south, rose splashing, but invisible, from the sea around us. The beating of their wings sounded like a waterfall. Unable to see us either, they flew just beside or close over our heads, and then the rushing of air through their wings echoed the song of a sudden high wind in a pine forest. Hours passed and the fog gradually lifted until we could finally see around the harbor and out to the islands beyond. Having secured three more seals, which would feed our dogs for another week, we swung about, heading for home.

Each day the temperature slipped lower, and there was a sense of urgency in the air. Much remained to be done before winter engulfed us, and we knew it was just over the horizon to the north. We all continued sealing, with varying success. The men hand-winched *Polar Bear* and *Aklavik* up on the beach beyond the reach of storm-shoved ice, slow work with a turnstile and block and tackle. That done, they set up our caribou-skin tent which I had so laboriously begun to patch.

The tent was eight feet wide, nine feet long, and seven feet high at the ridge pole, the walls being four feet high. The small door, about three feet high by two feet wide, was made of skin on a wood frame. The window was a piece of tightly stretched sealskin scraped free of hair and part of the skin to make it translucent. Unfortunately while patching the tent skins I had missed several small gunshot holes, through which the wind now whispered and windblown snow sifted, creating little white crystalline cones during the night. These quickly became puddles when the Primus was lighted.

I realized I'd have to stitch more patches over the holes on the outside of the tent. This necessitated pushing a needle with sinew thread through the edge of the patch and the tent, then going inside to pull it through and push the needle back out for the next stitch. I worked away at the task for an hour or two at a time until my fingers became too cold, then went into the dark, skin tent to work at other chores by kerosene lamplight until my fingers were warm enough to continue sewing.

I had no willow bed mat, which every good wife would have made for insulation from the gravel. Instead, I laid the polar bear skin, which Patsy had loaned us, hair side down on the gravel of our bed site. On top I laid the caribou skins, opened eiderdowns and our caribou-skin bags, as we had in our snow house. Large, smooth cobblestones held the front and one side of the bed skins in place while duffle bags lay between the other edges and the side and back walls of the tent.

The Primus box was set up on one side of the door along with the camp cookset and water bucket. A box with food supplies was placed beside them. On the other side of the door sat our enamel hand basin and towels. The daylight hours were gradually becoming shorter, and we found ourselves crawling into our inviting bed earlier and earlier in the evenings. The Primus and coal oil lantern warmed the tent enough for us to sit in our wool shirtsleeves, but when we awakened in the morning, hoarfrost usually covered the "ceiling." My first morning chore was to scrape the beautiful crystals into a tin plate with a spoon, before they had a chance to melt and wet the skins or drop down our necks.

It was now almost October and skim ice had begun to form on the sea. When you stood quietly by the shore and the water was calm, you could hear a sound like a whispered "shish" as the water became ice, and you could watch the elegant, flat crystals form and spread thinly over the water.

King William Island-Terror Bay. Our caribou-skin tent.

The little pond from which we took our fresh water also froze over, so we had to chop ice and try to keep a hole open by placing a snow block over the hole for insulation. During the night, a week after our arrival, winter came on the wings of a gale which blasted our tent and cast a thin blanket of snow over sea and land. When we looked out in the morning, the snow cover was still thin but there were drifts two to three feet high leeward of all obstructions. The young bay ice had been broken, piled upon itself, and pushed all the way to the mouth of the bay. However, the thermometer stood slightly below 0°F, so skim ice was again forming.

Link was busy making dog harnesses from strong webbing. A tedious task, it required a "palm thimble" and a big curved needle. There were eight places on each harness where crossing straps were stitched together and to the harness collars. Patsy showed Link how it was done and then whittled beautiful, perfectly shaped single trees, or dowels, from oak driftwood boards. These separated the side straps behind the dog's hind legs. Patsy used the brass ends of 12-gauge shotgun shells to cap and strengthen the ends of the single trees, to which the side straps, reinforced with leather, were screwed. Rings were fastened to the center of each single tree, to which the dog's trace from the main trace was hitched, so that the dogs pulled in pairs with a single lead dog. In the eastern Arctic a fan hitch was used instead, each dog having a separate trace fastened to the kamotik.

While Link was working on the harnesses, I began my lessons in caribou-skin "tanning." I had bought a wooden skin breaker/scraper, and planned to use my pocketknife to cut the skins. This would not have worked. Jorgen watched me using the wooden scraper, and later gave me a beautiful set of woman's tools he had made. They had a patina from many years of use and were, I think, those used by his first wife. The carefully reshaped caribou scapula had a wide, smooth, dull scraping edge, while the narrow end had been carved to fit the hand. It was used to "break" the skins.

This process split the outermost layer of skins into tiny sections that permitted them to "breathe" rather than remain airtight. Another tool, used for finishing the "tanning" process, was formed from a piece of caribou antler. One end had been carefully and precisely carved to fit comfortably in a woman's hand, while the other end held a slightly concave curved steel blade made from a steel sawtooth an inch and a half wide. For cutting the skins there was a beautiful ulu with a split-brass and ivory handle and curved steel blade similar to an old-fashioned hand food chopper. A big musk-ox tooth for sharpening the blades completed the set. With such perfect tools I felt sure I would inherit some of the skills of the woman, unknown to me, who had used them before me. I determined to strive to make her, and Jorgen, proud of me.

It is amazing how the skins of caribou fit the human frame. The back of the neck forms the hood of a kuletak (parka) while the back and sides form the kuletak's back. Front, sleeves, pants, mitts, and socks are also made from the caribou's skin. Their legs make the uppers of boots. Caribou hairs themselves are hollow but segmented, like bamboo, and as each tiny segment rubs against one's skin, it absorbs skin oil. Once filled with oil, the segment breaks off, exposing the next segment. The continuing process cleanses and gently massages one's skin all winter, and by spring, one's clothing is much thinner and therefore ready for the warmer weather.

The initial process in preparing a skin was "breaking." First, the skins were placed on the ceiling racks in the house for several hours to dry thoroughly. When they crackled when bent, they were ready to be worked. I sat on the floor with the two wives, trying to imitate their every movement. I slipped one edge of a skin, hair side down, between my outstretched legs,

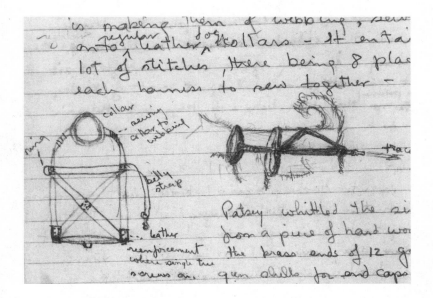

King William Island-Terror Bay. Diagram of the dog harnesses Link made for each of our dogs.

King William Island-Terror Bay. The wonderful set of woman's tools that Jorgen Klengenberg gave me in place of my inadequate ones.

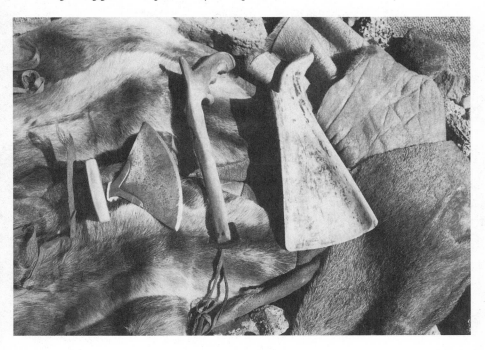

which I crossed to grip it while grabbing the free edge with my left hand. Then I pulled the skin up against the dull scraper, which I pushed downward and outward to the edge of the skin with my right hand. It takes, as Patsy said, "a great deal of beef," and I used a number of muscles in hands, arms, back, and legs that were unknown to me before.

I sat smiling and scraping with the two women for four hours, trying to copy them without appearing to do so, while they murmured to each other and giggled over jokes unknown to me. Finally, feeling that my caribou skin had reached about the same condition as theirs, I handed it to them for inspection. After close examination and many quiet comments, they handed it back with smiles, raised eyebrows, and inhaled breath signifying approval.

Feeling pleased and relieved that my efforts had passed the test, I started to get up. Instead I smiled what must have been a very silly smile. I was so stiff and sore from my toes, up my legs, up my back, up my neck to the top of my head, I was not sure I would ever be able to get up. And this was only my first skin! Visions of the remaining eight skins and bundle of leg skins floated tauntingly through my mind. How could I get them sewn into the necessary garments in time?

During the following ten days I worked feverishly on the skins. When I had finished breaking them, I went over to the house to see what the next step might be. This consisted of laying the skins out, hair side down, on the ground overnight to become damp, so that, by rubbing them between one's hands, the inner layer of rough, broken skin would be loosened for the final scraping. Then they were stretched across the hangers in the house until dry.

One worked much more gently and carefully at this stage in order not to cut the skin with the very sharp blade. Rather than the long sweeping strokes used in breaking, short strokes were required, over and over the same area from all directions until every bit of loose skin was removed and the underskin became as soft and supple as fine chamois. This time-consuming task was nevertheless very rewarding. Occasionally a section of the edge of a skin would be too thick and hard to scrape, and required gentle chewing until it became soft enough. The leg skins, which I would use in making our knee-high winter kamiks, had to be chewed all around the edges, especially the end that had been near the hoof. They actually tasted good, almost like unseasoned jerky.

Link finished the dog harnesses and learned the art of splicing rope and then made the central trace to which the individual dog traces were spliced. He also learned how to back his fishnet with the lines along the top and bottom of the net. With that ready, he tackled the task of sewing his two pieces of heavy canvas together to make the tarp we would use to wrap our load. He had a great time accomplishing this task, sitting on the floor in the house, yards and yards of tarp material spread around him, laboriously feeding it into a little hand-cranked sewing machine. It was his first experience using any type of sewing machine. The women were bent double with muffled laughter, watching him trying to feed the two edges of the bulky cloth evenly under the needle with his left hand, while cranking away with his right. He triumphed finally, with one side only a few inches longer than the other! A real accomplishment. I was proud of him.

I ran into a similar problem when I started sewing a double fur cover for the thermos bottle we would take on kamotik trips. I had watched the way the two women held the skins and handled the steel, triangular-sided furrier's needle while making their stitches. A thimble made from a piece of ugyuk skin was used on the first finger of the right hand and the stitches were taken at right angles to the two edges of the skins being sewn together. The edges were not overlapped, since that would make a ridge, but were held just touching. The edge of the skin closest to one's body was held between the thumb and third finger of the left hand, while the edge of the second skin was held against it by the first and second fingers of the left hand. This made it easy to move the two edges either forward or backward in relation to each other, or closer or looser. Three stitches were taken down through the top layer of the far edge and up through the top layer of the near edge, and then the sinew thread was drawn up. Simple enough, I mused.

Having cut what I felt was the proper-size, oblong piece of skin to fit the thermos, I began to carefully stitch the two long edges together edge to edge, not overlapping, to form the inner cover, which, like some of the clothing I would make, had the fur side inside. When I had stitched about halfway, I held it up to see how it looked and was horrified that one side was becoming longer than the other. Taking great care not to trim too much from the edges, I cut away my beautiful stitches and started over. Watching the length of the two edges carefully, I soon realized that the same thing was happening again. I thought about how I was holding the two edges and how I was pulling up the stitches, and decided that something was wrong with the way I was using the two fingers holding the underside of the two edges.

Taking the offending piece with me, I walked over to the house. Jorgen was there with the women, who were busy sewing. I showed him my problem and asked him to ask Mikigiak how she moved her two fingers that I could not see beneath the edges of the two skins. He looked at me with a funny expression—as well he might have—and spoke to his wife. Both women looked hard at me with questioning eyes and then at the skins in their hands. Then they sewed a few stitches, with faces puckered in concentration. After several tries, they looked at each other and at Jorgen and me. They giggled so much Mikigiak could hardly tell Jorgen that they didn't know what they did with their fingers; they just moved them and the sewing came out right!

A cup of tea seemed in order, after which I returned to the tent to wrestle with the problem. When I had finally worked out the right way to manipulate the edges with my fingertips and thumb and the proper tension to apply as I drew up the sinew, the edges came together perfectly. However, do not ask me to explain what I did. I do not know.

Time was slipping by too fast. One star-bright night near the middle of October, Link asked me to take a magnetic declination reading. By using the transit to observe the North Star, I could determine true north as opposed to magnetic north, which one gets by using a compass. This was needed because the North Magnetic Pole constantly changes its position. Link wanted to compare the readings with those taken earlier on Victoria Island. Also, we still needed to collect a suite of erratic stones to aid in determining the direction from which the last phase of continental glaciation might have come.

Link had to spare time every second or third day to take our dog team and travel with the other men out to the lakes to check the fishnets. Sometimes one or another of them would be lucky and have as many as twenty fish in his net, but the position of our net was not very favorable and we frequently had only three or four fish. We began to worry about food for our team as well as for ourselves. Meanwhile, the days sped by with Link away at the fish lake and me in the tent, working the skins and sewing. I despaired of ever gaining speed in sewing, but I was determined to make the stitches tiny and even.

Ayalik and Maneratsiak often came to have a cup of cocoa and a visit while I worked. They helped me learn how to say the names of everything I pointed to in the tent, but I found it impossible to write many of the guttural or aspirated sounds. Furthermore, as they could not speak English, I was not always sure that we understood one another, and later found out from Dr. Diamond Jenness, when we met him the following year in Ottawa, that this was indeed true. He had lived with the Inuit while on the Canadian Arctic Expedition, 1913–18, and was fluent in the language. We had some laughs over such mistakes as the one in which I had written the Inuktitut word for "big toe" as the word meaning the "chewed crimping" of the sealskin mukluk sole where it curved up *around* the toes!

By the middle of October the thermometer was registering −10°F and the polar wind made it seem much colder as it whistled around the tent, driving the fine crystalline snow into long, beautifully carved drifts called sastrugi. The crystalline structure of the dry, Arctic winter snow is different from that of the soft, moist flakes usually seen in warmer latitudes at low elevations. The Inuit have several names for snow which signify its quality— snow that is good for making snow-house blocks; snow that is not; snow good for sledge travel, and snow that is not; snow that pricks your face when driven by a high wind, as well as many others.

One day, after I had finally patched all the holes in the tent, and I was busy sewing as usual, the Primus stove refused to burn properly. I pumped it up, let out air, and used the little needle to prick and clean the burner. The lantern was not behaving either. It seemed to be dying, but had plenty of kerosene. I turned up the wick and trimmed it. The flame remained small. I became frustrated and pricked my fingers and could not seem to see the stitches. I kept on trying to sew and make the stove and lamp behave, becoming more and more frustrated. Then Ayalik and Maneratsiak opened the little door.

Oh blessed air! I could not gulp enough of it. The Primus roared to life. The lamp flame leapt up the glass chimney. The two boys exclaimed in fear, waving fresh air in with their hands as they knelt beside the little door. If they had not come for cocoa, I would not be writing this account of our life in the north. I should have realized what was happening. I later remembered that as a teenager I had thought Admiral Richard Byrd was pretty careless when he nearly asphyxiated himself in the same manner while staying alone near Little America in the Antarctic. Carbon monoxide is subtle, and lethal. I got up, took my pocketknife, cut a round hole in the top of the tent and from a piece of deerskin sewed a little angled chimney, which I stitched to the edge of the hole.

We had tried on several occasions to get our little radio transceiver to work so that we might hear Coppermine. Unfortunately, the battery had frozen and the nearest replacement was at least 500 if not 1,500 miles away at Coppermine or Yellowknife. Patsy's radio ran on a storage battery which needed recharging. He did not have a wind-charger, but he did have the good, long oak driftwood planks from one of the early expedition wrecks. From these he meticulously carved a perfect propeller blade and fin. Then he built a tower on the roof of the house to hold the blade and the charger, which he made by rewinding the generator from the *Aklavik's* auxiliary motor.

Patsy had an endless supply of ingenuity and ability, something we found true of most Inuit. Living in such an unforgiving environment they had long ago become adapted, both physically and mentally, in a manner that gave them the best chance for survival.

10 / *Learning about Inuit life*

September 20–December 8, 1940

*T*he early part of the last week of October was especially fine, clear and cold, the sun rising shortly after eight o'clock and filling the air with sparkling, frosty light. We wondered how long the near-perfect weather would last, and Patsy told us it usually remained good for a while after freeze-up. The men continued their trips to the fish lake and tried for seals at the edge of the sea ice until the bay was frozen over. After that, they tried to get them at the seals' breathing holes, a painstaking operation for neophytes and one that requires great patience. A piece of polar-bear skin was placed beside the hole on the ice for a man to stand on and keep his feet warm, for it was necessary to remain motionless. Any movement would alert the seal, and it would go to another of its breathing holes. A thin wand (carved from a long bone, or from a piece of caribou antler or wood) with a ring around the bottom for a float was placed through the saturated snow filling the hole. When the seal started to rise for air the water was disturbed, causing the wand to move. Forewarned, the Inuk speared the seal as its head neared the surface. If the point was well set, he pulled the seal up through the hole and onto the ice.

On October 29 the weather changed. A solid mass of low clouds moved in. We could actually smell the approaching snowstorm and doggedly hastened our preparations for winter. Link took one of the long wood rollers we had used when pulling the dory up the beach and cut it to make two stakes to bury in the snow as anchors for the long dog lines. The dogs' individual chains were fastened to this line. Before chains were available, dogs were allowed to run free when not in harness, the "boss" dog usually keeping the rest in order. Occasionally, however, the dogs mauled or even killed a child or woman.

Our preparations included cooking up a mixture of rice and mud with which to "mud" the steel-shod wood runners of our kamotik, since it was difficult to find and chip enough frozen mud to do the job alone. The mixture worked well, but we knew we would have to keep the dogs from getting close enough to chew the runners.

When we first arrived, Link had staked our team a short distance downslope from our tent, where we could keep an eye on them and where they could be easily fed. However, having seen the headlong speed with which the other teams took off, he figured we would never be able to guide our lead dog, Friday, in and out around the stacks of frozen seals, piles of driftwood, jolly boats, other kamotiks, oil drums, and a hundred smaller objects on the slope without coming to disaster. The only solution was to move the dog line nearer the bottom of the slope, thus giving the dogs an open run toward the frozen sea when we took off on a trip.

Generally the winter temperature keeps slowly sliding down the thermometer, with occasional brief hiccups, but the last day of October must have gotten its signals crossed. The mercury reversed itself, and the month departed on a surprising high, with a daytime reading of +28°F. The warm air brought snow that fell steadily all day and into the night, wrapping us in soft silence. With darkness, however, the mercury dropped again and was at −28°F by 10:00 P.M.! But our skin tent kept us warm and snug.

Patsy had decided to set out his trap line south along the coast as far as the site of the old Hudson's Bay Company post on Simpson Strait. After five days he returned discouraged. He had seen few fox tracks, no polar-bear tracks, and few seals—all suggesting a poor year ahead. There was still open water in the straits, apparently the result of continuing high winds. Jorgen had set out his traps along the coast to the north and said we would be welcome to accompany him sometime if we wanted to come along with our team. Mikigiak, Iglikshik, and Maneratsiak traveled with him to help with the traps and snow-house chores. We were very happy with the prospect, as it would provide an opportunity to see new country and collect geologic specimens.

I worked frantically to tan more caribou legs and skins and to sew skin mitts, socks, and long underpants, fur side inside, while Link reorganized the Primus box and made a wooden grub box for use on our kamotik. Our trip with Jorgen did not materialize, because Link developed a chest cold and decided he had better not go. After all the excited preparations it was a

King William Island-Terror Bay. Patsy icing his mudded kamotik runners.

King William Island-Terror Bay. Friday, our lead dog.

King William Island-Terror Bay. Pile of frozen seals for people and dogs. Patsy and Jorgen's storage caribou-skin tent in background.

King William Island-Terror Bay. Wind-drifted snow barchans on the bay.

disappointment, but the nearest doctor was 1,000 miles away, and Link was subject to bronchial problems.

The wind came up during the night, shaking the tent and sending the snow whistling past, piling it up in depressions and in the lee of obstacles like the house, tent, and even small stones. By the time we were up in the morning, the low ridges were bare and all the long drifts were deep, packed hard, and elegantly sculptured. Patsy, Jorgen, and Tulemaq cut snow blocks and stacked them around the tents and house, an excellent, cost-free form of insulation against the cold and bitter wind. We put them around our tent, too, and felt the difference.

By the end of the first week in November, it was dark by 3:30 in the afternoon and on clear nights the southern skies were alive with the aurora mysteriously weaving, gliding, fading, and glowing in endless motion. Since there had also been a period of radio blackout, we were interested to hear on Patsy's radio, November 6, 1940, that President Roosevelt had been reelected. How far away that world and all its man-made problems seemed.

One afternoon all the dogs started howling, and we went out to see if a polar bear was in sight. Instead, we were surprised to see two kamotiks approaching across the bay. It was Utuitoq and Aylikomiq, whom we had seen at the Royal Geographical Society Islands. Aylikomiq had brought his blind wife and little girl, but Utuitoq had left his wife and little daughter to keep the polar bears from destroying their camp! Tulemaq, who had set his traps out around Cape Crozier, had started that morning for the islands to visit them. They just missed each other as Tulemaq went up over the point while they came around the coast. Utuitoq and Aylikomiq had been unable to get many seals before freeze-up, and they came in need of meat, as well as deerskins for clothing. Our supplies were not much beyond our own needs, but we provided them with some of each, as did Patsy and Jorgen.

Aylikomiq reported seeing the tracks of three polar bears just beyond the entrance to the bay about six miles from our site. As a thank-you for the help we had given in September, Aylikomiq brought us a piece of caribou backfat and part of a leg of a polar bear he had killed with a .22 rifle on his way over. He told us, with Jorgen interpreting, that the bear was seen swimming in a lead between ice floes. Aylikomiq ran along the ice edge and shot at the bear's head each time it came up to breathe, until he managed to put a bullet into its brain through an eye. It was a big bear, and he had a dreadful time hauling it up onto the ice. He finally managed to get one end of a line around the bear's neck as it floated in the water and then fastened the other end to the main trace of the dog team.

The dogs had never pulled a bear out of water, and wanted to attack it. Aylikomiq struggled to keep the ice edge from cutting the line while he grabbed hold of one front leg of the bear and pulled, yelling all the time at the dogs to pull. Finally the carcass was dragged onto the ice, where Aylikomiq skinned and butchered it. Caching the rest of the carcass to be picked up on the return trip to the islands, he brought the two hind legs to share the kill with us all, as was the custom.

After everyone had tea, pilot biscuits, and jam at our tent, we walked over to the house for more tea and conversation, Jorgen and Patsy interpreting for us from time to time. We also listened to the weekly broadcast from Coppermine, which brought the outside world to us painfully (Chamberlain had died, the Greeks were holding their own, there had been a disastrous earthquake in Romania). We walked back to our tent through the beauty of the cold, silent night; the great, golden half moon hung against a cobalt sky, paling the aurora by its vibrant light.

Our full days were rushing by and we decided it was time to make our first solo excursion by dog team. It was not a disaster, but neither was it a huge success. We loaded the kamotik with everything we would take on a long trip, to find out how the sledge and dogs would behave when we did embark on one. With all lashings tight, we jumped on the load, pulled up the anchor, and the dogs, yelping happily, were off with a rush out the bay.

They moved along together well for maybe half an hour, but when we got into rougher ice the team slowed to a trot and then a walk. We jumped off the kamotik and jogged along, one on each side, endeavoring to keep it upright. It tilted erratically as it jounced over the irregular hummocks between larger and larger upended ice floes. Suddenly, as the kamotik moved up a slanting slab, it toppled over, abruptly stopping the team. "Using a lot of beef," as Patsy would have said, we finally righted it and started again.

Our old lead dog, Friday, was good but slow, so Link decided to try out his favorite, a young dog named Snap. This was a mistake. By simply lying down, Snap told us immediately and indisputably that he had no intention of getting into trouble with his teammates or Friday by occupying the leader's position. Neither friendly encouragement nor stern exhortation budged him. His expression was one of puzzled determination. Link gave in—he had to—and hitched up Friday again to continue ever so slowly on our way.

When we finally rounded the point and came out of the bay onto the gulf ice, our troubles really began. The wind and current had broken the ice and rafted it in crazy jumbles. The kamotik defied our diligent efforts by capsizing again and again, finally loosening the load. By then the sun, which hung low in the sky at our latitude of approximately 68° north, had set, and we decided to make camp. We were only a measly six miles from home and in an area that lacked good snow for building a snow house. We had little choice and were disgruntled.

It was dark by the time the dogs were staked out and fed, the little tent pitched, and snow melting in a pot on the Primus. Link built a snow shelter for the Primus just outside the tent door, so the steam from boiling water would not cover the inside of the tent with hoarfrost; even one's breath and body warmth frosted the single-layer tent at the –20°F temperature. When I dropped chunks of frozen seal into the pot of boiling water, hoping the aroma would not be wafted toward a hungry bear, the dogs looked up at me over the ends of their bushy tails, curled over their noses, but their stomachs were full and they soon slept.

It was a perfect night. The brilliant moon, almost full, made the snowy world sparkle. The rough ice took on all sorts of fantastic forms which glittered in the bright light. It was too easy to imagine polar bears padding silently along; we were camped where Aylikomiq had seen their tracks five days earlier. One swat of a bear's enormous paw would have totally demolished our tent, leaving us little chance to defend ourselves, but we had a rifle and knew our dogs would warn us, so we snuggled into our wonderful furry sleeping bags on our soft, warm caribou-skin bed and slept a dreamless sleep.

By the next morning we knew that a six-foot-square mountain tent, its sides slanting in from the two-foot-high walls to a center pole, had not been designed for occupancy by people dressed in bulky caribou-skin clothing, carrying bulky skin sleeping bags, duffle bags, and other paraphernalia. A snow house was the answer. We searched again for a suitable drift, but the snow was too light and powdery to make good snow blocks, so we decided to return home. Once the kamotik was loaded we were whisked away at a gallop. Headed home, the dogs improved their pace remarkably and it took us half as long to return as to go out. The kamotik itself seemed eager to be home, fairly bounding over the rough ice without capsizing.

The middle of November had overtaken us, and I was still "tanning" skins and sewing: a start on our caribou-skin socks, a pair of moosehide and canvas boots for Link, a moosehide case for the .22 rifle, a canvas case for the .30-30 rifle. All of this should have been finished much sooner. I had been told that Sedna, Spirit of the Sea, is angered if land-animal skins are sewn while one is camped on the sea ice, and that she might prevent one from catching any seals. I looked forward to the day when we would pack our wool socks, shirts, and underwear away and live in our new skin clothing, except for some Italian silk-knit undergarments I intended to wear under the skins.

A few days later we made another short daytime foray with the team, exploring a small river valley in the direction of the fish lakes. The land was so low and flat that a rise of 50 feet looked like a high hill. It was hard to keep on the winding river, for its course between low banks was leveled by drifted snow to almost the same flatness as the surrounding land. The following day a fierce storm blew in from the north, sending the snow drifting furiously before it, forming new sastrugi and recarving the old. We were glad we had decided not to camp out.

Patsy, returning from his trap line to the south, was caught in the blizzard. Heading into the storm he had become, as he said, "mixed up," and crossed his own track several times, not far from home. Losing one's direction is easy to do when traveling in zero-zero visibility, the temperature at −40°F, and the driving snow freezing on one's eyelashes and biting into one's eyes. Nevertheless Patsy's mood was high when he returned home. He had trapped forty-seven foxes when he thought he would be lucky if he got ten.

Jorgen had not had much luck to the north and brought his traps back. He found, as we had, that the high winds had jammed and piled the old ice up against the land, making kamotik travel very difficult. Hoping for better luck, he was going to set his traps out around Cape Crozier instead and again asked us to come along. Link was pleased to be able to check out that area for any indications of glaciation, so he re-iced our runners and we reorganized our gear for the trip before turning in.

Our alarm clock shrilled at 4:30 A.M. The wind had died and the dark night was still and cold. Link, as usual, reached out of his sleeping furs, lit the Primus, and put the big pot of snow on to melt for water before we got into our furs. Fortified by coffee, oatmeal, and frozen fish, our gear stowed and lashed on our kamotik, we were ready, with dogs clamoring, by 8:30 as Jorgen and Maneratsiak pulled up their anchor. The dogs threw themselves against their harnesses, yanking us all off the shore and away across the ice into the glimmering dark of the early Arctic morning. The blue-black sky, stretching away forever above us, was vibrant with scintillating stars. As always when we started out with our dogs, my heart lifted and I felt a surge of joy.

The ice was not very rough and the dogs were fresh and willing, so we skimmed along at a good trot. Finally Jorgen stopped to set out his first two fox traps. He anchored the free end of the trap chain in well-packed snow, on which he then placed and set the trap. Over it he laid a very thin block of snow, which he pared with his snow knife until he could see the dark suggestion of the trap through it. Next he laid a small piece of fish about three inches from the trap, banking the fish with snow and a large rock so that it could be seen or reached only from the side opening toward the trap. This usually ensured that the fox would step on the trap when trying to get the fish. We continued along the coast, stopping every mile or two to set out two more traps, and finally pulling up at sundown in the lee of a rise.

By thrusting in a thin bone wand, Jorgen tested the drifted snow and found that it was of the right consistency and texture to build a snow house. As soon as the dog lines were set out, Jorgen and Link began cutting snow blocks while Maneratsiak and I unharnessed, tied, and fed our dogs. By that time, the snow-house walls were up far enough for us to start chinking the cracks. The house was a comfortable twelve feet in diameter, and when it was finished the kamotiks were quickly unloaded.

When the kerosene lamp was burning brightly, causing the fresh snow crystals to glisten, Jorgen and Link handed in all our sleeping skins and bags. These I spread out on the snow bench for our beds, while Maneratsiak placed our respective Primus and grub boxes on either side of the entry. Jorgen and Link handed in two snow blocks, which I put in cooking pots on the Primus stoves to thaw for water. I then chopped some chunks of frozen seal meat off a large hunk to boil for supper. After supper, our stomachs full, dishes clean, and hot cups of tea in hand, Jorgen began to tell us what he claimed were true stories of people's encounters with polar bears.

One dark winter day an old grandmother was walking from her snow house to her son's. She had not gone far when a polar bear loomed up before her, rumbling loudly. She had nothing for protection except the stick she used for walking, so she yanked off one of her chunky, caribou-skin mitts and put it on the end of her stick. When the bear was only a few feet from her, he stopped a moment to growl again before attacking. She used the moment to lunge forward and thrust the mitt into the bear's open mouth, lodging it in the back of his throat, choking him. While he struggled to get it out, she hobbled fast as possible to her son's snow house and said that he should go out and see the bear she had killed. Of course nobody believed her and laughed loudly at her story, but she insisted it was true. To keep her quiet, her son finally went out and, finding the bear, rushed to tell everyone that old grandmother had indeed killed a bear. She, of course, was most pleased because she gained everyone's respect and admiration for being so clever.

A blizzard was roaring and screaming over the frozen sea one winter night, but the people were sleeping comfortably in their snow house at their sealing camp. Suddenly the man woke up, feeling that something was wrong. He heard sounds on top of the snow house. Jumping out of the bed skins, he grabbed his rifle from the entry tunnel and fired at the sounds. The bullet went through the snow dome and killed a polar bear who was leaning over the snow house about to smash it in.

Another family was not so lucky. A polar bear climbed onto a poorly made snow house, and it collapsed on top of the people. They were all killed by the bear.

By this time I began to feel a prickling at the back of my neck. I asked Jorgen if a bear had ever broken into one of his snow houses. "Yes," he said, "one stuck its head in the door-opening once, which was embarrassing because the gun, as usual, was in the entry tunnel." As he opened his mouth to continue the story, a big white face suddenly filled the open entry of *our* snow house. We all froze, then burst out laughing. Big Nero, with a pleased face, started to shoulder his way into the congenial warmth. Deciding to enjoy the companionship in the snow house, he had broken loose from the dog line. He must have remembered his time at Cambridge Bay when the RCMP men often let him stay in their house.

In the morning, Jorgen and Maneratsiak left to continue on the trap line, while Link and I took off to investigate the bedrock outcrops on the coast and nearby islands, which we found well smoothed. The surface was too weathered for us to be sure that faint scratches were in fact striae, but we found more erratics of granite and gneiss. We did find an old cairn on top of a low hill behind the snow house, but we do not know who built it and Patsy and Jorgen later said there was no message under it. Back in the snow house before dark, we lit the lantern and Primus, stuck some thin driftwood sticks into the snow blocks as drying racks for our mitts, socks, and kamiks, and then chinked up a few places where the wind was eating into the snow blocks, before preparing our evening meal of boiled char.

With rock samples and fossils packed and notes written, we snuggled into our sleeping bags. In the middle of the night Link's sleepy voice wakened me, saying he was sorry, but we had better move over, as the snow dome was sagging ominously over us. With much grunting, wriggling, and heaving we maneuvered our bedding and ourselves to one side, hoping the dome would not bury us. Neither Link's muffled snores nor a leaning bear brought it down, and first thing next morning Link piled up grub and Primus boxes to support the sag.

As I started to pull on my silk-knit underwear, I remembered Vilhjalmur Stefansson saying that with fur against the skin it was hard to be cold. I had been almost cold while traveling the previous day, and it was only –15°F, so I thought about that and decided to leave off the silks and try my furs next to me, as he and the Inuit wore them. His advice was as good in this as it was in everything he had told us. The skin clothing kept us warm and free of frostbite or frozen toes or fingers.

With breakfast and clean-up finished, we packed up, left the snow house, and headed for home, jogging off to examine more of the coast and islands, where deep snowdrifts made it hard to locate bedrock outcrops. Link had also told Jorgen that on our way home we would check his traps and pick up any foxes. Sometimes a trapped animal will chew off its foot to gain freedom, and frequently dies from starvation.

We had not gone far when we spotted a beautiful little white, furry fellow sitting quietly watching our approach. He had probably never seen a dog team or human being before. Most of our dogs were old hands at the trapping business, but Dumpy, the youngest, was greatly excited, howling, whining, and jumping against his collar while the others stood still with ears pricked, watching. Link reluctantly had to kill the poor beastie, a hard blow on his head to knock him unconscious and a quick twist of his thin little neck to make sure. The procedure was repeated at two more traps. We were very thankful that four years previously we had declined the opportunity to take over a trapper's line on the Porcupine River in the Yukon, since there was no need to do so and we really don't enjoy the killing.

Home again, dogs curled around full stomachs, and we, too, content after a plateful of beans, I suddenly realized while writing in my journal that Thanksgiving Day had almost passed! Thankful indeed, we hugged each other. Safe and happy, unlike so many others around our warring world, we had so much to be thankful for.

It was steadily becoming colder. When the temperature dropped to −32°F, the inside of our old skin tent and everything close to it became heavily frosted at night. Try as I would each morning I could not scrape all the frost off before the warmth from the lantern and Primus got to it and things began to get wet. Link told Jorgen about our problem and he brought a canvas tent which he and Link draped over the windward side of our skin tent. That, together with more snow blocks piled up around for better insulation, improved things considerably. To our delight, Jorgen and little Mary stayed with us for the evening meal, and we celebrated the occasion by eating the last dozen frozen eggs, duly boiled.

The crates of oranges, potatoes, and eggs we had brought with us were a great addition to our larder and we tried not to be greedy. That was a mistake, because the oranges and potatoes became inedible as soon as they froze. The eggs, however, were fine. They were also funny, as Ayalik and I discovered when I was carrying several from the supply tent one day. A precious egg slipped from my mittened hand, then bounced away like a ball. Puzzled, I put the others down carefully, picked it up, and dropped it again. It bounced better. I smiled and threw the egg on the frozen ground and to Ayalik's delight it bounced off crazily like a football.

When he brought it back I really slammed it down, which sent it leaping and bounding down the slope. Fascinated, I went for my geology hammer. Was it *really* an egg? When Ayalik had once more retrieved the thing, I hit it with the hammer. Nothing happened. Holding the egg firmly, I hit harder. The hammer bounced off it. Placing it on the ground, I took the hammer in both hands and hit the egg with all my strength, finally breaking it in half. I wondered then and am still wondering what those eggs were treated with before they left Edmonton on their long boat journey down the Mackenzie River, east along the coast, and on to King William Island.

That evening, as Link and I walked under the star-filled sky to the house, we thought how sad it is that people who live in big cities never know the magic of the sparkling heavens of a cold, clear night, nor do they ever experience silence. The news from Coppermine saddened us. Romania was being swallowed up by Germany, and Turkey seemed about to enter the war. Were we really on the same planet?

Life at Terror Bay continued undisturbed—in its own rhythm. Two days later Jorgen awakened us at 5:00 A.M. to say he was going to look at his fishnet and then continue on his trap line, and we were welcome to join him again if we wished. Link was anxious to look at some bedrock outcrops along the shore of the lake where Jorgen had set his net, so we jumped out of bed into our furs, turned up the Primus, swallowed a brief breakfast, packed our gear, loaded the kamotik, and hitched up the dogs. They were feeling fit and went along at a fine clip, continually overtaking Jorgen's team. Because they were doing so well, Link decided to try another dog, Brandy, in the lead. He was willing and the team kept up the good pace.

The hours slipped by slowly as we worked our way against a strong headwind and drifting snow, which took some of the joy out of running beside the kamotik. The land, flat and white as the winter prairie, stretched away to the horizon with nothing to cut the stinging bite of the north wind. By constantly putting first one, then the other mitten-warmed bare hand against nose and cheeks, we prevented them from freezing. We were relieved when, five hours later, we reached Jorgen's skin tent on the ice by a tiny island, halfway up the long lake, north of the regular fish lake. The thick-haired, late summer skins of the tent made it warm, comfortable, and frost-free on the inside. It was about the same size as our tent, but Jorgen had cut the walls shorter to make it less bulky to pack on the kamotik.

By the time everything was settled, dogs tied down and fed, fishnet pulled up and reset, and supper on the Primuses, it was already dark, yet only 3:00 P.M. By the end of November at latitude 68° north, the sun rises just above the horizon, moves along it for a while, then quickly disappears. Always, unless the sky is heavily overcast, the sunrise-sunset skies were breathtakingly beautiful, palest turquoise and lemon gold or fuchsia, soft blues, and salmon pink.

Sitting, snug, warm, and well fed on boiled char, holding cups of steaming tea, we spoke of the men from Sir John Franklin's last expedition a hundred years earlier, who had struggled over that frigid land in totally unsuitable clothing. How desperate they must have been—ill, slowly starving, and freezing to death. We felt almost guilty when we wriggled into our furry bed. Beneath our ears the lake ice boomed, groaned, snapped, and shuddered. Sometimes it seemed as though the ice would crack open and freezing lake water would inundate the tent. An eerie sensation to say the least. More than once, I could not refrain from slipping my hand out to be sure no water had seeped into our tent. Each time I was grateful and relieved.

The following morning we all headed north again, Jorgen and Maneratsiak to continue along the trap line for two days, while Link and I searched for bedrock exposures. Yet again we found the land buried under large, undulating waves of drifted snow, but bare rock showed in places and in others the snow cover was thin enough for us to dig down and collect hand specimens. Our dogs, glad to be off the dog line, galloped along like a bunch of pups. It was not often they had only two people to pull on an otherwise empty kamotik. As we sat there, zipping over the smooth lake ice, we remembered our conversation the previous spring when traveling with Sam. We had thought what fun it would be to have our own team, never dreaming that six months later we would be traveling behind our own seven dogs on King William Island! We hugged each other.

Back once more in the comfortable tent, our evening meal finished, Link decided to try to make Jorgen's big soapstone kudlik burn without smoking. It was a challenge. The oil must be persuaded to rise up the willow-fuzz wick in just the right quantity. After much gentle pressing of the wick with the specially carved stick, he managed to coax a good flame to run along the stone ridge evenly with little smoking. By its gentle, wavering light I continued the now-urgent business of sewing fur clothing, as content as any Inuit wife with a good hunter for a husband.

As our woolen socks, duffles, and insoles dried on the rack above the kudlik, I thought how much warmer our feet were going to be inside three pairs of fur socks, and I stitched faster. We spent two beautiful, peaceful days, searching for outcrops during the few, dim daylight hours and sewing or writing in the tent when the dark settled in. It now seemed natural to have supper at three or four in the afternoon and then nod off by six or seven and sleep until seven or eight the next morning. The second, and colder, night we almost jumped awake as suddenly loud cracking sounds rose up through the ice under our ears.

Jorgen and Maneratsiak brought back few fox skins, so we returned to Terror Bay the following day. Tulemaq and Patsy were also back from their trap lines. Patsy had made the more than 200-mile trip to the Hudson's Bay Company post at Gjoa Haven and brought messages and caribou meat from Billy Joss, the manager, who hoped we would come down to see him at the post before we returned to Cambridge Bay. We had considered that and it would have been fun and interesting, but Link decided he could not spare the time, for he needed to return to his work at Yale as soon as possible. Nevertheless, when Patsy said that we should start back to Cambridge Bay the following week, if we wanted to reach there by Christmas, we were shocked. It seemed impossible that we had been at Terror Bay nearly three months. We were beginning to feel completely at home and ready for the midwinter dark period, and now suddenly we must pack up and leave these wonderful, amazing, warmhearted friends.

While Link sorted and packed gear, I frantically sewed the last items of clothing. Mikigiak had made two fine pairs of mitts for Link, one with caribou-skin liners and polar-bear outers, and one with caribou-skin liners and dog-skin outers. She gave them to him the night before our departure, when we joined the families for a farewell dinner. Tulemaq had shot a polar bear a few days earlier and we all enjoyed the meat. We talked about the good trapping Patsy was having and wondered why there were fewer foxes to the north. Perhaps because there was not enough open water for seals, there would be fewer bears and therefore few foxes. In winter the foxes frequently follow the bears to feed on scattered scraps of meat.

The women and I smiled at each other a lot, and I asked Patsy to tell them how sorry I was not to be able to speak Inuktitut, and how much I appreciated their letting me watch them so that I could learn how to "tan" and sew the skins. This set them laughing good-humoredly, because it was funny that I had not learned such things as a child. They were kind enough to say I had done pretty well with the "tanning" and sewing, and Mikigiak said she did not mind cutting the skins for the shirts and pants and my kuletak so I could sew them. I did learn how to cut skins for mitts, socks, and boots.

Patsy asked us to join them for breakfast, thus allowing us to pack our cooking gear as well as everything else except our sleeping bags and skins, and this we did. Snug in our furs at last, by the soft glow of the lantern, I looked up at the top of the tent and wondered if I would ever scrape hoarfrost off the inside of a skin tent again. We had given the tent to Patsy, since we would no longer need it.

In the dark of early morning we went over to the house where a delicious and much appreciated breakfast of oatmeal, caribou meat, fresh bread, and coffee gave us energy for our journey. It was hard to pull ourselves away. Jorgen helped us lash the load on our kamotik, and we started off at seven o'clock with Patsy and Maneratsiak. Tulemaq, who was starting out on his trap line again, joined us for a while. It was December 8, and Patsy figured we would get to Cambridge Bay in plenty of time for Christmas. He said it should take us no more than eight days, even with some rough ice in Victoria Strait.

11 / Attempt to reach Cambridge Bay with Patsy
Retreat
Travel with Jorgen and family to Perry River
December 16–27, 1940

*T*he first pale light of dawn began to brighten our way as we waved good-bye at 7:45 and our teams trotted out onto the ice. A tight feeling gripped my chest and moisture froze on my cheeks. A glance at Link told me he felt the same way. Without fully realizing it, we had slipped into the routine of our friends' lives, which flowed in rhythm with the turn of the seasons. Each day had brought its challenges and rewards, in seminal ways, and deepened our respect and love for these amazing, warm, and generous friends. They had unobtrusively helped us in a thousand ways, always with a smile. When a problem arose, their first reaction was often amusement, after which they focused their energy on finding a solution. There was no time to waste on anger or self-pity.

We traveled steadily by daylight while it lasted, then by the light of the waxing moon that rose over the edge of the frozen Queen Maud Gulf about 5:30 that evening. A headwind was cold on our faces as we followed the coast south out of Terror Bay. The ice was fairly smooth most of the way, outside the band of rough ice shoved up against the land. At Cape Crozier we turned west, heading for the Royal Geographical Society Islands, and Aylikomiq and Utuitoq's camp. Having stopped once briefly for tea and pilot biscuits, we reached the small islands about 6:30 and saw the soft glow of the snow house. When their dogs began howling excitedly, Aylikomiq and Utuitoq came running out to greet us, embracing us with welcoming sniffs (the Inuit do *not* rub noses, they sniff!), and helping us with our teams. Our poor dogs were exhausted. We had come about 50 miles.

The snow house was the largest and most complex one we had seen. The main unit was about 15 feet in diameter with a perfect, high dome, all the blocks cut as truly as the stone blocks of a cathedral. The second unit, in

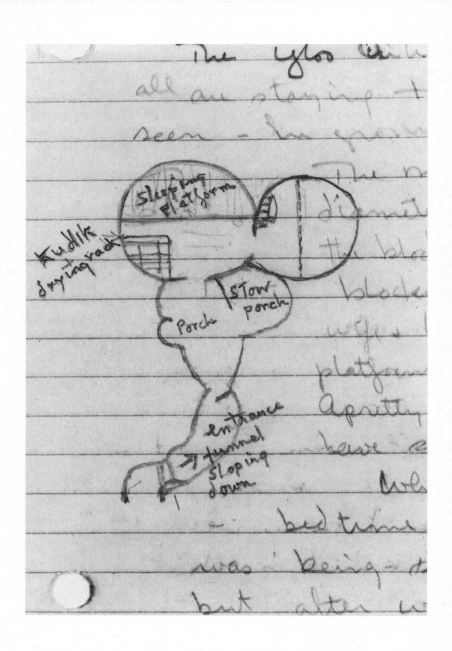

Geographical Society Islands. Plan of large double snow house.

which Utuitoq and his family lived, was joined to the first by a beautiful, open arch about 4 feet high. A few feet from the entrance, the entry tunnel made a right-angle turn toward the snow house, then sloped gently down for 12 feet and opened to two small half-domes, one on each side. One was a storeroom for frozen seals and fish. The other had a shelter for a bitch with tiny pups, all comfortable on an old piece of caribou skin. Two guns in caribou-skin cases leaned against the snow-block wall, where they remained cold yet within easy reach should a polar bear climb onto the dome.

After a welcome supper of boiled seal meat, pilot biscuits, and tea, Link and I sat on the snow bench beside the others listening to their soft, sibilant conversation, catching familiar words now and again and yearning to understand the rest. What a tremendous difference it would have made. From near the kudlik, Aylikomiq's wife picked up a hunk of something and passed it to her husband. He bit into the edge then cut off a piece with his hunting knife and passed the rest on to the others. I tried to figure out what it might be. It was a moldy looking, grayish green of indeterminate shape. After Patsy had a bite, he handed it back to Aylikomiq.

I asked him what it was. "Summer fish," he replied, explaining that both fish and seals were buried under beach gravel, where they remained until needed. It might be one or two years old! I said I should think it would be poisonous, and asked what it tasted like. Smiling, he said, "Roquefort cheese." I thought about that, then asked if I might try it. "Of course," he replied, "but you have to swallow it." When he told Aylikomiq I would like a bite, he and the others were both surprised and pleased and passed it over. I bit into it and discovered that he was right. If I had been given some on a cracker, I would have thought it was Roquefort.

The snow bench, wide as it was, could not hold all of us at night. Aylikomiq, his wife and little girl, Patsy, Link, and I were to sleep side by side on the bench, while Tulemaq and Maneratsiak would put their sleeping skins and bags on the floor, a much colder place. When I went out to brush my teeth, I stopped, amazed. Very small colored flares were shooting up at a point on the horizon. That was impossible, but as I watched, wondering, a brilliant, scintillating light momentarily appeared. A planet was rising over the southern rim of the frozen sea. Perhaps the cold clarity of the air over the sea ice, or some kind of atmospheric effect, caused the colored light.

A strong, cold wind was blowing the next morning when we left the hospitable Inuit's camp. Aylikomiq told Patsy that there was open water and very rough ice in Victoria Strait between the Royal Geographical Society Islands and Victoria Island and that we would have to travel very far south, almost to the mainland coast, in order to reach Cambridge Bay. However, Patsy felt we could probably get through, so we set out, trotting along over good ice until early afternoon when we came to the older, rafted ice.

The going became slower, the kamotiks tipping precariously more and more frequently, and the wind increased steadily, driving low, dark clouds ahead of it. Although it was only 2:00 P.M., Patsy opted to make camp. The snow was not as hard as it should be for snow blocks, but I tied and fed the dogs while the men put up a small snow house, draping a tarp over the dome to keep the wind from eating through the chinks between blocks. Supper of small fried caribou steaks and hot tea warmed us, and we were more than ready to slip into our fur bags.

It was a cold, clear, and wind-still morning with pale dawnlight just seeping up the southern horizon as we broke camp and hitched up the teams at 8:15 A.M. Heading west for Jenny Lind Island, we worked through the rough ice in short order. The ice was relatively smooth for several hours, and we wondered where the really bad ice and open water that we had been warned about might be. By 1:00 P.M., however, we entered the jumbled confusion of great, thick upended and jagged blocks of ice that had been shoved up and over each other at improbable angles, to heights of at least 30 feet. I recalled paintings of early Arctic expedition ships beset in such ice. I had always thought them to be exaggerated, but they definitely were not.

Patsy said that it could be worse, but we wondered, as we tried to help the dogs get through, pushing, hauling, and shoving the kamotiks, which frequently became jammed between the incredible slabs of ice. Often we had to chop the kamotiks free with the ax. Again and yet again they toppled over as they rose upward behind the struggling dogs and teetered on the drunken angles of the shattered floes.

There was little time to think, but I do remember wondering, as I was wedged against massive ice, one foot caught and the kamotik pressing down against me, how long it would be before one of us suffered a broken leg. There are no words to convey the sense of shocked futility and helplessness that momentarily overcame me then as, unable to move, I looked up at the towering, chaotic angles of the ice rising all around us. Link came to my rescue by chopping the ice to free me.

December 16–27, 1940 ✶ *186*

As darkness approached, we stopped at a spot in the lee of an immense upended floe, just wide enough to pitch the little tent and make a shelter out of the canvas load cover. The exhausted dogs lay down where they stopped, rousing almost reluctantly to swallow a chunk of blubber before curling up in harness. We had seen three sets of polar-bear tracks, and just before we stopped to make camp the dogs had begun yelping and trying to pursue a bear they apparently smelled nearby, but it did not appear. In the twenty-nine years during which we have traveled in different areas of the Arctic, we have seen only fifteen bears.

After supper we left the tent to see if there was a way through the incredible ice. The night was perfect. The moon and stars overhead were brilliant, and pale aurora veils were weaving, gliding, and drifting across the dark blue sky. It was −30°F and calm. In the silence, the icy forms loomed in ghostly, gleaming light all around us. Patsy went ahead, and when he returned he said the ice on all sides looked pretty tough and the only way that looked possible was the way we had come. He was frustrated and said he would look again the next morning when the light was better before deciding what to do.

Upon awakening we found that the sky had turned threatening. Dark, snowy clouds moved low overhead. The nearly black clouds to the north and west reflected open water. Patsy climbed a high ice pinnacle, and said he could see no way we could continue without risking the kamotiks and exhausting ourselves and the dogs. As it was, he'd had to shoot a dog that had injured a leg and was unable to go farther. I felt guilty at putting the dogs through such struggles, and tried to make myself realize that this was part of their natural lives. The working dog has incredible stamina, and after a frozen fish or chunk of seal meat or blubber and some sleep he is ready to go on again.

Patsy said that if we felt we had to try to get through anyway, we would have to leave behind the kamotiks and take only food and bedding, which we could roll up in his bearskin for the dogs to drag. We might have to walk almost to Perry River, as Utuitoq had said. We realized that we must instead return to Terror Bay and later go to Gjoa Haven with Patsy when he looked at his trap line. We would hope to find an Inuk there to guide us to Perry River and thence to Cambridge Bay.

Hitching up the dogs, we struggled back along our tracks through the brutal ice, finally reaching the relatively smooth area where we had camped, but we didn't stop. Patsy's dogs were still in good shape, seasoned by long trips on the trap line. Our poor dogs, however, had only been on relatively short trips. We had not realized that they needed to be "broken in" before taking a long journey. Soon, Patsy and Maneratsiak disappeared ahead in the heavily drifting snow which also quickly obscured the dog and kamotik tracks. Our old lead dog Friday plodded on, nose to the snow, as though he knew where he was going, for which we were grateful, since Patsy's tracks were nowhere to be seen. Every once in a while we would catch a glimpse of a footprint or of a brief runner track, which mightily encouraged us, but as the drift became ever heavier we could only just see Friday, and really had no idea where we were heading.

Suddenly Friday made a sharp turn up across a low pressure ridge into some rough ice. We thought he might have smelled a bear, for we could not imagine that Patsy would turn into rough ice when the going was smooth ahead. Link stopped Friday, leading him back to the place where he had turned, and told him to go in the direction we had been headed before. He looked at us with a questioning expression and walked slowly forward, tail down, looking back over his shoulder for directions. This being quite un-like his usual behavior, we quickly decided that maybe Patsy *had* gone into the rough ice, so we again turned the team around to backtrack. Friday's tail went up, his nose down, and he trotted eagerly back to the place where he had turned into the rough ice, and without hesitation did so again. He continued to follow the invisible trail and, some hours later, gratefully re-lieved, we caught up with Patsy and Maneratsiak, who had at last stopped to wait for us. We made a small snow house and, after eating some boiled seal meat, fell into our sleeping skins for a brief rest.

Four hours later we were off again, unexpectedly meeting Aylikomiq and Utuitoq, en route to their trap line around the small islands near Petu-lik. They were equally surprised. We all stopped and sat on our kamotiks, Patsy and our friends discussing the rough ice. Hot tea from our thermos bottles was wonderful, as always. (The heat slides down one's throat to the stomach with a thump, then seems to flood through the body and out to the fingertips and toes. A most delicious sensation when one has been jog-ging along for hours beside the kamotik at −30°F to −40°F.) Patsy decided we would press on for home rather than sleep, so again we embraced our friends, trusting they would ultimately find their way back to Pelly Bay.

About halfway to Terror Bay, as the last dim light in the southern sky was fading, a huge moon rose. Partly flattened, it looked like a great, squat and deep orange lantern hesitating on the horizon. Then as it climbed up from the rim, regaining its proper roundness, it became an enormous, gleaming silver disk hung against a startlingly blue sky. The snow and weird ice forms became pale pink with purple and blue shadows. I felt like Alice in Wonderland, so unreal did it all seem.

As the moonlight brightened, we came upon an abandoned snow house where we stopped for a cup of tea and a brief respite for ourselves and the dogs. I would have curled up happily in my sleeping bag, had it been suggested, but Patsy sensed impending bad weather and said we must continue. So we pressed on. When we neared the coast a few hours later, a strong wind sprang up, sending the fine snow up and up until it enveloped the icy world. The moon's light, which still glimmered through, made the fine, icy crystals glint with myriad tiny soft lights. I finally became too weary to run beside the kamotik any longer, and although I hated to add my weight to our dogs' task, I flopped down on the load and lay on my back for a few miles, watching the sparkling snow crystals through the long wolverine fur around the hood of my kuletak.

I had once again been jogging along mechanically for some time in the shimmering light when the two schooners on the shore and the little house upslope gradually took form through the snow-filled air. We could hear Jorgen's dogs as they set up a wild howling chorus. Jorgen and Ayalik dashed out of the house expecting a bear and could scarcely believe their eyes. They ran down the slope to embrace us and help us unharness, tie up, and feed our poor dogs, who were too exhausted to eat. The dogs had brought us nearly 70 miles since early morning.

I have never known what time it was when we reached home, but it was noon before we awakened the following day. When we looked out of the tent, we could just barely distinguish the house through the smothering snow. Patsy was right. The first really fierce blow of the winter had whirled out of the north. Thankful that we were not still out on the ice, we pulled up our hoods, bent against the wind, and hurried to the house.

After much discussion with Patsy and Jorgen, it was decided that we would accompany Jorgen and Mikigiak to the Hudson's Bay Company post at Gjoa Haven, where we would be with Billy Joss for Christmas, and hopefully find an Inuk who would then guide us to Perry River and perhaps on to Cambridge Bay. By evening the next day, however, Jorgen and Mikigiak, who had never been to Perry River, decided this would provide a good excuse for making the trip, and they would be there for the Christmas festivities. Moreover, Jorgen was not catching many foxes on his trap line, and the amount of credit at the Hudson's Bay Company we agreed on in exchange for guiding us would come in handy for him.

Because Jorgen had never crossed Queen Maud Gulf to Perry River, he took Link's map to the shore and stood for a long time looking out over the bay. Actually he was studying the sastrugi, noting particularly the orientation of the longest ones, which form parallel to the prevailing wind. When he had memorized the angle at which we should cross the sastrugi in order to reach a point on the coast about 25 miles east of Perry River, he was prepared to start. It was still blowing the following morning, but since it was already December 17 and we would have the wind behind us, Jorgen decided we should leave if we had any hope of crossing Queen Maud Gulf in time to reach Perry River for Christmas.

At Jorgen's suggestion, we harnessed our dogs behind his, leaving our little kamotik as well as Dumpy and our bitch Arluk with Patsy, who wanted Arluk to put a new bloodline into his team. She was small, had a good coat and feet, and was intelligent and a good puller. Dumpy was really not a useful sledge dog, for he was clever enough to pull only as much as was needed to keep his trace up. Still, it was hard to leave them both and take Patsy's old leader and another old dog in exchange.

Jorgen's big kamotik was loaded more than waist high by the time all frozen seals, looking like fat logs, and the boxes of rock specimens, the grub and Primus boxes, duffle bags, and fur sleeping bags and skins were lashed on. It took a good jump to sit on the load for the usual yelping rush away from home and out onto the bay ice. As we drew away, leaving another bit of our hearts in that corner of the Arctic, the mournful howling of Arluk and Dumpy and of Patsy's and Tulemaq's dogs drifted through the swirling snow, growing ever fainter.

The heavy drift continued all day. It was impossible to keep the snow out of one's face, no matter which way the head was turned or bent. By the time we stopped to make camp, we resembled automated snowmen. Frost crystals had formed on every eyelash, every eyebrow hair, and on all the fuzz on our faces. It felt odd, for our eyelids tended to stick together when blinking and our skin felt stiff. We looked at each other and took time out for a good, hearty laugh, which warmed us up. We stopped early, at 12:30 P.M., to build a snow house. Because there were no deep drifts, Jorgen cut the snow blocks horizontally instead of vertically. His method worked admirably, and an hour later we were out of the wind.

This was really the first time Link and I had traveled by dog team with an Inuit family, and we were interested to see how life flowed in their snow house. Little Mary was happy and quiet, and all family conversations were subdued. I watched Mikigiak out of the corner of my eye and admired her economy of movement as she arranged her Primus stove, cook pot, and a few other necessary items, then placed the block of snow Jorgen handed her into the pot to melt for cooking water. I did the same on our side of the snow house, but it somehow took me longer.

In the morning we awoke to find a fine day with a light breeze. In the soft dim light, pastel shades tinted the luminous sky and snow-covered ice. After tea and porridge and while I was still taking care of our cooking and eating implements, I was astonished to see Jorgen break a large hole in the side of the snow house, then step out through it and turn to Mikigiak, who handed their grub and Primus boxes, sleeping bags, and skins out to him. One more lesson learned. I put on full speed to catch up, and managed to have everything ready when needed. The kamotik was soon packed, and Jorgen, Mikigiak, and Link were tightening the lashing on the load when the ugyuk-hide bottom line around the kamotik broke.

With amused expressions, discussion, and laughter, Jorgen and Mikigiak began to unload. We joined in the task. Everything had to be taken off so that Jorgen could splice the line. Then all was once more loaded and the covering tarp carefully pulled over. This time, the lashing lines were tightened with caution, but still not gently enough, for the old line broke again. Jorgen and Mikigiak leaned back against the load convulsed with laughter.

"It's pretty funny," Jorgen said when he had recovered himself enough to speak, "because I'm not sure I can fix the line so it'll hold. If it doesn't, the dogs will have to drag as much of our stuff as we can tie up in the polar-bear skin, and maybe some things can be tied over their backs. We'll have to pack as much as we can on our own backs, and leave the rest on the ice." With a rueful smile, he continued, "It'll be a pretty long walk, and everyone at Perry River will laugh like crazy because we didn't have a spare line. I'll have to borrow a small kamotik at Perry and then come back to try to find my big kamotik, unless a tide crack's swallowed it." When they laughed again, we joined them, trying to learn to appreciate the funny side of our predicament.

Jorgen's reaction to such a situation was typical of the Inuit we knew, and I have been grateful for the lesson I learned from it. I suspect that through the millennia those who could laugh at trouble and then find a way to overcome it survived, while those unable to do so perished. It is a pretty good way to operate, if one stops to think about it.

The mending of the line was done with exquisite care, and the final tightening of the lashing with extreme caution. The old line held all the way to Perry River. Once again the patient dexterity and perseverance, which I observed in most Inuit, saved the day.

We had been traveling pretty much southwest, and the going had been relatively easy. Most of the open tide cracks were narrow enough for the lead dog to jump over, with the team following. But there were also places where the wind and currents broke the ice to form tide cracks and then squeezed the edges together, lifting large slabs up on end to form long pressure ridges up to fifteen feet or more high. The longer the edges were under pressure, the wider and higher the ridges became. Sometimes a way for the dogs and kamotik could be chopped right through, but often we had to travel beside a ridge for some distance before finding a place where it was not too high and jumbled to cross, or where we could chop a way through for the kamotik.

It was hard work and a bit scary at times, as the slabs of ice were steep and jammed at all angles. In some places there were unexpected openings between slabs where a misstep could have become a rollercoaster slide into open water. Occasionally we came to a wide stretch of fairly smooth ice with but a few big sastrugi. We would sigh with relief and take turns sitting on the load for a few minutes, bantering about people who were too weak to run. The dogs responded to the easy going by trotting faster.

We were making good time over such an area one day, when the twilight faded before we could find a snowdrift deep enough to cut snow blocks. With a twinkle, Jorgen finally said, "We will just have to use the tent for shelter, but that's OK, because we can sleep *really* close together to keep warm." While he and Link set out the dog lines, chipping holes in the ice for the stakes and freezing them in with urine, Mikigiak and I set about unhitching our dogs as usual.

I took hold of Friday's trace and tried to unsnap the metal clasp, but found that my thumbs would not work properly; they simply folded in against my palms. I had not realized they were so cold, but with the temperature at −40°F or −50°F, the strong wind caused severe wind chill and my poor thumbs had just given up. I could neither push nor grasp with them. I should have kept my thumbs in the palms of my hands where they would have been warmer. I did not dare use my teeth for fear my lips would freeze to the metal. I had an awful, frustrating time getting the harnesses off without thumb power. Once I had accomplished the task and fed our dogs, the tent was up and it was my turn to prepare supper.

Link and Jorgen had built a low shelter of snow blocks for the Primus stoves just outside the tent, as there was not room inside—besides, they would have frosted the tent. This arrangement was fine, but I had to get a lantern lighted so I could see what I was doing. While I was wrestling with the harness problem the lantern had been standing by the tent, snow had blown into its chimney, and the coal oil was almost frozen. I cleaned out the snow, tried to dry off the wick, and was looking for my match case when Jorgen handed me a lighted match. While I was huddled over the lantern trying to keep the little flame from blowing out as I held it against the wick, Jorgen said, "Better get it lighted. Last match."

A sudden, unthinking sense of panic flooded over me. I *knew* it would not catch with one match, but I was too tired and cold to realize he was teasing me. Panic became despair as the match went out. I just knelt there. Then Jorgen, laughing softly, handed me the matchbox. I looked up to see a mischievous smile on his face. He had won that round handily. Regaining my sense of humor, I laughed with him.

Another day we traveled in an almost complete whiteout. To see ahead better, Jorgen and Link ran a little to either side of the leader, barely visible to Mikigiak and me. Suddenly both men slammed, spread-eagled in an almost vertical position, against the invisible icy face of a pressure ridge block. The dogs piled up on top of each other between them and began fighting. Mikigiak and I grabbed hold of the kamotik and dug our heels into the snow, futiley trying to stop it, while Jorgen and Link got their legs under themselves again and began shouting at the dogs, yanking them apart, then separating and untangling them.

In the whiteout, they had all run headlong into the unseen pressure ridge, which even the lead dog had not sensed, or perhaps he had kept going because Jorgen, running beside him, had failed to direct him to turn or stop. When everything was straightened out, we had a good laugh, then proceeded along the barrier until at last we found a place where we could chop our way through.

We had been traveling five days and felt we must be nearing the mainland coast, when out of the opaque gray nothingness of the fog there loomed a darker area. It turned out to be an island. As we continued, another island and still others appeared. We wound our way among them and it became difficult to know whether we were actually following the general coastline or going into one of the very numerous bays.

The wind died away and the temperature rose, melting the icing on the runners. This made pulling very hard, and our progress slowed to about half speed when the mud runners began to crack. A chunk fell out and was lost before we realized it. As soon as we saw the gap, though, we stopped and unloaded the kamotik. Jorgen mixed some tea leaves together with smashed hardtack biscuits and made a thick paste by adding a man's ever-ready natural hot water. The gap was patched, immediately freezing solid. After a little smoothing and icing, the kamotik was righted, repacked, and we were off again.

Earlier than usual, Jorgen decided we had better make a snow house and trust for better visibility in the morning, in the hope we might be able to determine where we were. He had stopped the team to check a nearby snowbank for snow block quality, when the dogs suddenly lunged ahead, breaking the main trace and leaving only four of our dogs hitched to the kamotik. Link dashed after the others and threw himself on the end of the trace. That stopped them for a split second but they lunged again, leaving two dogs with Link. Mikigiak and I yelled, and Jorgen dashed in a shortcut to head them off. Luckily he was able to catch the rest of the team when they momentarily stopped to fight. Maybe they scented a polar bear, a white fox, or an Arctic hare; we will never know. The dog lines were staked out and we laughed a lot, discussing what we might have done had they gotten away.

I had frequently wondered how Mikigiak was able to carry four-year-old Mary on her back, all day, every day. To be sure, she rode most of the time, but she was a tiny woman and Mary a big child, showing something of her grandfather's Viking genes. While we chinked the snow blocks as the men set them, I noticed that Mikigiak winced occasionally, straightening her back as she tried to reach up. Later, when supper was cleaned up, we sat to-gether on the sleeping bench, sewing patches on the worn moosehide of the mukluks, a frequent necessity. I put my hand on her back briefly and asked if it ached. She understood my question and raised her eyebrows with the inhaled "iyeh," in the affirmative. I wished that I could offer to carry Mary to relieve her occasionally, but my kuletak was designed more like a man's, with a small hood and no room for carrying a child.

Supper that evening gave us a really good laugh. Trying to think of something to vary the fare of seal meat and frozen fish, I decided to com-bine our last tin of bully beef with our last bit of cornmeal. It smelled good as it cooked, and had a hearty, thick consistency when I served it on our tin plates. Jorgen and Mikigiak politely accepted my offering, and we all took a bite. Their faces were pictures of self-control. An Inuk does not insult his friend by refusing to eat what is given him. Link and I looked at each other and tried a second bite. It was impossible. It had the consistency of slightly set, yet still gooey cement, with an indescribable flavor all its own.

We looked at Jorgen and Mikigiak, wrinkling our noses in a negative re-action, then burst out laughing. We all laughed for at least five minutes, sputtering as we tried to describe the mess to each other. I took all the plates and was about to throw the stuff out of the snow house when Jorgen said, "Wait, it would be great for runner repair!" And so it proved to be.

A couple of days later we crossed an old kamotik track and passed an old snow house, and in half an hour were overtaken by an inland Inuk who was trapping along the coast. He told Jorgen that a group of Inuit, camped at the mouth of a river some miles to the west, were also going to Perry River but intended to take an overland shortcut, saving a day. That sounded good, so Jorgen followed the directions. However, after an hour's travel up a big bay without discovering any sign of a camp or new track, he thought it best to head back north until we were outside the islands. Once out, we turned west again, our way lighted by the glowing colors of the southern sky.

Some hours later we found a recent track which we happily followed, until it suddenly led up onto an island. Since there was no good snow, and darkness had fallen, we put up the tent. It was December 22 and Jorgen was getting anxious about reaching the post for Christmas. He didn't know how far east of Perry River we were, and the irregular coastline was screened by islands, one of which was Flagstaff where the post was situated. Jorgen feared we might pass Perry River without recognizing it. Moreover, he could not understand why there were no fresh kamotik tracks, since many Inuit were sure to be heading for the annual gathering of the People. Puzzled, we stopped to build a snowhouse and had our evening meal. Then Jorgen took his flashlight and went out to search for a track, any track, that might lead us to Perry River. He finally found one, and said we should start very early next morning.

We were off at 3:30 A.M. by the wan light of a quarter moon. Jorgen ran ahead until he located the track, which we confidently followed to its unexpected end at a snowhouse. An Inuk with his wife and child were just preparing to leave. After a short conversation Jorgen arranged that we would go ahead and they would catch up. This they did and we continued on together until reaching rough ice, just before dark. When the Inuk had to stop to re-ice his runners, we lost each other. Jorgen climbed a big slab of ice but could not see them and decided that we should make camp.

When the dog lines were staked out, Jorgen and Link started a snow house, as usual, while Mikigiak began to undo the load, and I started to tie up the dogs. The snow house was half built and most of the dogs curled up waiting for supper when an Inuit team appeared out of nowhere. After a couple of minutes of conversation, the couple and Jorgen began to laugh. The Inuk wanted to know why we were building a snow house when the Hudson's Bay Company post was maybe four miles away just beyond a couple of islands!

We all had a good laugh and reversed our procedures, repacking the kamotik and putting the very unwilling dogs back in harness. They growled and snarled and almost had to be dragged back to the center trace for hitching, because they had never been treated in such a manner before. Poor things, they hardly had time to catch their breath and had no supper, and were now expected to hit the trail again. I wished that I could make them understand that it was only for a short trip. We started off, and Jorgen again laughed, "That partly built snow house'll be a real puzzle to people who pass it. Everyone is going to stop to figure out why anybody would begin a snow house if they're not going to use it. Who could have done this, they'll ask? Why?" He told us later that he overheard several people at Perry River discussing the problem, but he had just smiled.

An hour later we rounded an island and saw the lights of the post house and the beautiful, softly glowing domes of the numerous snow houses. All

Mainland coast, Perry River. Angalalik's boat, the Hudson's Bay Company post buildings in the background.

the teams began to howl as we approached, and people came running out to see who was arriving and to help stake out the dogs and start a snow house. Everybody laughed and talked at once, and again we regretted our ignorance of the language.

Angalalik, who had traded at Perry River for many years, took Mikigiak, Mary, and Jorgen to his house, while Link and I went up to the post. Patsy had told Billy Joss at Gjoa Haven about our plans, and Billy had alerted Angus Gavin by ham radio, so we were expected. But, arriving at night as we did, we took Angus and his wife Phyllis by surprise. Nevertheless, we were greeted most warmly, both in manner and in fact, since the snow-block covered house was heated to well over 80 degrees by a big coal range. Dressed in double caribou-skin clothing, we almost passed out. By sitting on the floor under a window, where it was slightly cooler, I managed to survive.

"Raw," untanned caribou-skin clothing is ideal in cold places, but it does have a definite aroma when heated. Phyllis disappeared for a few minutes, and returned with an armful of her own "civilized" clothing, together with towels and soap, saying that a nice hot bath awaited me in the kitchen. I retrieved my bra and silk-knit underclothes from my duffle bag and headed to the kitchen. There I doffed my furs and stepped into the big, round zinc washtub of steaming water. What a novel and delightful sensation! I scrunched myself down into the water, almost sloshing it over the sides. How long was it since I had enjoyed that bath at Coppermine—nine months? Well, we had done as the traditional English gentleman did in far lands; we had learned to "bathe in a tea cup."

The soapsuds were fairly flying about as I lathered myself from head to toes, when suddenly I got that funny feeling of being watched. Looking up to my right I was astonished to see a row of happily grinning faces! Angus had built a bench in the entry room and put a big window in the kitchen wall so that the people in their furs could sit and watch Phyllis working in her kitchen, without coming into the hot house. They were enjoying the free show to the full.

My first impulse was to grab a towel. Instead, I smiled through the soap bubbles streaming down my face, and scrubbed my head and body more vigorously. After a good rubdown with the big towel, I donned my own underwear and the clothes Phyllis had loaned me and rejoined the others in the living room. Angus prepared Link's bath for him, and I alerted him to the situation.

Except for trading for food staples or other necessities or visiting the missionaries, the people did not really have much contact with Caucasians. They seldom visited in their homes, except to listen to the Christmas and Easter programs from Coppermine, times when messages could be sent to absent family members or friends. Because the Inuit families were out on the land alone or in small groups for much of the year, they naturally enjoyed visiting with other Inuit when they came together. In spring, summer, and early autumn, when it was daylight all 24 hours, visiting might be enjoyed at any time, and in winter when days and nights were dark, if people met while on their trap lines or hunting, they were accustomed to visit freely.

This made a problem for the Caucasians who lived pretty much by the clock. To have visitors arrive while they were sleeping annoyed them, and, being used to privacy, there were many times when they did not want visitors. Furthermore, the Inuit usually dressed in their caribou-skin clothing, which gave off a strong odor in the heat of the houses.

It did feel very odd and quite uncomfortable to have hard, tight shoes on my feet and to have my body confined in flimsy clothing again, but I greatly appreciated Phyllis's generosity in lending me her own clothes. Angus did the same for Link, as none of us could have endured the skin clothing in the heated house. Jorgen, Mikigiak, and little Mary soon joined us for a delicious supper and lively conversation. We also listened to Angus as he kept his several radio skeds. All of us sent greetings to friends or relatives along the coast, and Link and I sent Christmas messages to our families Outside, the first direct word they'd had from us since September.

The next day was very special. A line of light at the horizon would let people know that the sun would soon return to break the winter's darkness, and even though the coldest days were still to come, spring would also return. We celebrated by going to the post store with Angus to find gifts for our host and hostess, for our good friends and traveling companions, Mikigiak, Mary, and Jorgen, and for all those back at Terror Bay. Later, Phyllis and I visited while she knitted a sweater and I sewed patches on our fur socks, mitts, and boots in preparation for the next leg of our journey. We expected that it would take us five or six days to reach Cambridge Bay. Later, when Angus and Phyllis had gone to bed, I cut bells and angels from the silver foil of cigarette papers and chocolate bars and put them on the table for decoration, along with our presents for Phyllis and Angus.

Christmas Day dawned clear and a cold −45°F. When we sat down for breakfast we were, of course, all "very surprised" to find bright parcels on the breakfast table. Link received a fine striped blue shirt, and I a fine green sweater. I also found a new silver wedding band like the ones the Inuit wore, and which I still cherish. We joined a chorus on the radio singing Christmas carols, and after the breakfast dishes were washed we went out to watch the Inuit kamotik races. By 1:00 P.M. a dozen teams were ready to line up. When one team started to move up into position for the takeoff, all the other yelping, howling dogs leapt after them and there was complete pandemonium—jumping dogs, careening kamotiks, and shouting Inuit.

One team got away without a driver and went tearing down the slope, crossing two dog lines, and then leaping broadside over a big kamotik, which abruptly halted them as their kamotik rammed the other. Angus had

Mainland coast, Perry River. Inuit teams lining up for annual Christmas race.

planned to start the race with a rifle shot, but the gun had frozen, so he had to shout above the bedlam. As each Inuk pulled up his snow anchor, the leaping, straining teams fairly flew down the long slope at top speed, obviously enjoying the competition. Everyone stood cheering their favorites, laughing and chattering in great good humor and excitement until the teams were almost lost to sight.

We then returned to the house for a bite and to listen to the annual Coppermine Christmas broadcast. However, we were all disappointed, because poor atmospheric conditions interfered with the reception. Moreover, the motor for the transmitter at Coppermine stopped functioning about halfway through the broadcast, abruptly ending the program. An hour later we went out again to see which team was to be the winner and to watch the footraces, which Jorgen lost by a nose. Back at the post, Phyllis had been busy in her kitchen. When we rejoined her, she loaned me a handsome red bouclé dress she had handknit, together with a green leather belt, flowers, and shoes, while she donned a similar blue outfit. She was both master knitter and chef.

Christmas dinner was a banquet we deeply appreciated—delicious soup, stuffed canned chicken, fresh potatoes, peas, green and red jello, and Christmas cake, all topped off with champagne. Our taste buds were overwhelmed! Jorgen, Angalalik, and a number of other Inuit came to visit after dinner, and we called Billy Joss and Scotty Gall on the ham radio to wish them a Merry Christmas. We wondered what our families were doing, and hoped that they had enjoyed the day as much as we had. Angus and Phyllis suggested bridge, so we played a few rubbers before turning to our sleeping bags in the wee small hours.

Being with the Gavins was a good reintroduction to Outside living, and we greatly appreciated their hospitality. It would have been a pleasure to linger, but we planned to reach Coppermine by the end of January, and it was necessary to hurry on to Cambridge Bay. When we spoke to Alec Eccles on Wilmot Island via ham radio on Christmas Day, we learned that Amos Cockney was with him and would be happy to escort us to Coppermine from Richardson Island off the southwestern coast of Victoria, where he lived with his stepfather, Ole Andreasen. We especially looked forward to meeting Ole and hoped he would tell us about his long treks over the ice with Stefansson in 1914.

12 / To Cambridge Bay
On to Ole Andreasen's
at Richardson Island
December 28, 1940–February 16, 1941

*W*e had decided to start for Cambridge Bay on December 28. Two Inuit, Ohokok and Aytok, planned to visit there and were willing to take us and all our duffle, since they were carrying minimum loads. Link was especially sorry to have to leave Snap, who had frozen his flank and was not in good enough shape for the trail. Angus said he could use him and promised to take good care of him.

The morning of the 28th dawned gray and relatively warm, with a light southeastern breeze. Jorgen and Mikigiak loaded their kamotik as we readied ours. Link had bought one good young dog to replace Snap and two others who seemed in good shape. All our dogs were hitched behind Aytok's team. It was very hard to wave good-bye to Mikigiak and Jorgen. Having spent so many warm, instructive, and happy times together, we had become very fond of them. They had been so good to us and so patient with our total ignorance about how life was lived in the Arctic winter. Their warm good humor under some frustrating situations emphasized for us the advantages of a humorous perspective in dealing with life's vicissitudes. The lessons have served us well.

Little Mary, peering out from the side of the hood by her mother's face, smiled her bewitching little smile, big black eyes shining. She had been so good through all the long days, riding hour after hour snug against her mother's back inside the furry kuletak. She had never fussed during the eight days of our journey.

With a last halloo to Angus and Phyllis, Angalalik, and the others, the anchors were pulled up, and away we went. The two teams settled into a steady pace, slowly eating up the miles over fairly good ice until about 4:30 P.M., when we stopped to build a snow house. With three men cutting

Mainland coast, Perry River. The author and Phyllis Gavin.

blocks, it went up quickly. By the time I got our dogs tied up and fed I had to rush the snow-block chinking so that I could start melting snow for water to boil the frozen char and make tea. After supper plates were cleaned, Link and I sat a while, writing and remembering, before slipping into our fur bags. The next day was calm, clear, cold, and so very peaceful. Only the lilting song of the runners and an occasional command to a lead dog by one of our companions broke the silence. Nothing else was alive and moving, to the very edges of our visible world.

Aytok, deciding that his three-month-old puppy should learn the art of kamotik travel on his own feet, dropped him off the load. Gradually he fell farther and farther behind us until he was just a little black spot on the ice. The teams were stopped then, and we waited for him to catch up, whereupon we started off again. Finally, after a couple of hours, the poor puppy just sat down when he was dropped and began to howl. That time Aytok picked him up and dropped him on a caribou skin on the load. I think the puppy was already asleep before he collapsed in a furry heap. It seemed cruel, but like marathon runners, he had to be trained to the point of exhaustion. If a puppy could not develop the necessary stamina, he was not kept.

We made a detour when crossing over a point, because Aytok wanted to obtain a specimen of mineralized quartz from the bedrock for Link, perhaps thinking the gleaming pyrite to be gold. Occasionally we stopped to measure the orientation of glacial striae and to collect bedrock specimens from some of the many small islands that fringe the coast. A low curtain of dark clouds gradually obscured the sky, and the world once again became an opaque gray void. Rough ice or islands beyond a hundred feet were lost to sight. Our pace seemed to slow down.

Moderately rough ice and tide cracks slowed us even more, because with virtually no visibility it was not possible to maneuver around them and still maintain an adequate sense of our location or direction. Ohokok and Aytok decided to make camp early, and when I opened my journal that night I suddenly realized that it was New Year's Eve! I had not really thought about seeing the Old Year out in a snow house on the frozen Arctic sea. I whispered "Happy New Year" to Link, who looked up surprised. We smiled, remembering other years. Our contented silence was broken only by the soft murmuring of our companions.

In the morning we awakened to find a beautiful but very cold day, the thermometer standing at −48°F. We had been traveling along the southern coast of Melbourne Island and were glad when we passed its western end and the small islands beyond. From there we could look north across Dease Strait and see the gleaming white cliffs of Cape Colborne, which the Inuit called Ikpukshak.

Our joy was dampened, however, for poor Aytok had developed a dreadful chest cold and lost his voice. Link and I were afraid he might come down with pneumonia, but he and Ohokok thought it was very funny. When he tried to shout directions to his lead dog, no sound came forth and he had to run up and shove the astonished dog to one side or the other to avoid small rough ice chunks that might dump the kamotik. Aytok's kuletak was old, its hair short and thin, and he had bought a miserable pair of imitation-fur gloves with little warmth in them. Worrying about him, I gave him both aspirin and my spare wool shirt, and Link offered his storm mitts, all of which Aytok accepted with a surprised and delighted smile.

The aurora borealis was spellbinding as we neared the coast of Victoria Island. One moment sheer curtains were swinging and rippling as in a light breeze; the next, streaking from all sides toward the zenith in great flames of red, yellow, blue, and green, they veiled a young quarter moon hanging wanly in the sky, its beauty lost in the fury of the aurora. We made camp just east of the little bay where we had taken cover from the storm in September while with Patsy on the *Aklavik*.

In the morning our companions decided to hitch all the dogs to one kamotik, leaving the second one at the snow house for their return trip. Later, as we crossed a point at the height of land, the dogs suddenly took off at top speed, tearing headlong down the slope. It was impossible to slow them, although all four of us were hanging onto the kamotik and sliding feet first, heels digging into the snow as hard as possible. Finally the kamotik dumped as it hurtled over a hummock and the team was jerked to a sudden stop. We had just caught our breath, when a few moments later, an Inuk, the cause of their abandoned behavior, appeared over a hilltop, then came to greet us. He said he was camped on the sea ice and had been hunting ptarmigan inland, but without luck. His appearance reminded us that we were about to rejoin the little group of friends at Cambridge Bay.

Later, as we rounded Cape Colbourne and were crossing the outer bay, we met four teams leaving Cambridge Bay. We all stopped for a visit and mug-up. We had not been long on the way again when Louis Kaglik met us with the RCMP puppy team, so Link and I rode with him the rest of the way home. At the post we found Scotty and Isabel just stirring, as the New Year's Eve party had lasted until 4:00 A.M.! We continued the short distance to our base near the Catholic mission, where Father Delalonde and Father Raymond were getting ready to leave for Coppermine in a few days. They had recently returned from a long journey to their mission at Burnside Harbour, near the bottom of Bathurst Inlet. From Burnside they had visited with the inland Inuit, crossed the land to Labyrinth Bay on Queen Maud Gulf, and so back to Cambridge Bay. They were the first Caucasians known to have made that overland crossing without an Inuk to guide them.

Corporal Duncan Martin offered us a spare room at the RCMP detachment for the few days we expected to be at Cambridge, which we gratefully accepted. We stayed with Isabel and Scotty for supper, and they brought us up to date on world happenings since our departure in September. Our future, like that of so many others, had become uncertain. We also caught up with the local news and spoke to the Gavins via Scotty's ham radio. It was great to be with old friends again, and we felt truly at home as we set out in the calm night to cross the frozen bay to the barracks half a mile away.

Suddenly we were buffeted by a strong wind. In moments the air was filled with horizontally driven snow. Remembering tales of men lost and frozen in just such sudden onslaughts, we turned back over the ice to re-trace our steps while we could still see an occasional glimmer of light from Scotty's window as the dim world rapidly became invisible in the drifting snow. Scotty and Isabel had become worried about us, and, relieved by our return, provided us with sleeping bags and blanket.

The following morning was calm again, unlike some of the people. Aytok and Ohokok were getting ready to return to Perry River; Einar Far-volden, a trader for Slim Semmler, was packing up to leave the country; Reg Goodey and the two priests were organizing for the trip to Coppermine; and everyone was rushing about collecting last-minute necessities. All this took several hectic days but the various kamotiks were finally loaded and the teams took off down the bay.

The morning after their departure, I awoke with a fever, throbbing toothache, and swollen face. I remained in my sleeping bag. Had I cracked a filling while crunching frozen fish or meat? I remembered the tales of how bad teeth were dealt with in the north. Visions of empty liquor bottles and large black pliers danced menacingly across my fevered brow. I shuddered, pulling my sleeping bag up around my face and willed the pain, fever, and swelling to vanish. That took two days, during which time I remained out of sight as much as possible, lest someone should get "itchy fingers" on my behalf.

Link decided to make a quick trip to Anderson Bay. He wanted to know if the fossiliferous specimen of rock that I had found on the beach there was an erratic, or from local bedrock. Identifying the fossils would give him the age of the bedrock. Louis Kaglik and Havioyak agreed to take him out, and three days later they returned with a rucksack full of rock specimens. Duncan found a stout wooden box in which we packed them so they could be shipped out with the *Fort Ross* the following summer.

Duncan and Reg Goodey had been so kind that I wanted to do something in return for our keep at the detachment. Since Mary Kaglik took care of all the housekeeping, I offered to assist Dunc in the weekly chore of making eight loaves of bread. A neophyte at this, I followed instructions carefully until I had an enormous mass of heavy dough which we took turns punching down and folding over and over. Finally we covered it with an attigi and set it on the upper shelf of the coal range to rise. The dough rose only a little, but we put the pans in the oven anyway.

When Dunc said the bread should be ready we took a pan out. The loaf felt as heavy as stone and proved to be equally hard. We tried to cut, break, and saw the little loaves. It was impossible. Finally, hating to waste so much food, Dunc threw them to the dogs, who fell upon them eagerly. The following day they were still gnawing on them. We started a new batch of dough with double the regular amount of yeast. It rose to great heights, seeming to grow as we worked it, and we wondered how it would bake.

This time all the little loaves rose right up to the top of the oven, where they stuck. Dunc had to use the long snow knife to cut them free, and they proved as light and airy as spun sugar. I was greatly chagrined by my failure, but we laughed as we ate what Scotty called "cheat-the-belly-bread," more air than substance. The following week I again used the prescribed amount of yeast and redeemed myself by producing a great batch of fine-textured loaves. Perhaps the first yeast was too old.

When Amos finally came in from Wilmot Island and asked if we could wait a couple of days longer while his dogs rested, we of course agreed. Mary Kaglik had finished making our new, beautifully sewn caribou-skin pants, mitts, socks, boots, and a shirt, which we needed for our journey to Ole Andreasen's at Richardson Island and on to Coppermine. She had also dressed a doll for me in a kuletak made from the perfect tiny skin of a caribou fetus.

On the day we had planned to leave, we awoke to find a frigid gale blasting face-freezing snow before it and causing near-zero visibility. Relieved to be where we were rather than stormbound on the trail, we waited for several days for the storm to subside. Link became concerned. Since we were already a month behind our scheduled departure date, he sent a message to Canadian Airways asking that a Norseman pick us up at Richardson Island rather than Coppermine.

Dunc insisted that we take a batch of hearty pemmican for the trail, so we boiled a mixture of beans, rice, canned tomatoes, and ground caribou meat. When it was ready we formed the pemmican into blocks and put it out to freeze. Link bought a big tin of slab bacon from Scotty. We planned to eat the lean part for breakfast and soak hardtack biscuits in the frying fat.

When frozen those made great lunch snacks and gave us energy. Dunc said we must also take a sack of doughnuts. I had never made doughnuts; nevertheless, we mixed up a colossal amount of dough and melted a huge pan of lard. With the lard boiling gently, I formed circles of white dough and dropped them ring by ring into the bubbling fat. When each was done, I forked it out to cool, then tossed it into a gunnysack, until that was full. Doughouts had never been my favorite snack and I felt I would never again want to see, let alone eat one. But they did taste good on the trail.

We had agreed to hitch our remaining dogs behind Amos's team, except for Tuk, who was middle-aged and had certainly done more than his full share for us. Isabel wanted a pet dog, and we knew he would respond to her warm care. We felt he deserved a good home rather than a precarious future. When the day dawned, bright and wind-still, we loaded the kamotik and bade our friends farewell. The rising sun spread a golden path across the frozen bay before us. Poor Tuk. When he realized we were going without him, he stood on his hind legs pawing the air frantically, howling his anguish at being left behind. Looking back to wave to the now tiny figures standing by the house, I could see Mount Pelly looming like a dream on the horizon, so beautiful in the dim morning light. Once again tears froze on my cheeks.

The pulling was very slow at the outset, the snow hard and gritty as wet sand. It was −40°F when we started, but without a breath of wind it did not feel cold. We jogged along beside the kamotik in the bright rays of the low sun. The song of the runners and jingling harness bells hypnotized me, and for a moment I could again believe I was traveling with an Inuk a thousand years ago, when the realm of "civilized" man was still half a world away. The day was clear, and darkness did not fall until after five, so we continued west along the same coast we had traveled with Sam Carter in the spring. We were halfway to the Finlayson Islands before we built a snow house.

We noticed that one of the dogs we had purchased at Perry River was not pulling, but rather just trotting along in a listless way. Amos thought the problem was "dog sickness"—usually fatal. That evening, instead of eating his piece of seal meat, the dog just stood still, eyes half closed. As I watched he appeared to shrink and then fell over stiffly on his side—dead. We felt quite helpless. There was nothing we could have done to help or save him, and we worried that others of the team might have contracted the sickness.

Two days later, the young dog we also brought from Perry River did develop the sickness, but instead of just weakening he suffered terrible cramps, yelping in pain. Link and I decided it would be best to put him out of his misery, but Amos said that dogs that get sick in that manner sometimes recover, and since he was so young we should give him a chance. We tied him behind the kamotik and it was very hard but we accepted Amos's advice and the dog did recover a few days later.

The weather deteriorated. With our heads bent against the wind, and the driving snow crystals biting our faces as we jogged, we wondered how soon we would reach the seal camp. There we knew shelter awaited us. Suddenly stones appeared through the snow beneath our feet. Without realizing it we had edged inland onto the low-lying coast. Link chipped out a few erratics, and then we swung the team around and backtracked until we were again on the sea ice, our mud runners thankfully still intact.

This inadvertent digression lengthened our journey, and we were relieved when the dogs quickened their pace. Soon we too heard the welcome, full-throated chorus of the Inuits' dogs at the sealing camp. Straining our eyes through the dusk and the driving snow, we saw three softly glowing snow domes. As we approached, the people came out and greeted us warmly. They helped us stake out and feed our dogs, then showed us the snow house they had built for us. We were surprised to see that the oddly flat dome was supported by one horizontal two-by-three-inch board laid across the snow house from side to side and supported by another. It appeared sound, so we hastened to spread our sleeping skins on the snow bench and melt snow for tea and boiled char.

When the meal was finished, Amos said he was going over to visit with his friends and invited us to come with him. We thanked him and said we would but had a few things to arrange first. We were still holding our teacups when we were suddenly blasted by snow.

For a moment we stood stunned, hip deep in snow, too astonished to move, each holding a snow-piled mug. Our snow-house dome had collapsed upon us! How comical we looked by the flickering light of the snow-capped kerosene lantern. We laughed. I could just see us in cartoon—"Intrepid Arctic travelers enjoying their evening cup of tea." Half buried in the broken snow blocks, the blizzard driving icy snow crystals into our suddenly exposed and freezing faces, we shivered and, pulling up our furry kuletak hoods, scrambled to action. Link heaved broken snow blocks over the remaining snow wall while I clambered out to get Amos. Stooping through the long, low entrance tunnel I found them sitting on the edge of the snow bench happily visiting over mugs of tea. When I asked Amos if he would give us a hand, because our roof had collapsed, he translated for the others and everyone jumped up, pulled on their kuletaks, and we all scrambled out.

Link climbed out of our snow house to help Amos cut new blocks to rebuild the top of the walls, while the two women and I climbed in to clear the interior of loose snow. The two other men ran to an enormous snowdrift, into which they furiously dug, finally retrieving a big tarpaulin from their buried cache. This they stretched across the top of the rebuilt walls to act as a roof, then another row of snow blocks was placed around the edge to hold the tarp down.

Half an hour later our house was cleared. The caribou-skin bedding and sleeping bags were shaken out and replaced on the snow bench; our duffle bags, Primus stove, lantern, and cooking utensils were recovered and cleared of snow, and all of us were back in the other snow house laughing, talking, and warming up with hot tea. The Inuit told Amos that when they built our snow house, the storm-driven new snow had not had time to become firmly packed, as it must be to make good building blocks. To compensate, they had made the dome higher and more conical than normal to allow for shrinkage. It sagged anyway. When this was discovered, they placed an eight-foot long two-by-three across the center from wall to wall, supporting it and the sagging dome by a vertical seven-foot two-by-four. The support had worked for a while!

Weary from traveling, we left our hosts and returned to our repaired snow house. Though quivering in the wind, the new tarp roof seemed secure, so we slipped into our sleeping bags. In the middle of the night something aroused me. I pushed my head out of the top of my bag and heard a soft flapping sound. By the lantern's dim light I could see a cone of snow on top of it, one on Link's bag, and another on Amos's. Even as I spoke to Link, whose head was beside mine, the flapping became urgent, and one corner of the roof tarp lifted ominously. Link struggled out of his sleeping bag and shook Amos, who jumped into his pants, boots, and kuletak and was out the door in an instant, while Link pulled on his fur long johns and grabbed hold of the loosening tarp, which he held down while Amos piled on more snow blocks along the outside wall top. Secure again, we all laughed and snuggled in our bags to finish out the night.

By morning, the storm had abated. We continued our journey, checking the geology whenever the low-lying land was sufficiently snow-free for us to see bedrock. We checked the direction of striae, crescentric fractures, or abrasion, which indicated direction of glacial movement.

Two days later, as the light waned and the drifting snow became tinged with faint lavender and pink, the dogs suddenly quickened their pace again, ears and tails on the alert. We could not see far through the drifting snow and wondered if a polar bear were near. Amos put one hand on his rifle—then three teams materialized. Reg Goodey and the two Inuit teams were on their way back to Cambridge Bay from Coppermine. Everyone began talking at once, and we decided to make camp and enjoy a good visit. Amos, Reg, and Link started a snow house for us while I took care of the team and chinked between the snow blocks, as usual. I noticed that one of Friday's flanks was frostbitten and made a mental note to make a caribou-skin shield for him before sleeping.

The five Inuit were busy building a big snow house 50 feet away, all of them cutting and placing blocks while animatedly exchanging news. As soon as the house was up, the Primus stoves and lanterns were lit and Amos went over to join the others. Reg, Link, and I were putting the finishing touches on our house when a loud "whoosh" made us jump and turn. There was a moment of shocked silence followed by peals of laughter as the Inuit stood up, hip deep in snow, shaking their kuletaks. The whole snow house had collapsed on them! We knew exactly how it felt, and after we all stopped laughing, we helped to clear their belongings of snow while they began to build a new house. This time they went about the job carefully, almost silently, making sure the blocks were correctly placed.

In the morning, after breakfast and warm handshakes, we went our opposite ways. Hours later, as the last light failed in the frosty air, a glimmer of light in Ole's house and the faint howling of dogs told us we had almost reached the end of our journey. We looked forward to meeting Ole and his family, but the knowledge that we would have to leave our dogs behind when we departed weighed on our hearts. We had not yet decided what to do about them. The two survivors from Perry River were in good shape, even the one who had been sick; since they had been bred by Inuit, they and

En route along coast from Cambridge Bay to Ole Andreasen's home on Richardson Island. Stop for a visit and "mug-up." Link with passing Inuit at −45°F.

Richardson Island. Ole Andreasen, Susannah, and the little girls.

the others would be useful to Amos or one of his stepbrothers. But Friday was too old to pull for another year, and with his flank frostbitten he would be unable to work again for some time.

The whole family came out to welcome us: Ole, his wife Susannah and son Jasper, with his two little girls, and Amos's wife Agnes, who was Ole's stepdaughter. Agnes unhitched and fed Amos's dogs, while Amos helped me with ours. Jasper, Ole, and Link unloaded the kamotik and we all carried our gear and boxes of rock specimens up to the house. Like most Arctic houses, this one had a closed porch or entry in which everyone beat and knocked the snow from kuletaks and boots with a hardwood stick. Beyond that was another unheated entry where outer garments, boots, mitts, and all manner of gear were kept. From this space one entered the main room, which was approximately 24 feet square. As in Patsy's house, each family had a curtained living space with a high platform. The big coal range stood against one side wall, which had a southern exposure with a view out over Coronation Gulf. A row of towel hooks hung on the entry wall, against which stood a washstand and basin and a six-by-three-foot, short-legged Japanese-style dining table, which was placed in the middle of the floor at mealtime.

I thought of our apartment in New Haven, Connecticut, which, while small, was filled with so many things, and realized how free we had been during the past eleven months. Why, I wondered, do we burden ourselves with so many possessions? We could better use the same money to travel, to see far lands, to meet and learn to know other peoples; to become world citizens. As I glanced around wondering where we should place our things, Ole said we might put our sleeping skins and bags on the floor under the window, between Amos's area and the wall with the three living areas. We were out of the flow of traffic and had not displaced anyone, for which we were grateful.

Ole confirmed that Coppermine expected the plane to arrive on February 15, weather permitting. That would just give Link and Amos time to make a run along the coast as far as Lady Franklin Point and back. I remained at Ole's collecting erratics, specimens from nearby bedrock outcrops, and checking for striae and other indications of glacial movement.

Also, I wanted to surprise Link by making him a pair of house slippers from some special caribou leg skins I had saved for the purpose. I chewed the edges until they were soft enough to scrape, and when the skin was finally all white and supple, I cut and sewed them, which took me a couple of days. I was pleased with the results.

Susannah spoke no English, but asked Ole if I would show the slippers to her. I had prepared and sewn them as carefully as possible, making sure the small stitches were even and never went all the way through the skins, so I did not mind. After examining them carefully, she asked through Ole what fur I was going to sew around the tops. I pulled a piece of wolverine fur from my bag. She smiled, and then rummaged through a sealskin pouch for a strip of beaver skin, which she first held around the top of the slippers and then handed to me. Ole said she wanted me to use it, as it would look nicer than the wolverine. This was true, but I was loathe to accept it, for I knew it would be difficult to replace. She insisted, so I stitched it on the now really handsome slippers. We were both happy, and Link was pleased when I gave them to him. He still has them.

One of Ole's daughters-in-law had died, leaving two little girls about three and five years old who wondered who we were. At first they were very shy, but after a couple of days they inched nearer while I sat on the floor sewing. With their straight black hair, shining black eyes, and bright red cheeks, they reminded me of a favorite Japanese girl doll I'd had as a child. We exchanged many smiles and finally they crept close to me, laying their heads on my lap, where they fell asleep. The poor little things were longing for a mother to care for them and had apparently decided that maybe I was going to be the one. After that, they stayed close to me and followed me whenever I moved about, sitting on either side of me when we were at table.

One day, when I went out to collect bedrock samples, they tagged along behind without my realizing it, and I had gone some distance before anguished wails made me jump. They had no kamiks on, the hair inside the feet of their caribou-skin tights had worn thin, and the tights were too short for them. With the temperature at −40°F, their little feet were freezing! I gathered them up, one weeping child under each arm, and returned to the house. Putting them down, I mentioned to Ole that maybe their feet would be frozen unless someone repaired their leggings. Motherless children and orphans sometimes had a bad time, with no one taking responsibility for their welfare, especially if they were girls. In earlier times, as in ancient China, baby girls were disposed of at birth if the family already had a daughter or if a suitable little boy was not available to name as the promised husband.

Again I set out walking through the snowy world, inspecting all the snow-free rock exposures and knocking off occasional hand specimens. When I returned from my survey, Susannah looked up from her sewing and smiled. She was busy putting new feet on the girls' tights. When the little ones had pulled on their repaired clothing, they came to me, all smiles, and Ole followed them, bringing something with him. It was Susannah's Dance Hat, which he said she wished me to have. The hat was beautifully sewn from very narrow, pie-shaped strips of alternating white and dark brown, short-haired caribou skin, separated by still-narrower strips of red-dyed, hairless skin, while a thin strip of wolverine fur was sewn around the edge.

I was deeply touched, for a Dance Hat was a cherished possession that was worn on suitable occasions throughout one's life. I so wanted to express my appreciation of her gift, to talk with her, to ask her a thousand questions, but could only say *kuannapuk*—thank you very much—and hope that my expression and voice would convey something of my deep feelings.

We had been at Ole's four days and I was busy making a pair of slippers for myself when Ole asked me if I had ever been around to help a woman when she had a baby. I confessed I had not and asked if someone was expecting. He said yes, Agnes was, at any moment. Since I was not experienced in midwifery, he went out to fetch an old Inuit grandmother living in a snow house nearby. I had wondered if Agnes might be pregnant, but it was hard to tell, for the full, long duffle attigi with its cotton cloth cover effectively concealed her figure. That morning she had washed a tubful of clothing, kneeling on the floor, and had just finished kneading a big pan of dough for eight loaves of bread, when she abruptly climbed onto her platform and pulled the curtain across the opening. Ole returned with the old Inuit grandmother, who climbed up and disappeared behind the curtain. A few almost inaudible whispers drifted out. Then, about fifteen minutes later, the high, shrill wail of a newborn filled the room. The event of birth was met with equanimity, just as were all facts of life. No more time than was essential was allocated to them.

Link and Amos returned the following evening, and when Ole kept his radio sked with Coppermine, we learned that if the weather cleared there, the plane would arrive the next day. We would have to prepare a runway on the bay ice. After breakfast, Ole, Amos, Link, and I went down to the shore, taking four shovels and a dozen sacks of coal with us on the kamotik to mark the borders and wind direction.

A light breeze chased wisps of snow through the bright blue shadows cast by the long, gleaming, pink-tinged sastrugi, many of which we would have to remove. First we placed the sacks in two parallel rows about fifty feet apart, making an arrow point at one end to show the wind direction. Then, chopping, smashing, and shoveling the sastrugi, we slowly cleared a strip. As we finished, three hours later, glowing from the exercise, the wind died down and it became calm. Looking out after lunch we saw that the wind had risen again and was busy piling ridges *across* our strip. There was only one thing to do; go down and make a new one.

By the time we had relaid the coal sacks and cleared off the hard-packed snow, it was so late we were sure the plane would not come that day and we would doubtless have to do our work all over again the following morning. Walking back to the house, Link and I stopped to speak to our dogs. Link had talked with Ole and Amos, who said they would be glad to have them, but Link had finally decided that the kindest thing to do for Friday, our faithful old leader, would be to shoot him. We could not take him Outside with us and, if we left him, Ole or Amos would have to shoot him. A non-working dog could not be kept. It was a hard decision, but Link got his rifle and a big frozen fish, which he let Friday get really involved in eating before ending his life with an unexpected bullet in the back of the skull. A cruel but also loving reward for faithful service and friendship.

The "sked" with Coppermine that evening told us that the weather to the south had cleared and the plane would surely be in to pick us up the following day. Feeling rather sanguine about this, we laid out our sleeping gear again, and after a delicious supper of boiled potatoes and caribou meat, Amos played many cowboy songs on his old hand-wound Victrola, his favorite being "The Red River Valley," which he played over and over. Whenever it comes to mind I can feel again the welcoming atmosphere of Ole's home and of the family who took us in, and out of the generosity of their hearts fed us and enriched our lives with their friendship. We left our remaining food supply with them.

The following day dawned clear, with a stiff breeze carving the sastrugi and sending the loose snow swirling. When we went down to look at the runway, we found that the fickle wind was blowing strongly across our strip and had drifted snow over our coal sacks. Feeling sure that the wind would change direction again, we joked about how strong our arms were getting and bent our backs to the shovels. It took a couple of hours of hard work each time we had to shift the coal sacks, which we had to do again in the late afternoon.

The sun had slipped down near the edge of the world and we all thought it was too late for Alf to come. As we were teasing each other about having to clear the snow again in the morning, we looked at the glowing copper ball that seemed to hesitate at the horizon, and there, in its middle, for a moment, appeared a black speck. Frantically we worked to level the remaining ridges of snow before the Norseman roared overhead, critically examining the results of our labor.

The little plane circled, slid down from the sky, and bounced along our runway, finally coming to a stop. Alf had decided that he had better come over while the weather was good at Richardson, because we could always take off, even if it snowed, as long as it was clear enough to land at Coppermine. Looking at our boxes of rocks stacked in the outer entry, he said we should load them before supper so that we could get an early start in the morning, weather permitting. Amos hitched up his team to haul the boxes and after they were safely loaded in the Norseman, Alf and Pat brought their sleeping bags into the house and we shared our bedding skins with them.

During supper Ole told us about his journeys over the ice with Vilhjalmur Stefansson, and the changes that had come to the Arctic since the advent of flying. Ole had first met Stef when the latter had stopped at Ole's trapping camp on the Arctic coast, east of the Mackenzie River, in 1912. Stefansson asked Ole in 1914 if he would be willing to accompany him, Storker Storkerson, and several others on a kamotik journey of exploration. They planned to start from Collinson Point on the Alaska coast and go northward over the frozen Beaufort Sea to latitude 74° north, then east to Banks Island, where a supply ship was expected to meet them. Ole agreed to join the expedition.

That 700-mile journey, which took them from mid-March to mid-September, demonstrated they could "live off the sea as well as the land." They took basic rations with them, depending on shooting seals and polar bears while on the ice, and caribou, musk-ox, Arctic hare, and ptarmigan

Richardson Island. Boarding the Norseman for Coppermine and Yellowknife.

on the land. Three months after their return to base camp at Sachs Harbour on Banks Island, they set forth again, discovering Brock, Borden, Meighen, and Lougheed Islands.

This journey further vindicated Stefansson's belief that Caucasians as well as Inuit could adapt to the "friendly Arctic." Most important, his travels and discovery of new lands contributed significantly to establishing Canada's claim to that sector of the triangle of islands extending from the mainland coast toward the Pole. Ole was a quiet, modest man and his description of these extended journeys over unknown sea and lands made them sound quite matter of fact, whereas they were extraordinary.

In the morning, we were up early for a quick look at the weather. Not too bad. Oatmeal, Arctic char, bread, and coffee were soon ready, and we all sat down on the floor around the low table for the last time. Amos had cranked up the old Victrola and once again the strains of "The Red River Valley" filled the room. With breakfast over, Alf stepped outside. Returning, he said it was flyable, so we hugged the little girls and Susannah and Agnes, and grasped Ole's and Jasper's hands—how could we thank them—

then loaded our duffle on Amos's kamotik and dashed down the slope to the plane. All gear on board, we squeezed Amos's hands and climbed into the Norseman.

We were in luck. Or were we? It was hard to know. There, in that remote corner of the globe, was peace, serenity, friendship. Outside, the "civilized" world was tearing itself apart. I felt a chill around my heart as I looked at Link. If the United States entered the war, he would sign up. But he needed time to write his dissertation on the data we had gathered. Our future, like that of thousands of others, was filled with uncertainties.

Our flight to Coppermine over the austere expanse of the frozen Coronation Gulf was uneventful, our stay brief, and our leave-taking overshadowed by the war, as was our flight south and arrival home. But one thing *was* certain. Our lives had been infinitely enriched by the many friends we had made across the Arctic. We had learned much about geology, but even more about life. Everywhere we traveled, the people welcomed us and helped us in a thousand ways. They shared their knowledge eagerly, hoping it would make our travels easier and perhaps help us to avoid dangerous mistakes. They welcomed us in their homes and snow houses, they gave us needed tools and showed us how to use them, they taught us the ways of Arctic life, and, most precious of all, they accepted Link and me as we were and gave us their friendship.

L'envoi

*L*ink received his doctorate in June 1942 and immediately joined the Armed Forces. He was sent to the eastern Canadian Arctic as an observer on the Hudson's Bay Company supply ship *Nascopie*. This reinforced his desire to continue his geological studies in the Canadian Arctic. To my delight, this has resulted in many field seasons in Northeast Greenland and Arctic Canada. Link's geological studies during the years covered by this book were published by the Geological Society of America.

We are grateful to the Canadian government's Polar Continental Shelf Project and the Resolute Hamlet Council for making it possible for us to continue work during recent field seasons in the Resolute area of Cornwallis Island.

Acknowledgments

Without my husband Link's encouragement, patience, and assistance with the manuscript, this book would not have been written. I am also deeply indebted to George H. Hobson for his kindness in writing the Foreword. Dr. Hobson was the first director of Canada's Polar Continental Shelf Project and has spent considerable time in the Arctic. I am also grateful to the late Robert F. Legget for his helpful suggestions regarding this manuscript and its publication; and to Judith and Norman Laska, John Bockstoce, Stuart Jenness, and Dorothy Jean Ray for careful editing of the manuscript and for asking many helpful questions, as did our friend Anneka Stuiver and our daughter Nuna Cass, our son Land, and daughter Sila.

Without the help of Patra Leaming and Kim Moloney, who spent endless hours deciphering my handwriting while typing the many "reworkings" of the manuscript, over a period of several years, it would never have been published.

I am very grateful to C. Floyd Bardsley of the Department of Geological Sciences at the University of Washington (now retired), for drafting the maps, an essential part of this book.

Link and I remember with gratitude the late Charles Camsell, former Deputy Minister of Mines and Resources, and other friends in the Canadian government at that time, who made it possible for us to work in the Arctic. I am also greatly indebted to the late Diamond Jenness and Vilhjalmur Stefansson for their warm friendship and generous sharing of knowledge gained during their years of travel in the Canadian Arctic.

With warm appreciation we remember the late W. R. "Wop" May and his wife Vi. Wop facilitated our flights to, from, and in the Arctic, and they both became dear friends. We remember our fine pilots Harry Winnie and the late

Rudy Huess, with whom we flew in 1938; also the late Alf Caywood, who was our pilot in 1939, 1940, and 1941, and who, with his wife Evelyn, remained dear friends; also Ernie Boffa, who flew Erling Porsild, John "Pete" Jenness, and us to various locations on Victoria and Banks Islands in 1949. We treasure the longtime friendship of Pete and Ernie and their wives, Mary and Nettie.

We remember with deep appreciation the late Hudson's Bay Company managers who assisted us in so many ways and for their friendship over many years: F. R. (Ray) Ross and his wife Lillian, at Read Island, and E. J. "Scotty" and Isabel Gall, at Cambridge Bay; Jock Kilgour and Bill Calder, at Baillie Island and Holman Island. We recall with much pleasure Christmas at Perry River with Post Manager Angus Gavin and his wife Phyllis.

We also think of the kindness of Captain R. J. "Shorty" Sommers of the Hudson's Bay Company supply ship the *Fort Ross*, and of Sergeant Henry Larsen, F.R.G.S., Commander of the Royal Canadian Mounted Police schooner *St. Roch*; also Corporal Scott Alexander, Corporal Duncan Martin, and Constable Reginald Goodey, who were stationed at Cambridge Bay.

I wish to express our appreciation of the warm and ready helpfulness of all of our Inuit friends. Particularly we remember the warm and patient kindness of George Porter and his wife Martha Nulaik, his half brother David Piktukana, and Ikey Bolt and his wife Etna Klengenberg, with whom we made long trips on their schooners. They made it possible for us to see and study many areas we would otherwise not have been able to visit.

We shall always feel deeply indebted to the late Patsy Klengenberg for his willingness to take us to King William Island, and to him and his brother, Jorgen, and their wives, Iglikshik and Mikigiak, for their warm friendship and for helping us learn the ways of living on the land, and for guiding us on long journeys over the ice.

We remember with gratitude and pleasure those with whom we traveled by kamotik: Amos Cockney, Sam Carter, Penuktuk, Kopun, Mary Kaglik, Joe Kaglik, Georgie Carter, Ohokok, and Aytok.

We also remember the warm hospitality of the late Ole Andreasen, his wife Susannah, son Jasper, stepson Amos Cockney, and stepdaughter Agnes, with whom we stayed at Richardson Island.

We remember with appreciative warmth the late Father Raymond de Coccola, OMI, and Father Roger Buliard, OMI, both of whom shared their knowledge of the Arctic with us and assisted us in many ways, and who remained close friends, as did the Reverend Harold Webster and his wife Edith.

Glossary

Inuktitut words were defined by the Inuit we met; spelling of some of the words varied from region to region. Most geologic terms are based on *Glossary of Geology,* Fourth Edition, ed. Julia A. Jackson, American Geological Institute, 1997. Most other definitions are based on *Webster's New World Dictionary,* 1984.

active layer   A surface layer of ground, above the permafrost, that is alternately frozen each winter and thawed each summer; it represents seasonally frozen ground on permafrost. Its thickness ranges from several centimeters to a few meters.

aiyakok   A game usually comprising a seal flipper into which a number of small holes have been drilled, attached to a pointed spindle by a string of plaited sinew. The objective is to hold the spindle and swing the flipper with the intent of impaling it in on of the holes.

attigi   A parka.

barograph   A barometer that makes a continuous record of changes in atmospheric pressure. It usually consists of a special type of aneroid barometer.

bedrock   A general term for the rock, usually solid, that underlies soil or other unconsolidated, superficial material.

Brunton compass   A compact pocket instrument that consists of an ordinary compass, folding open sights, a mirror, and a rectangular spirit-level clinometer, which can be used in the hand or on a staff or light rod for reading horizontal and vertical angles, for leveling, and for reading the magnetic bearings of a line.

candle ice Disintegrating sea or lake ice consisting of ice prisms oriented perpendicular to the ice surface; a form of rotten ice.

cephalopod A marine mollusk belonging to the class *Cephalopodia*. Fossils include straight to curved forms. Octopuses, squids, and cuttlefishes are common living cephalopods.

crescentric fracture A crescentic mark in the form of a hyperbolic crack, of larger size (up to 10–12 cm long) than a chattermark; it is convex toward the direction from which the ice moved (its "horns" point in the the direction of ice movement) and it consists of a single fracture without the romoval of any rock.

ctenophore Any of a phylum (*Ctenophora*) of sea animals with an oval, transparent, jellylike body bearing 8 rows of comblike plates that aid in swimming.

deerskin In the Canadian Arctic a name commonly used for a caribou skin.

duffle 1. Hudson's Bay Company heavy wool blanket cloth used for attigis, duffles, and mitts. 2. The whole of transportable personal possessions.

duffle bag A large cylindrical cloth bag, especially of waterproof canvas or duck, for carrying clothing and personal belongings.

duffles Boot liners made of Hudson's Bay Company heavy wool blanket cloth.

erratic A rock fragment carried by glacial ice or by floating ice, deposited at some distance from the outcrop from which it was derived, and generally though not necessarily resting on bedrock of different lithology.

esker A long, narrow, sinuous, steep-sided ridge composed of irregularly stratified sand and gravel that was deposited by a sub-glacial or englacial stream, flowing between ice walls or in an ice tunnel of a stagnant or retreating glacier, and was left behind when the ice melted.

flying contact (aircraft) Flying low enough to see the ground at essentially all times.

geocryology The study of ice and snow on the Earth, especially the study of permafrost.

geomorphology The science that treats the general configuration of the Earth's surface; specifically the study of the classification, description, nature, origin, and development of present landforms and their relationships to underlying structures, and of the history of geologic changes as recorded by these surface features.

glacial abrasion   Mechanical scraping and wearing of rock surfaces by solid rock particles transported at the base of the glacier.

glacial striae   Long, delicate, finely cut, commonly straight and parallel furrows or lines inscribed on a bedrock surface by the rasping and rubbing of rock fragments embedded at the base of a moving glacier; usually oriented in the direction of ice movement. Also found on rock fragments transported by the ice.

Hessian   A coarse cloth used for bags. The kind used by the Hudson's Bay Company for baling furs and similar to burlap, but of jute or hemp and more finely woven.

ice blink   A relatively bright, usually yellowish or whitish glare in the sky near the horizon or on the underside of a cloud layer, produced in the polar region by light reflected from a large ice-covered surface, which may be too far away to be visible.

ice shove (ice push)   The lateral pressure exerted by the expansion of shoreward-moving ice.

Inuit   Eskimos. Inuit is the name preferred by the Native people themselves. Inuk is the singular.

inukshuk   The profile of a standing person formed by stones laid on each other. Such profiles are often erected on higher ground to deflect caribou in a direction favorable for hunting.

Inuktitut   The Eskimo language.

jolly boat   A ship's small boat.

kamiks   Skin boots.

kamotik   Heavy dog-drawn sledge.

kudlik   An oblong shallow dish carved from soapstone and used as a seal-oil stove or lamp. The wick is formed of pinches of willow fuzz along the top edge.

kuletak   Outer parka, usually made of caribou skin.

lead   Any fracture, water opening, or long narrow strip of ocean water through sea ice (especially pack ice), navigable by surface vessels, and sometimes covered by young ice; wider than a lane.

lemming   Any of a various small arctic rodents (genera *Lemmus* and *Dicrostonyx*) resembling mice but having short tails and fur-covered feet. Some species undertake spectacular mass migrations at peaks of population growth, ultimately crowding into the sea to destruction.

limestone A rock consisting mainly of calcium carbonate, often containing fossil remains of sea animals, such as mollusks, corals, etc.

magnetic declination The angle formed by a magnetic needle with the line pointing to true north.

Norseman (aircraft) Canadian light, single-engine, fabric-covered airplane with short landing and takeoff capability, on land with wheels or skis and on water with floats.

patterned ground A group term for certain well-defined, more or less symmetrical forms, such as circles, polygons, nets, steps, and stripes, that are characteristic of but not necessarily confined to surficial material subject to intensive frost action. The material is classified according to type of pattern and presence or absence of sorting.

Paulin altimeter A precision field instrument to measure differences in altitude from differences in atmospheric pressure temperature.

pingo A conical mound of soil-covered ice (commonly 30–50 m high and up to 400 m in diameter), raised in part by hydrostatic pressure of water within or below the permafrost of Arctic regions (especially Canada) and of more than one year's duration.

raised beach An ancient beach occurring above the present shoreline and separated from the present beach, having been elevated above the high water mark either by local crustal movements (uplift) or lowering of sea level.

sastrugi Irregular ridges up to 5 cm high, formed in a level or nearly level snow surface by wind erosion, often aligned parallel to the wind direction, with steep, concave or overhanging ends facing the wind; or cut into snow dunes previously deposited by the wind.

sediment Solid fragmental material that originates from the weathering of rocks. It is transported or deposited by air, water, or ice or accumulates by other natural agents, such as chemical precipitation from solution or secretion by organisms, and forms in layers on the Earth's surface at ordinary temperatures in a loose, unconsolidated form (e.g., sand, gravel, silt, mud, till, loess, alluvium).

shikshik (or siksik) A ground squirrel.

Sila Inuit Spirit of the Weather.

single tree A wooden dowel fastened between the ends of the side traces of a sledge dog's harness and the central snap to the main trace.

"sit down"   A term commonly used for landing an aircraft under less than ideal conditions.

"skeds"   Term used by amateur radio operators and others when referring to radio schedules.

skim ice   First formation of a thin layer of ice on the water surface.

sledge   A rugged sled made from two 6-foot to 18-foot planks 2x6 inches to 2x12 inches wide, lashed about 2 to 3 feet apart by 3-inch-wide cross boards.

snow barchan   A small crescentric or horseshoe-shaped snow dune with the ends pointed downwind.

snow knife   A knife similar to a butcher's knife but with a longer blade.

"socked in"   Zero–zero visibility for aircraft landings.

solifluction lobe   An isolated, tongue-shaped feature, up to 25 m wide and 150 m long, formed by more rapid solifluction on certain sections of a slope showing variations in gradient. It commonly has a steep front (15°–25°) and a relatively smooth upper surface.

sorted circle   A form of patterned ground whose mesh is dominantly circular, with a sorted appearance commonly resulting from a border of stones surrounding finer material; developed singly or in groups. Diameter: a few centimeters to more than 10 m; the stone border may be 35 cm high and 8–12 cm wide.

stratigraphy   The science of rock strata. It is concerned not only with the original succession and age relations of rock strata but also with their form, distribution, lithologic composition, fossil content, geophysical and geochemical properties-indeed, with all characteristics and attributes of rocks as strata; and their interpretation in terms of environment or mode of origin and geologic history. All classes of rocks, consolidated or unconsolidated, fall within the general scope of stratigraphy.

Thule people   The Thule people, believed to be the direct ancestors of the present Inuit, moved eastward from Alaska about 900 A.D.

till   Dominantly unsorted and unstratified drift, generally unconsolidated, deposited directly by and underneath a glacier without mixture of clay, silt, sand, gravel, and boulders ranging widely in size and shape.

tomcod   A small, codlike saltwater food fish.

trap rock   Any dark-colored, fine-grained igneous nongranitic rock, such as basalt or diabase.

trap line   A series of traps (for trapping fox or other animals); hence the route along which such a line of traps is set.

tuktu   Caribou.

ugyuk   Bearded seal. May be 6 feet or more long.

ulu   An Inuk woman's all-purpose knife characterized by a semicircular blade.

umiak   A large open boat made of skins stretched on a wooden frame, used by Inuit for transporting goods and traditionally rowed by women.

Appendix: Intinerary and People Met

1938

We left *Edmonton* July 17. Pilot *Harry Winnie*. Stopped at *Fort McMurray*. Met RCMP *Nevin*, who was on his way out from *Aklavik*. Landed at *Fort Smith* and saw the *Distributor* at the dock. Met pilot *North Sawle*, who said *Charlie Gilham* was at *Coppermine*.

Yellowknife: Met pilots *Rudy Huess* and *Con Farrell* and mechanic *Duncan McLaren*. Stayed at *Corona Inn*. Met young *Fellows*, who was typing out "The Prospector" news sheet. Met pilots *Jack Crosby* and *Mert Wales* and RCMP *Inspector Cork*.

July 18: Flew to *Coppermine*. Met HBC *Post Manager Nichols*, his wife and two-year-old daughter, and HBC *Apprentice Art Figgures*, *the Reverend Harold Webster*, wife *Edith*, and baby *Marguerite*. Radio Chief *Mr. Deacon* and wife, his assistant *Oliver Howey*, RCMP *"Red" Abraham*, HBC *Inspector Copland*, and assistant *O. M. Demment*.

July 18: Landed at *Cambridge Bay* 7:30 P.M. *Captain C. T. Pedersen's* ship, *Nigalik*, was at anchor, and *Mr. Bartlett*, *Charlie Smith*, *Pete Brandt*, and *Rudolf Johnson* of *Pedersen's Canalaska Trading Company* were on the beach to greet us, as well as *Corporal W. D. Kane*, all of whom we had met at *Herschel Island* in 1936. Also his assistant *John Cheetham*. Also on the beach were *Charlie Gilham*, *the Reverend and Mrs. Roceby-Thomas*, and *Mr. and Mrs. Frank Milne of the* HBC.

July 20: Returned to *Coppermine*.

July 21: Flew over *Bernard Harbor* and *Charity Island* and crossed the *Strait* to overfly *Read Island*, continuing across *Wollaston Peninsula* almost as far as *Prince Albert Sound*, which was full of ice. Returned to *Read Island*,

229

where we met *Post Manager Ray Ross*, wife *Lillian (Lin)* and baby *Raymer (Buddy)*. Also *Mr. Chitty* of the *Canalaska Trading Co.* Met Inuit people *William* and *Lena Kuptana* and children *Phillip* and *Margaret*. Another son, *Donald*, was at *Aklavik* with tuberculosis. *Lena* was *Nellie Kunellik's* niece. (*Nellie* we met at *Herschel Island* in 1936.) *Avarana* and wife *Lucy* and children *Peter* and *Edith*. *Avarana's* son-in-law *Gabriel Katutuk*, a *Coppermine Inuk*. *George Porter* and wife *Martha Nulaik* and children, *Georgie* (seven), *Mary* (three), and *Walter*, (four months). *Pat Kunellik*, *Nellie's* son. *Luke* and *Lila Maluksuk* and son *Andrew James*. *Arthur Watson's* boat the *Audrey B.* anchored with *Slim Purcell*, *Bill Storr*, *Luke Angalalik*, young *John*, and *Count Gontran de Poncins*, who was going to winter on *King William Island* at *Gjoa Haven*.

August 4: Left *Read Island* on the *Fox* with *George* and *Martha Porter* and children, *Pat Kunellik* (*Nellie's son*), *Joe* (from *Walker Bay*?), *Luke*, and *Lila*, with three-month-old *Andrew James* and eighteen dogs.

August 5: Reached *Ulukhaktok*. *David Piktukana's* place. *David* was *George's* half brother. *David's* schooner the *Sea Otter* was not there and *David* was not home. *George Porter's* father was a whaler and friend of *Captain C. T. Pedersen*. He and *Pedersen's* son *Teddy* were at school together at the *Jesse Lee Home* in *Dutch Harbor, Alaska*. *George* joined the *U.S. Armed Forces* and was sent to *Camp Merritt, New Jersey*, for training in 1917. He started overseas but bacame sick and was sent back, later being attached to the *Lafayette Division*. The *Armistice* was signed before he was sent over again. He could have stayed Outside, but decided he preferred the free lifestyle of the Arctic.

August 9: Left for *Ikey Bolt's* place called *Sikosuilak*, "the place that never freezes," in *Minto Inlet*. There we met *Ikey Bolt*, *Diamond Klengenberg*, and *Tommy Goose*. Continued on up *Minto Inlet* to a river and high hill called *Niakoknajuak*, "big round head." There we met old *Jack Nukatlak*, whom *Ikey* said was about ninety years old and whose older brother remembered *Collinson's* expedition. Also his wife *Annie Ottoayuk*.

August 11: Reached *Walker Bay*, stayed until 12th. Met *Charlie Rowen*.

August 17: Reached *Silas Kangegana's* place by the *Smoking Mountains* at the bottom of *Franklin Bay*, and met his wife and two adopted children. *Silas's* wife thought I was her daughter *Margaret*, who had gone Outside to become a nurse. *Silas's* wife was married to a whaler earlier. Left *Silas's* for *Baillie Islands*, but ice forced us to return.

August 19: Left for *Baillie Islands*. A shaman, old *Kutakok*, who was at *Silas's*, joined us. At *Baillie Islands* we met the HBC *Post Manager Jock Kilgour*, his apprentice *Art Figgures*, and HBC *Post Manager Charlie Rowen* from *Fort Collinson*, who was relieving *Kilgour* and the Inuit *Tunaomik*. Father *L'Helgouace* from the *Anderson River Mission* stopped by en route to *Cape Bathurst*. *Rowen's* schooner was the *Adanac*.

August 24: *Fort Ross* arrived. *Captain R. J. "Shorty" Sommers*. Crew on *Fort Ross* were: *Len Adey*, mate; *J. Piercey*, chief engineer; *W. Starks*, bosun; *H. James*, A.B.S.; *W. Smith*, A.B.S.; *W. Short*, cook; *S. Sydenham, "Sparks."* Aboard were *Mr. Chitty* from *Read Island*, and *Owen Hanson*, who was en route to *Fort Collinson* at *Walker Bay* where he and *Kilgour* were to be. *Ernie Donovan* was en route to *Read Island*, and *Reverend Nicholson*, to *Coppermine*.

August 25: Sailed on *Fort Ross* to *Fort Collinson*, *Walker Bay*.

August 26: Reached *Fort Collinson*.

August 27: Departed for *Read Island*.

August 28: Arrived *Read Island*.

August 29: *William Kuptana* and *Lena* were there. Pilot *Rudy Huess* flew in with *W. R. "Wop" May* and *Mr. Ken Muir, manager engineer* at *Camalaeron Mine* on *Gordon Lake*. We return to *Coppermine* with them.

August 30: Left for South.

1939

July 20: Took fellow graduate student *Preston Cloud* north with us. Left *Edmonton* for *Coppermine* with the *Reverend Harold Webster*, wife *Edie*, and one-and-a-half-year-old *Marguerite*. *Mr. French* going to *Great Bear*. *W. R. "Wop" May* going to *Coppermine*. *Mert Wales* pilot. Pilot *Rudy Huess* in hospital.

At *Yellowknife* met *Richard (Dick) Finnie* and wife, *Con Farrel*, *Tom Moore* from *Harvard*, *"Doc" Fred Jolliff* from *Princeton*, *Bert Airth* (mining engineer). Saw *Ken Muir* at *Thompson Lake*.

At *Great Bear* met *Manager E. J. Wallie* and wife *Ginger*. Also *Dave McDonald* (accountant), *Campbell* (underground), *Al Black*, *Clem Bucher* (mill), and *Mr. and Mrs. Muskett; Al Torgerson*. Also *Bishop Fleming*, *Father Roger Buliard*.

July 23: Arrived *Coppermine* at 9:45 P.M. RCMP *T. E. Shillinton*, RCMP

Doug Kane, *Father LeMère*, Anglican *Reverend Nicholson*; *Slim* and *Agnes Semmler* (traders), *Art* and *Tiny Watson* (trader), *Mr. and Mrs. Deacon* (weather), *Oliver Howey* (weather), *Slim Purcell* (trader), *Ralph Jardine* (HBC), *Miss Brown* (exchange teacher from *South Africa*), *Johnny Norberg* (trader), *Chips Leonard* (trader).

July 27: Went to *Read Island* with *Slim* and *Agnes Semmler* via *Cape Krusenstern*, where we left *Agnes* and two children. *Annie* (?) was there.

July 28: Arrived *Read Island*. *Ray, Lillian*, and *Buddy Ross* (HBC), *Henry Jensen*, trader for *Slim Semmler; Bill Storr* came. *Mr. Chitty*.

August 2: *Ikey Bolt's* wife *Etna Klengenberg*, and children *Jane* and *Walter Bolt*; *Avarana*, wife *Lena*, daughter *Naomi; Pootuk*, wife and two boys, *Pudnuk* and *Ketuk*. *Tadlidiak*, wife *Margaret*, little daughter *Naomi*, and baby *Illipsiak*. *Ikey* said *Read Island* is really *Katanayuk*. The real *Read Island* is 15 miles west and was sometimes called *Linklater Island*. Its Inuit name was *Affeketuk*.

August 7: Left with *Ikey* and family plus *William Taptuna* for *Okallik Islands*. Dropped *William* and *Pres Cloud* there. Also *Ikey's* family.

August 9: Left *Read Island* for *Ulukhaktok*. Picked up *Pres* and *William*.

August 10: Reached *Ulukhaktok* 11:00 P.M. *Jock Kilgour* (HBC), *Owen Hanson* (HBC), *George Porter* with wife *Martha*, daughter *Mary*, sons *Georgie* and *Walter*. *Moses, Father Raymond de Coccola*, and *Father Lucien Delalonde*.

August 16: *Fort Ross* arrived. *Skipper "Shorty" Sommers, Mate Len Adey, Chief Piercy, Bosun Starks, Sparks Graham Sturrock*, HBC Inspector *Mr. Copland, Bill Smith*, the new HBC apprentice *Robert McIsac*, going to *Gjoa Haven; E. J. "Scotty" Gall* and wife *Isabel* (HBC) going to *Cambridge Bay, Phyllis McKinnon* en route to *Perry River* to marry HBC *Post Manager Angus Gavin*.

August 18: Left *Ulukhaktok* with *Ikey* together with *George Porter* for *Minto Inlet*. Reached *Ikey's* place, called *Sikosuilak*, at 3:30 A.M. on the 19th.

August 19: *George* took *Tommy Goose* and *Jimmy* to tear down the HBC warehouse at *Walker Bay* to be rebuilt at *Holman*. We met *Andrew* and *Bob Klengenberg* and *Billy Banksland* again.

August 20: Went up *Minto Inlet* to *Kuujjuua River*, where we found: *Jack Nukatlak*, whose brother remembered the *Collinson Expedition;* his wife *Annie Ottoayuk; Louie Onnayak;* his wife *Lucy Ottoayuhok; Phillip Aogak;*

Mark Emigak, his wife *Otyah; Dennis Avahannia* (son to *Mark*), his wife *Martha* and children *Mary* and *Pete, Adam Ekyukseak; Fred Kutlak.*

August 21: Returned to *Niakoknajuak—Omanahok,* where we found *Adam Ekyukseak's* daughter, *Elsie Alekamik,* whose husband is *Ikey Bolt's* adopted son *Mathew Malqokok,* and their children *Margaret Tagik, Joe Appiana, Roy Ennuktalik,* and baby *Evakluk.* Also *Adam's* son *Joseph Negeonak* (had tuberculosis). Also *Henry Aolatuk,* his wife *Eva Mapauk,* and son *William Kakyon.* Mrs. *Jennie Klengenberg,* her son *Andrew,* and his wife *Joan Okalik,* who is *Henry Jensen's* daughter and their adopted child *Martha* or *Martina Aviligak,* who is *Diamond Klengenberg's* daughter; *Bob Klengenberg* and his wife *Lily Akanasiak* and their baby *Akepgak.*

August 24: Left for *Ulukhaktok-Holman* at 9:00 P.M. *Bob, Lilly,* and baby *Okepgak Klengenberg* and *Joseph Negeonak* accompanied us.

September 3: Left for *Tuktoyaktuk* on *Fort Ross.*

September 5: Arrived *Tuktoyaktuk.* Met *Johnny One Arm* and *Mr. and Mrs. Sedgewick* of HBC.

September 10: Arrived at *Read Island* and offloaded, then picked up *Ray* and *Lin Ross,* who were being moved to *Coppermine.*

September 11: Left *Read* for *Coppermine.*

September 13: Left *Coppermine* for South.

1940

March 27: Arrived *Coppermine* at 9:15 A.M. *Ray* and *Lin* and baby *Buddy Ross, Johnny Norberg,* the Reverend *Harold* and *Edie Webster, Deacon* and *Howey* (radio), *Yates* and *Shilly* (RCMP). Arrived *Cambridge Bay* at 2:10 P.M. *Scotty* and *Isabel Gall* (HBC), *Reginald Goodey* (RCMP), *Einar Farvolden* (trader for *Slim Semmler*); Father *Raymond de Coccola;* Reverend *Nicholson; Kopun; Amos Cockney, Sam Carter, Mary Kaglik, Joseph Kaglik.*

April 2: RCMP Cpl. *Scott Alexander* returned from a long inspection trip by dog team.

April 8: *Johnny Norberg* stopped off en route to *Coppermine. Mary Kaglik's* sister *Annie,* who had fainting spells. A very old woman, beautifully tattooed on face, hands, and lower arms. *Sam Carter's* son *Georgie,* and *Jo* (son of *Kaglik?*). At seal camp met several local people; one mother's name was *Molly* and her baby was called *Margaret.*

April 28: *Taipana* and wife *Micheliagak* came in. They had been fishing and hunting; also *Paniyoyuk* (sp?).

May 22: *Kaituk* came in from hunting.

June 6: At our camp at *Mount Pelly*. *David Paniyoyuk*, his two little sisters, father, mother, and his uncle *Kopun*, with his three-year-old son *Adam* and mother stopped by en route to a fish lake.

June 22: *Penuktuk*, his wife *Hadlelah* and three boys and his brother *Taipana* came visiting.

August 9: Left by plane, pilot *Alf Caywood*, for flight across center of *Victoria Island* to *Holman Island post*. There saw *Ikey* and *Etna Bolt* and *Jane*, HBC Post Manager *Jock Kilgour*, *Bill* (assistant), *Father Buliard*, *Tommy Goose*, *Nukotlak* and his old wife, from *Minto Inlet*, *Jimmy* and *Jacob* from *Minto Inlet*. *David Piktukana*, his wife and son and *George* and *Martha Porter* and three children.

August 10: Flew to *Coppermine* and met the *Fort Ross* . Met HBC Inspector *Paddy Gibson*.

August 15: *Donald Kaglik* fell into the hold of the *Fort Ross*, dislocating his shoulder and injuring something in his pelvis. He went to *Aklavik* with the *Fort Ross*.

August 16: *Slim Semmler* and *Johnny Norberg* returned from *Tuktoyaktuk* in the *Eagle*. *Chips Leonard*.

August 26: *David Piktukana* and *George Porter* and three Inuit families arrived with forty-three dogs, from *Holman* on *Sea Otter*. *Father Raymond de Coccola*, *Father Delalonde*, and *Father L'Helguace* came with the schooner *Lady of Lourdes;* en route to mission house at *Bathurst Inlet*.

August 27: Left *Coppermine* for *Cambridge Bay* with *David* and *George*, and *Norman* and *Harry* and families. Went ashore at *Tree River* (Aug. 29). *Chips Leonard* also there, fishing.

August 29: Left *Tree River* for *Wilmot Island*, where *Alec Eccles* was in charge of *Patsy Klengenberg's* trading post.

September 7: Left *Wilmot Island* for *Cambridge Bay* with *St. Roch*, Skipper *Henry Larsen*, Mate *Jeek Farrar*, Corporal *Bill Peters*, Corporal *Duncan Martin*, who was relieving *Scott Alexander* at *Cambridge Bay*, and others.

September 8: Arrived *Cambridge Bay*. Met *Patsy Klengenberg*, wife *Iglikshik*, son *Ayalik*, nine years old, widowed daughter *Ikilik* plus baby daughters, *Iviguak*, three years old, and *Ohokok*, three months.

September 13: Left for *Terror Bay* on *King William Island* with *Klengebergs* on *Aklavik*.

September 17: Reached *Royal Geographical Society Islands*. Found two families from *Pelly Bay: Utuitoq* and *Aylikomiq;* the latter's wife was blind; they had a little girl.

September 21: Left the *Islands* for *Terror Bay*. Met *Jorgen Klengenberg* and his wife *Mikigiak*, four-year-old *Mary*, and adopted twelve-year-old son *Maneratsiak*. Also *Tulemaq*.

December 9: Left *Terror Bay* with *Patsy* and *Maneratsiak* for the *Royal Geographical Society Islands*.

December 10: Left *Islands* for *Cambridge Bay*.

December 12: Turned back by impassable rough ice and open water in *Victoria Strait*.

December 13: Continued back—very long day. Reached *Terror Bay*.

December 14: Rested.

December 17: Left *Terror Bay* for *Perry River* with *Jorgen, Mikigiak,* and *Mary*.

December 23: Arrived *Perry River*. HBC Post Manager *Angus Gavin* and wife *Phyllis*. Inuit trader *Angalalik*. Met *Harry* and *Norman* again.

December 28: Left *Perry River* for *Cambridge Bay* with two Inuit, *Ohokok* and *Aytok*.

1941

January 2: Arrived *Cambridge Bay*. Stayed at RCMP.

January 26: Left *Cambridge Bay* with *Amos Cockney*, stepson of *Ole Andreasen*, for *Ole Andreasen's* at *Richardson Island*.

February 6: Arrived *Ole Andreasen's* home at *Richardson Island*. Met *Ole* and wife *Susannah*, *Ole's* stepdaughter *Agnes*, who was *Amos's* wife, his son *Jasper*, and his two little girls. *Jasper's* wife had died.

February 16: Flew South.

Bibliography

Franklin, John, Captain R.N., F.R.S., and Commander of the Expedition. *Narrative of a Journey to the Shores of the Polar Sea, in the Years 1819, 20, 21, and 22.* With an Appendix on Various Subjects Relating to Science and Natural History. Illustrated by Numerous Plates and Maps. Published by Authority of the Right Honorable The Earl Bathurst. London: John Murray, 1823.

Hearne, Samuel. *A Journey from Prince of Whales's Fort in Hudson's Bay, to the Northern Ocean: Undertaken by Order of the Hudson's Bay Company, for the Discovery of Copper Mines, a Northwest Passage, Etc., in the Years 1769, 1770, 1771, & 1772.* London: A. Strahan and T. Cadell, 1795.

Huntford, Roland, ed. *The Amundsen Photographs.* First USA Edition. New York: Atlantic Monthly Press, 1987.

Jenness, Diamond. *Physical Characteristics of the Copper Eskimos.* Report of the Canadian Arctic Expedition, 1913–18. Volume 12: The Copper Eskimos. Part B: Southern Party, 1913–16. Ottawa: F. A. Acland, Printer to the King's Most Excellent Majesty, 1923.

Larsen, Henry A., Sergent, F.R.G.S., Commander. *The North-West Passage, 1940–1942 and 1944: The Famous Voyages of the Royal Canadian Mounted Police Schooner "St. Roch."* Vancouver, B.C.: City Archives, 1948.

Mirsky, Jeannette. *To The North! The Story of Arctic Exploration from Earliest Times to the Present.* New York: Viking Press, 1934.

Stefansson, Vilhjalmur. *My Life with the Eskimo.* Illustrated. London and New York: Macmillan, 1913.

———. *The Friendly Arctic: The Story of Five Years in Polar Regions.* Illustrated. New York: Macmillan, 1921.

Index of Geographical Names and Locations

Coppermine, hamlet on Coronation
Gulf, Arctic Coast; government base
for central Canadian Arctic, 5, 9, 10,
12, 15, 16, 24, 25, 28, 29, 37, 48–51, 66,
68, 71, 73, 76, 78, 125, 133, 135, 139, 143,
179, 198, 199, 201–19 passim; itinerary
for, 229, 231, 233
Coronation Gulf, between Arctic mainland coast and Victoria Island, 5, 9,
13, 24, 69, 133, 139, 213, 219

Darnley Bay, on mainland coast, 42
De Salis Bay, on southeast coast of
Banks Island, 40
Dease Strait, separates Kent Peninsula
from Victoria Island, 17
Dolphin and Union Strait, separates
Wollaston Peninsula, Victoria Is-
land, from the mainland Arctic
coast, 5, 25

Finlayson Islands, west of Cambridge
Bay, Victoria Island, 78, 103, 208
Flagstaff Hill, at Walker Bay, 37
Flagstaff Island, 1940 location of Perry
River Hudson's Bay Company, 195
Fort Collinson, a Hudson's Bay Com-
pany Post at Walker Bay, 36, 231
Franklin Bay, mainland coast between
Cape Parry and Cape Bathurst, 42,
230

Gjoa Haven, south coast of King
William Island; a Hudson's Bay
Company Post, 9, 16, 29, 187, 197,
230, 232
Great Bear Lake, northwestern Northwest Territories; site of El Dorado
radium mine, 5, 16, 51, 71, 72, 73

Great Slave Lake, Northwest Territories,
5, 9, 10

Herschel Island, west of the mouth of
Mackenzie River, 3, 4 19, 28, 153, 229
Holman Island, small island at mouth
of Prince Albert Sound, Victoria Is-
land; site of Hudson's Bay company
Post in 1939, 32, 124, 127–28, 134, 232,
234
Horton River, empties into Franklin
Bay, 42

Jenny Lind Island, southeast of the
southeast coast of Victoria Island,
150, 186

Kent Peninsula, on Arctic coast east of
Coppermine, 16, 17, 123, 124
Kings Bay, eastern cove of Ulukhaktok
(Holman) Bay, Victoria Island, 57
King William Island, east of Victoria Is-
land, 4, 7, 16, 17, 146, 153, 199, 230, 235
Kuujiuua River ("full of fish"), a good
camping place, 34, 61, 232

Labyrinth Bay, mainland coast, at base
of Kent Peninsula neck, 205
Lady Franklin Point, Victoria Island,
south coast, west of Richardson Island, 213
Letty Harbour, on mainland coast, 42

Minto Inlet, northwest side of Victoria
Island, 25, 34, 37, 51, 57, 60, 230, 232,
234
Mount Bumpus, northeast of Wollaston
Peninsula on Victoria Island, 25, 49,
129

Index of Personal Names

Abraham, "Red," RCMP, 16, 229

Adey, Len, mate on *Fort Ross*, 69

Alexander, Scott, RCMP corporal, Cambridge Bay, 83, 95, 98, 101, 121, 123, 143, 233

Anderson, Rudolf M., leader of southern party of the 1913–18 Canadian Arctic Expedition, 7

Andreasen, Jasper, Ole Andreasen's son, 213, 218

Andreasen, Ole, Stefansson's companion on northern journeys of 1913–18 Canadian Arctic Expedition, 79, 202, 207, 211, 212–15, 235

Andreasen, Susanna, Ole's wife, 212–18, 235

Angalalik, Luke, Inuit trader, Perry River, 197, 201, 202, 230, 235

Aylikomiq, from Pelly Bay on Simpson Peninsula, 151, 152, 171–73, 183, 185, 188, 235

Aytok, Perry River, 202–4, 206, 235

Banksland, Billy. *See* Natkusiak

Bartlett, Mr., trading manager for Captain C. T. Pedersen, 19, 229

Bolt, Etna (Edna), 126, 129, 234. *See also* Klengenberg, Etna (Edna)

Bolt, Ikey, Inuit trapper and fur trader from Point Hope, Alaska, xi, 34, 36, 51, 54, 57, 60, 61, 126, 230, 232, 234

Bolt, Jane, daughter of Etna, 129, 232, 234

Boyd, Louise, leader of expeditions to Greenland on Norwegian sealer *Veslekari*, 4

Brandt, Pete, member of Pedersen's crew, 19, 229

Buliard, Father Roger, Roman Catholic missionary, 51, 57, 61, 126, 128, 231, 234

Byrd, Admiral Richard, 164

Calder, Bill, Hudson's Bay Company Post manager, Holman, 126

Cameron, Pat, co-pilot for Canadian Airways, 73, 76, 124, 129, 133, 217

Carter, Georgie, son of Sam Carter, Cambridge Bay, 84

Carter, Sam, Inuit trapper, Cambridge Bay, 84, 85, 97, 101–3, 149, 206, 208, 233

Caywood, Alf, pilot for Canadian Airways, 73, 76, 124–26, 129, 133, 217, 234

Index of Ships/Schooners

Library of Congress Cataloging-in-Publication Data
Washburn, Tahoe Talbot.
  Under Polaris : an Arctic quest / Tahoe Talbot Washburn.
    p. cm.
  A McLellan book
  Includes bibliographical references and index.
  ISBN 0–295–97761–2 (alk. paper)
  1. Washburn, Tahoe Talbot—Diaries.   2. Inuit—Northwest
Territories—Victoria Island—Social life and customs.   3. Inuit—
Northwest Territories—King William Island—Social life and
customs.   4. Victoria Island (N.W.T.)—Description and travel.
5. King William Island (N.W.T.)—Description and travel.   I. Title.
E99.E7W383   1998   98–29158
971.9′7—DC21   CIP